PLEIN

AIR

Contents

Works

Installations

Texts by
Aram Moshayedi

The following is a brief natural history of ferns contained by pictures. There are more than fifty species of common ferns in Vermont, reducible to the typologies of their fronds. Inherently full of compositional potential, the expansive and diffuse leaflets are naturally unfixed, thin and delicate, easily rustled, fluttering. And though botanical studies have attempted to fix the outline of their shapes to a static mode of representation and a standardized vocabulary that is clear and legible, their temperament evades permanence. The elements of this feathery plant are never made wholly visible, despite the evocativeness of their Farrah Fawcett-like qualities. The ferns of Hartland, Vermont, are at their best when existing as images of themselves, represented absences, silhouettes of time, environmental afterimages. Rendered into a series of individual studies in natural appearance, they give very little by way of classification. They are pictures of pictures, post-painterly, post-photographic, post-naturalistic, post-ferny, as if it were possible to capture the ethereal ghosts of ferns that whither and wilt when bathed in too much sunlight. The shadows of ferns, rendered in outlines of aqua blue, shades of fuchsine, roseine, goldenrod yellow—the colors of Big Stick cherry-pineapple popsicles—leave their traces in the dark of night, when the air is moist and full of dewy particles that blend and merge the random selection of artificial pigment into one another. The sun is too much for these creatures, making the processes of selection, composition, and coloration into accidents of nature, freak occurrences under the protective cover of darkness. Time—approximately the duration of a single night that the large drop cloths were left outdoors—affords the process by which the images of ferns in Hartland, Vermont, come into being. More than being representations of a particular moment, place, gesture, or species of plant, the drop cloth surfaces are markers of this duration, part and parcel of a genealogy of process-based artworks, accented by random flicks of color. These are billowy images of residue, the stuff that leaves only a trace of leaves, but there is no hand, no witness, and no presence needed for their completion. The breathy atmosphere and lush green conditions of New England impress themselves onto the surfaces. And where there were once the fronds of specific ferns haphazardly strewn about, there is little of their weight beyond their outlines and shapes.

HARTLAND, VT

9.
Untitled (Hartland, VT, Ferns 12V), 2013
Pigment on canvas
132 × 93 inches
(335.3 × 236.2 cm)

11.
Untitled (Hartland, VT, Ferns 11V), 2013
Pigment on canvas
132 × 93 inches
(335.3 × 236.2 cm)

12.
Untitled (Hartland, VT, Ferns 7V), 2013
Pigment on canvas
132 × 93 inches
(335.3 × 236.2 cm)

13.
Untitled (Hartland, VT, Ferns 9V), 2013
Pigment on canvas
132 × 93 inches
(335.3 × 236.2 cm)

15.
Untitled (Hartland, VT, Ferns 3V), 2013
Pigment on canvas
132 × 93 inches
(335.3 × 236.2 cm)

17.
Untitled (Hartland, VT, Ferns 4V), 2013
Pigment on canvas
132 × 93 inches
(335.3 × 236.2 cm)

18.
Untitled (Hartland, VT, Ferns 10V), 2013
Pigment on canvas
132 × 93 inches
(335.3 × 236.2 cm)

19.
Untitled (Hartland, VT, Ferns 1V), 2013
Pigment on canvas
132 × 93 inches
(335.3 × 236.2 cm)

21.
Untitled (Hartland, VT, Ferns 6V), 2013
Pigment on canvas
132 × 93 inches
(335.3 × 236.2 cm)

22–23.
Untitled (Hartland, VT, Ferns 4H), 2013
Pigment on canvas
138 × 162¼ inches
(350.5 × 412 cm)

24–25.
Untitled (Hartland, VT, Ferns 5H), 2013
Pigment on canvas
138 × 162¼ inches
(350.5 × 412 cm)

26–27.
Untitled (Hartland, VT, Ferns 2H), 2013
Pigment on canvas
138 × 162¼ inches
(350.5 × 412 cm)

28–29.
Untitled (Hartland, VT, Ferns 1H), 2013
Pigment on canvas
138 × 162¼ inches
(350.5 × 412 cm)

30–31.
Untitled (Hartland, VT, Ferns 3H), 2013
Pigment on canvas
138 × 162¼ inches
(350.5 × 412 cm)

32–33.
Untitled (Hartland, VT, Ferns 6H), 2013
Pigment on canvas
138 × 162¼ inches
(350.5 × 412 cm)

34–35.
Detail of *Untitled (Hartland, VT, Ferns 6H)*

36.
Detail of *Untitled (Hartland, VT, Ferns 11V)*

37.
Detail of *Untitled (Hartland, VT, Ferns 4V)*

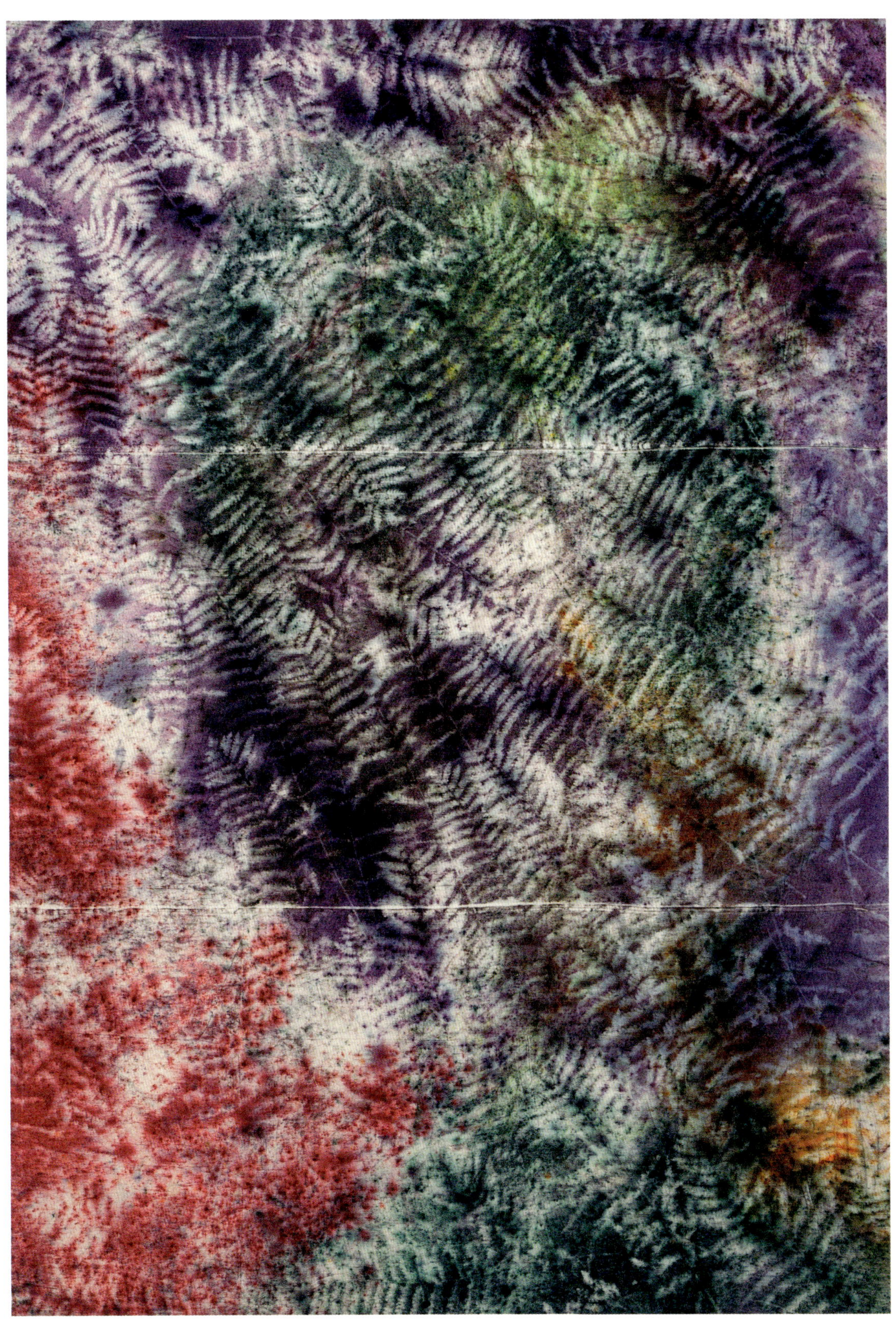

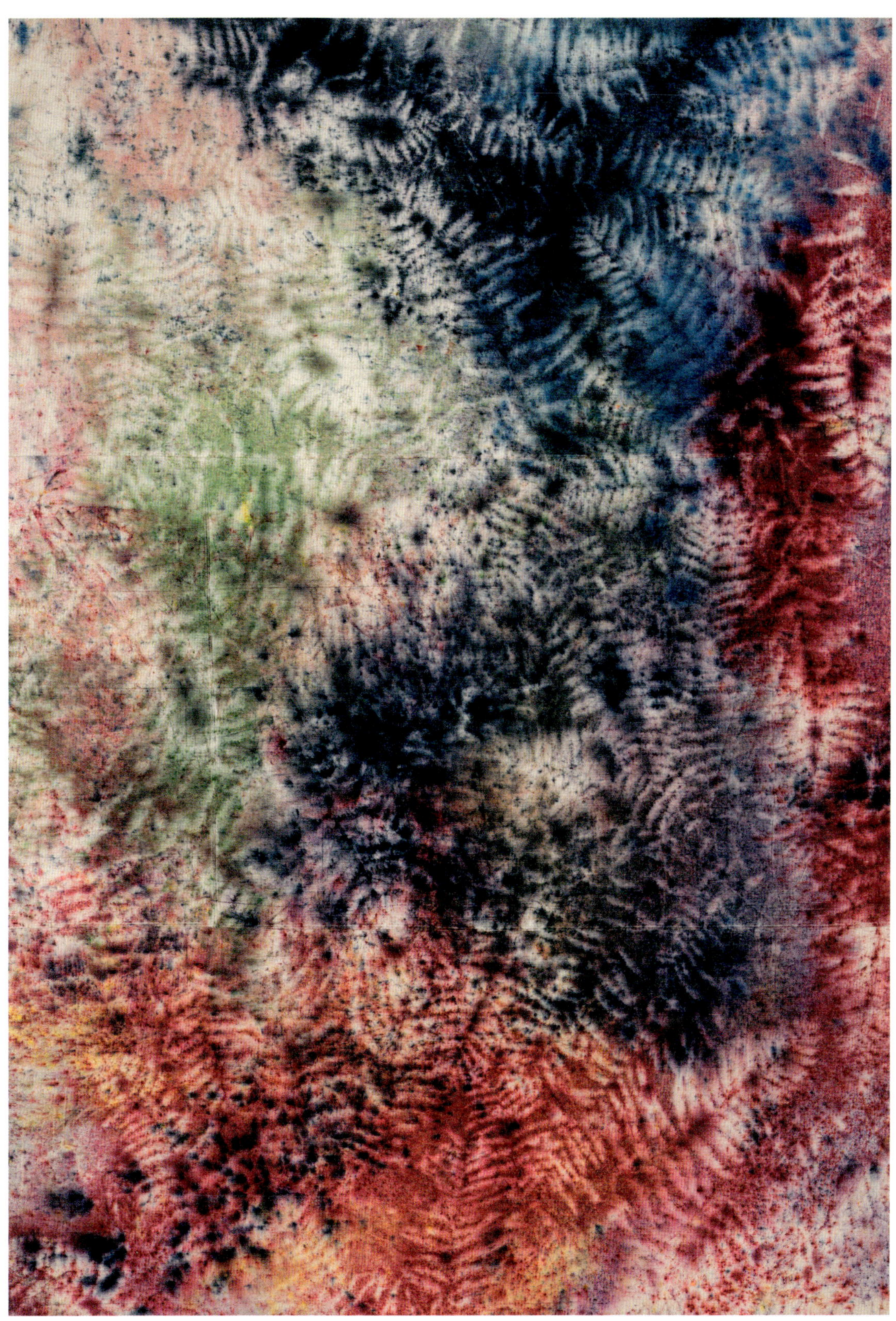

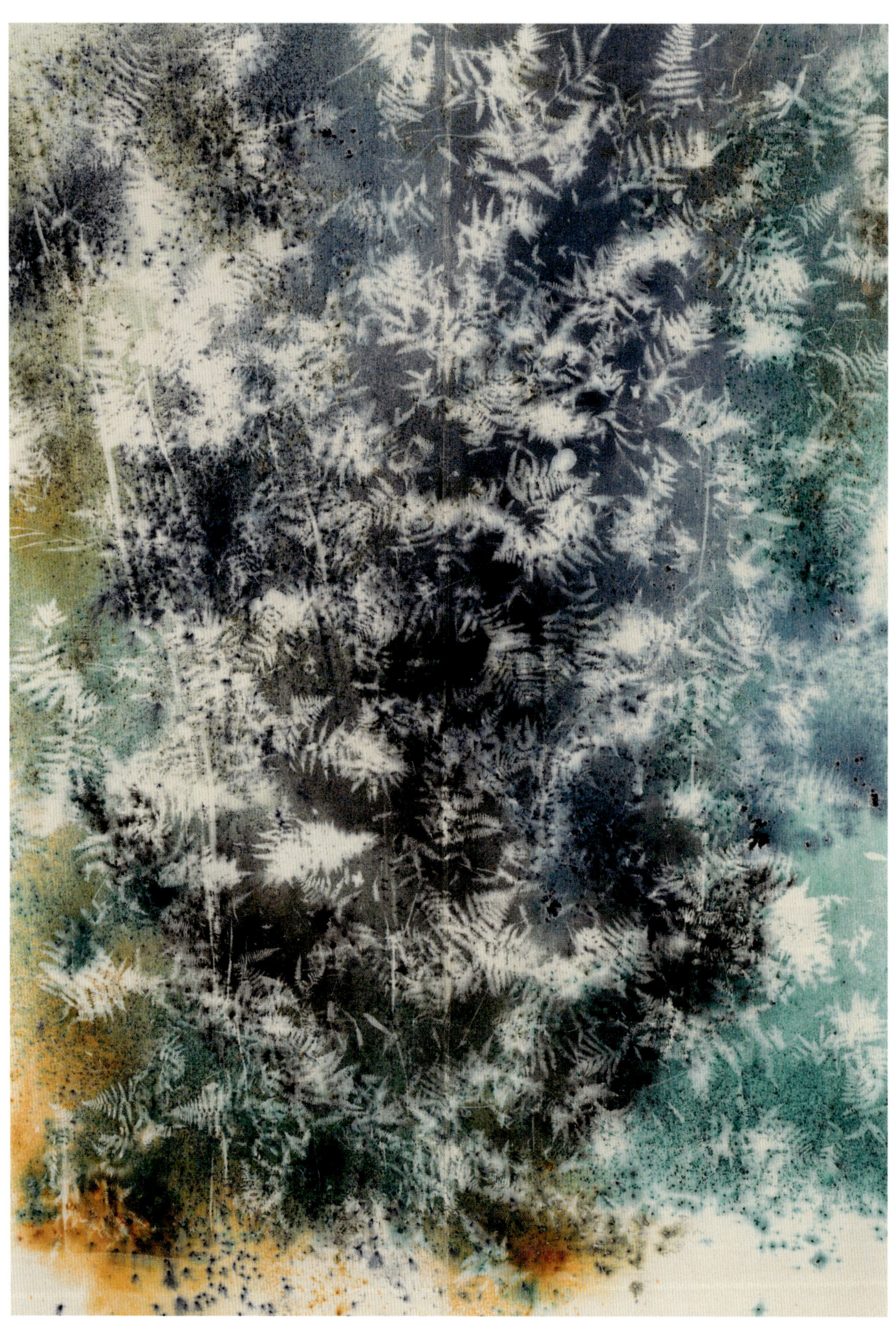

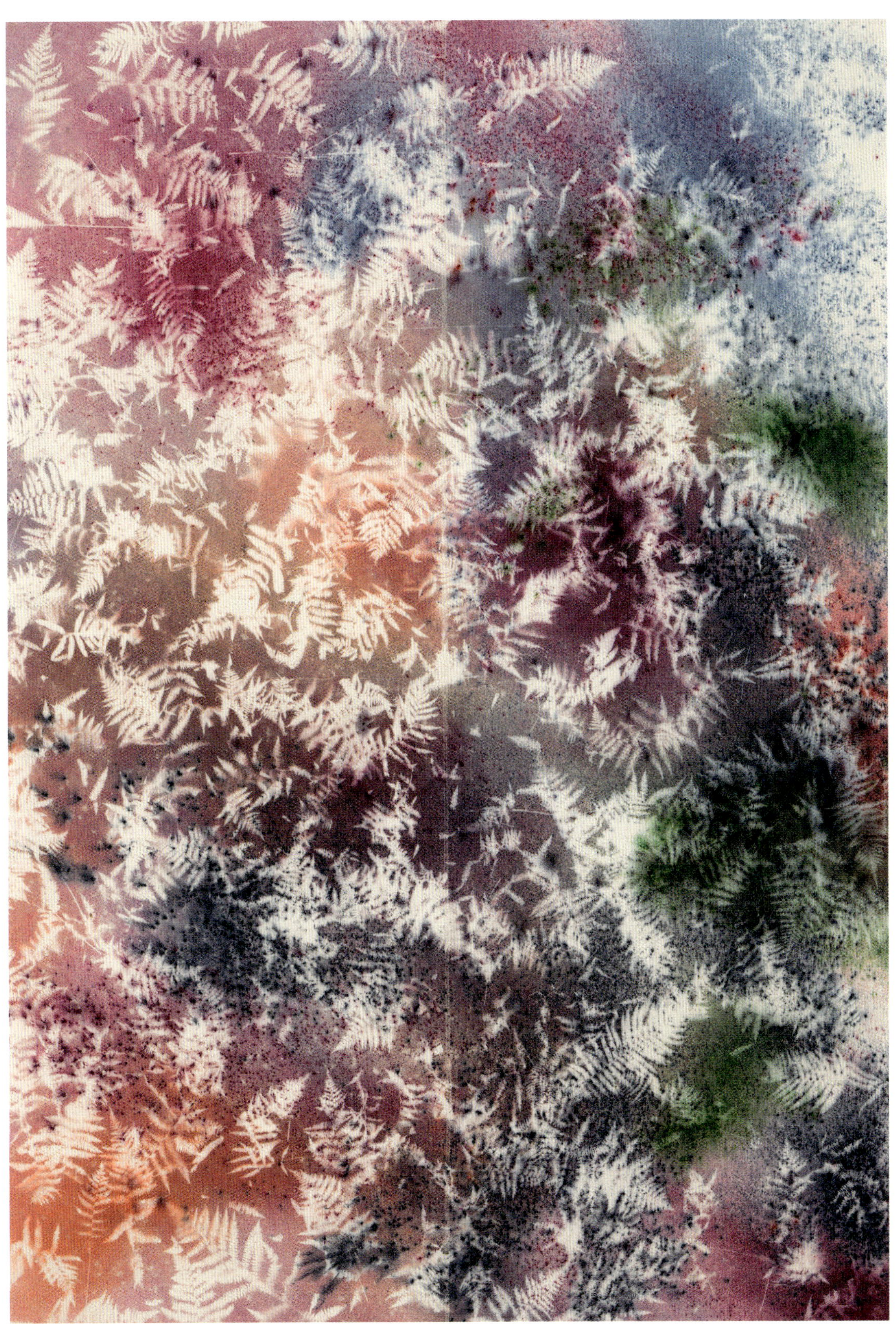

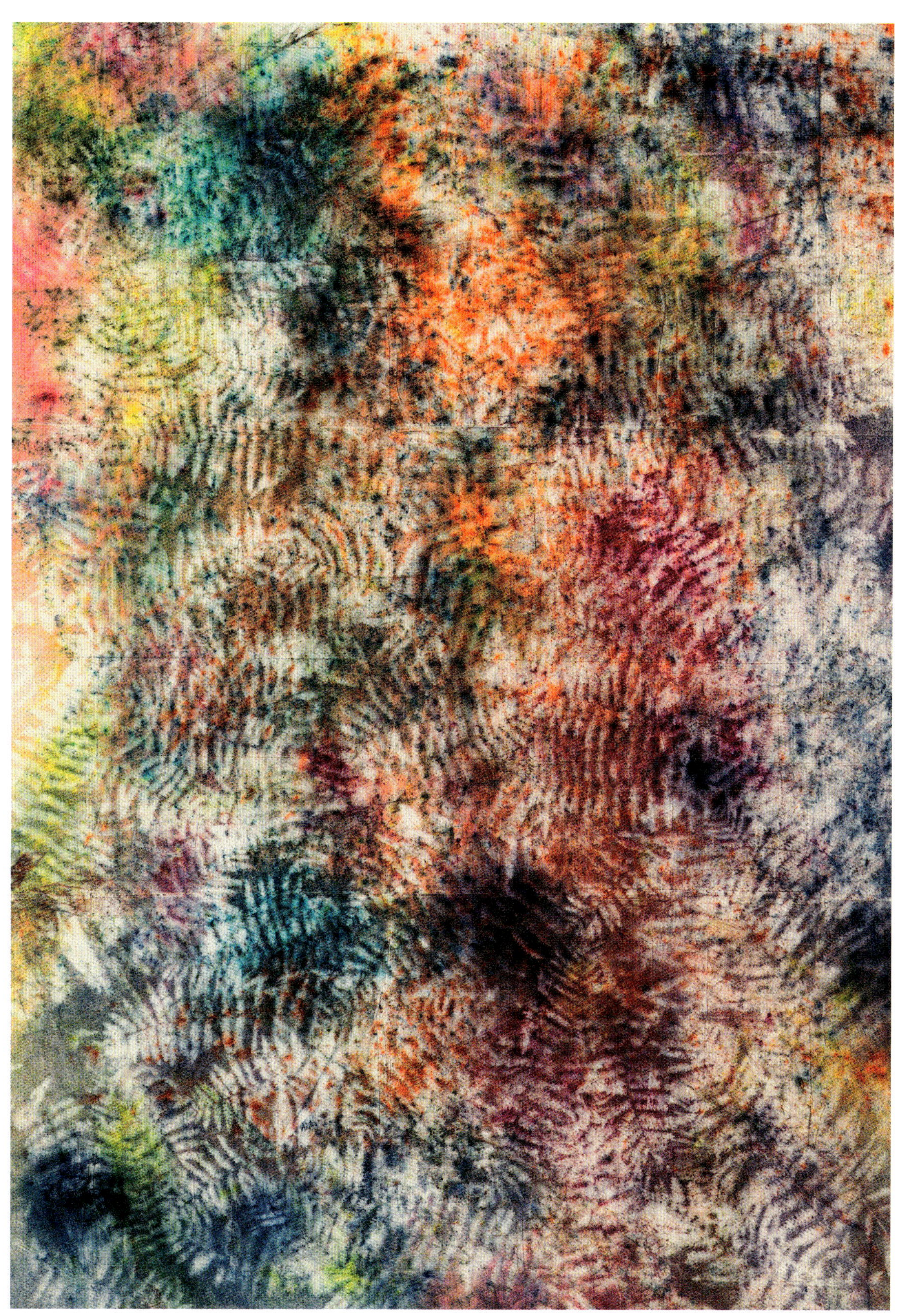

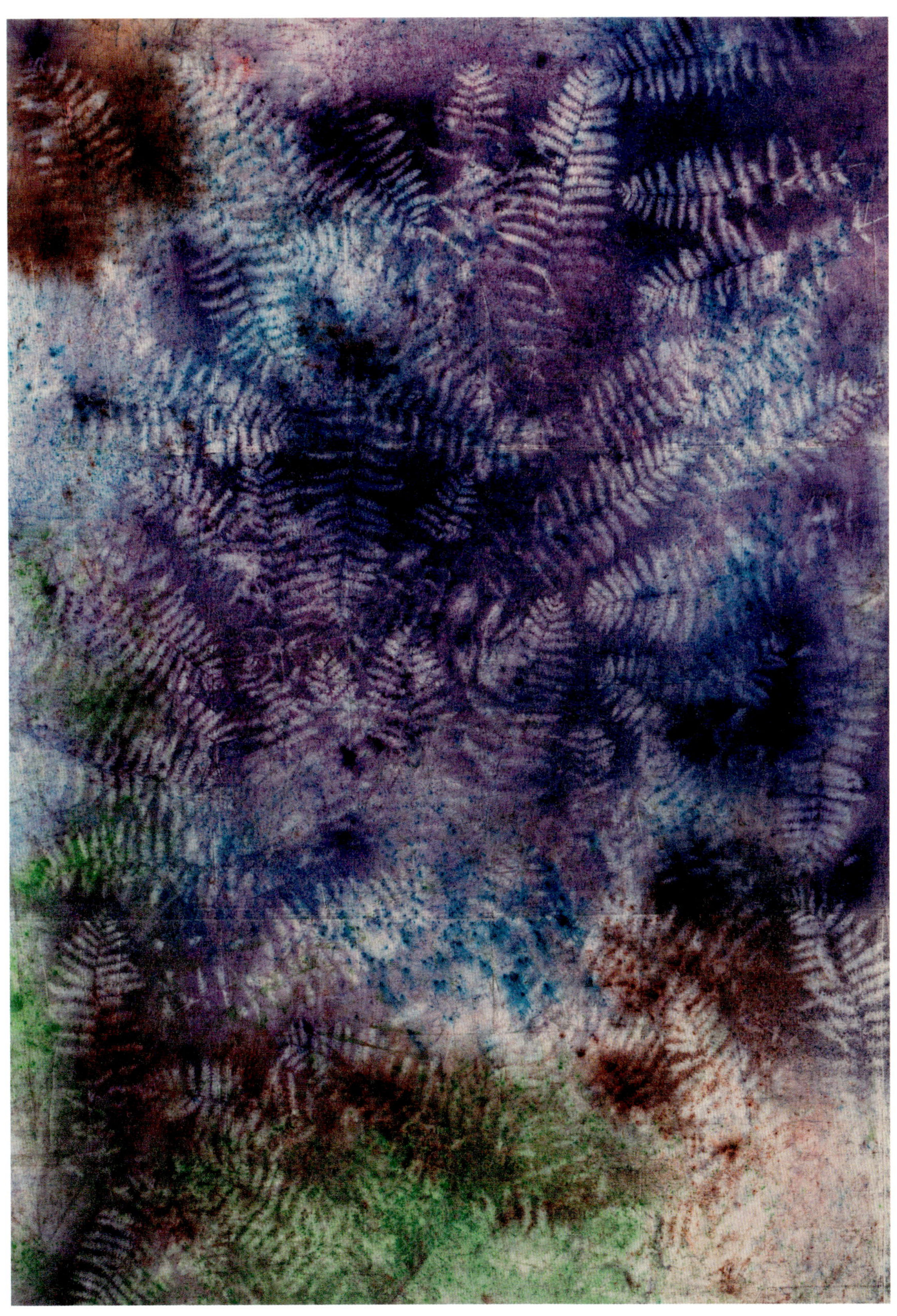

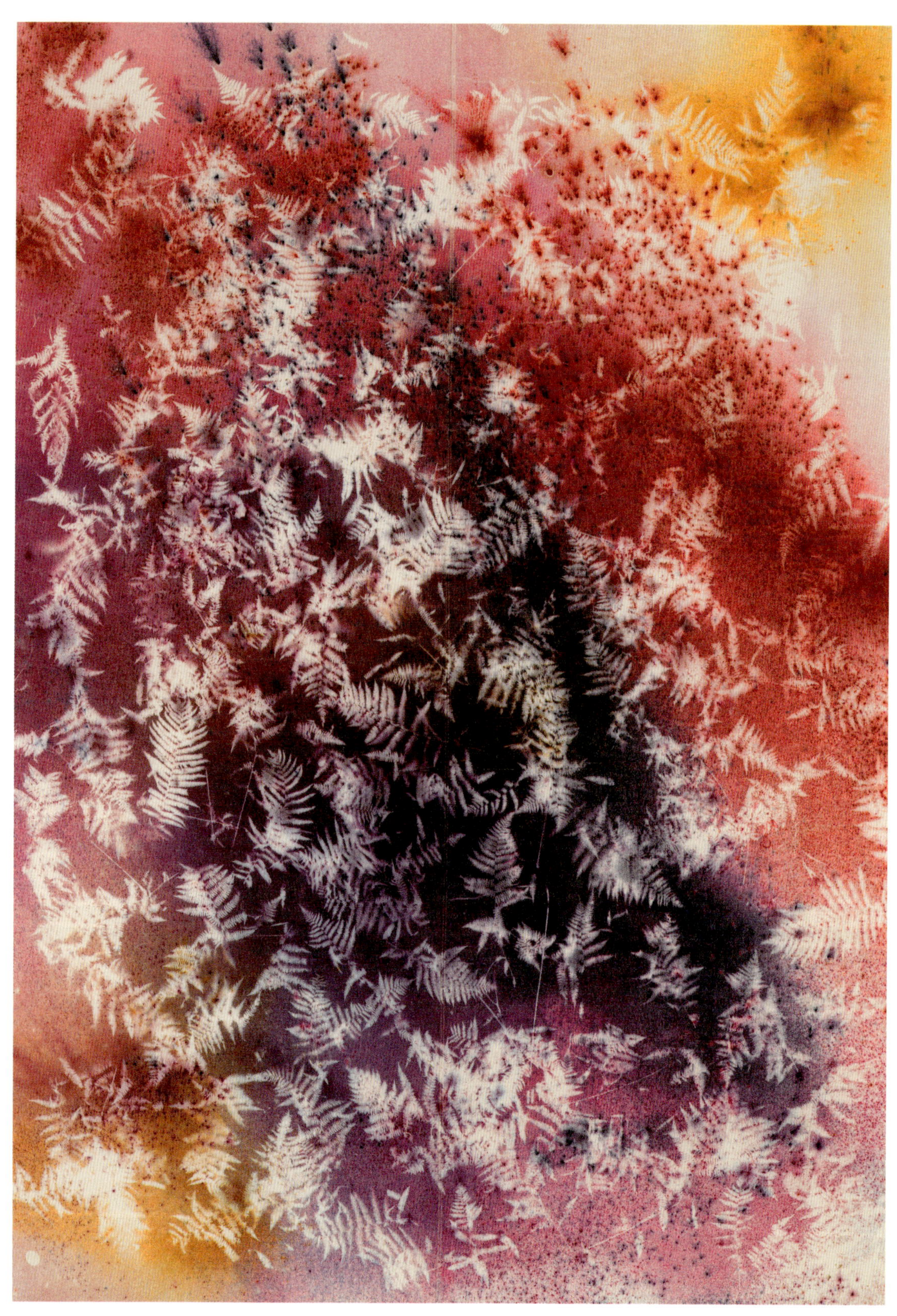

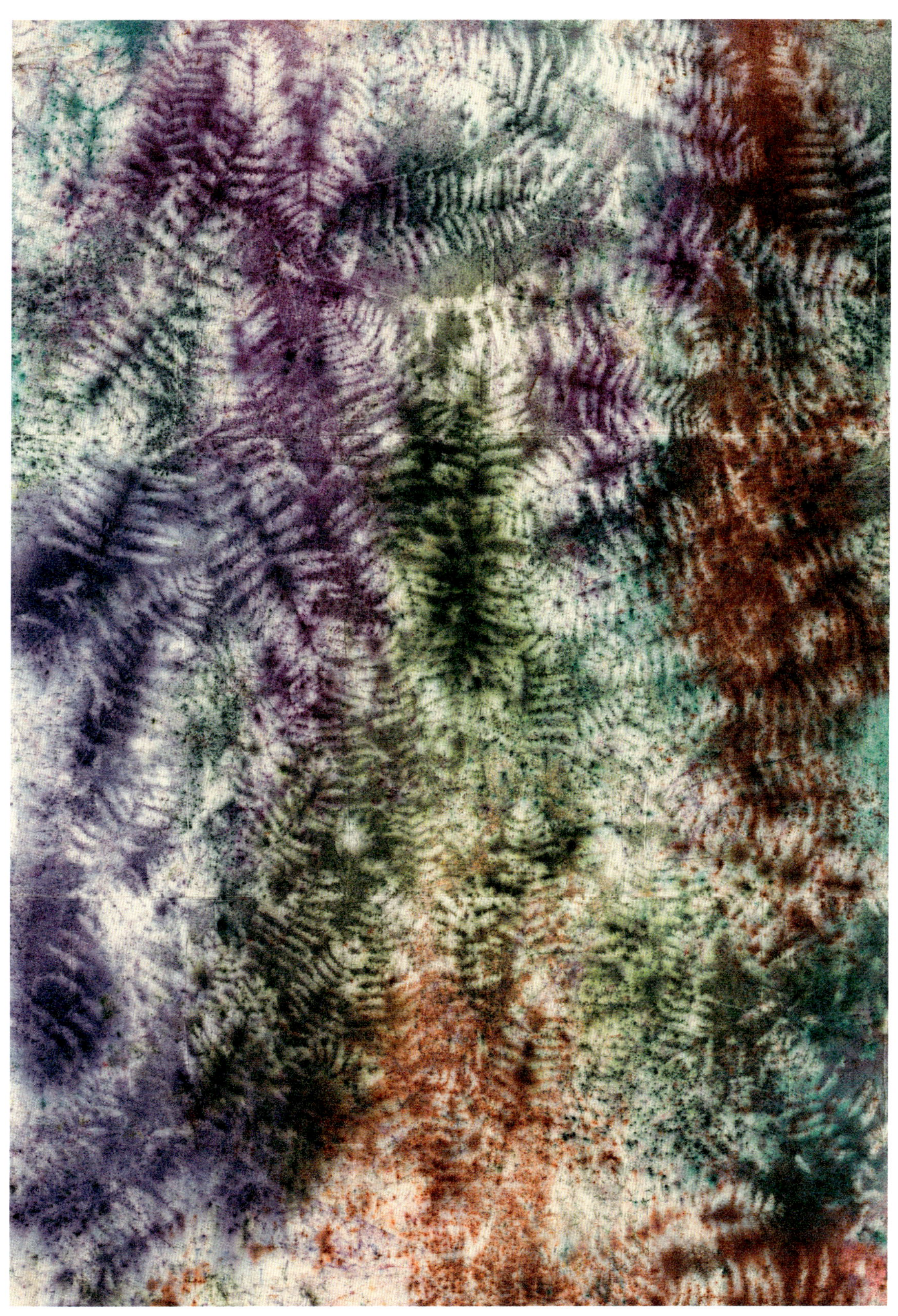

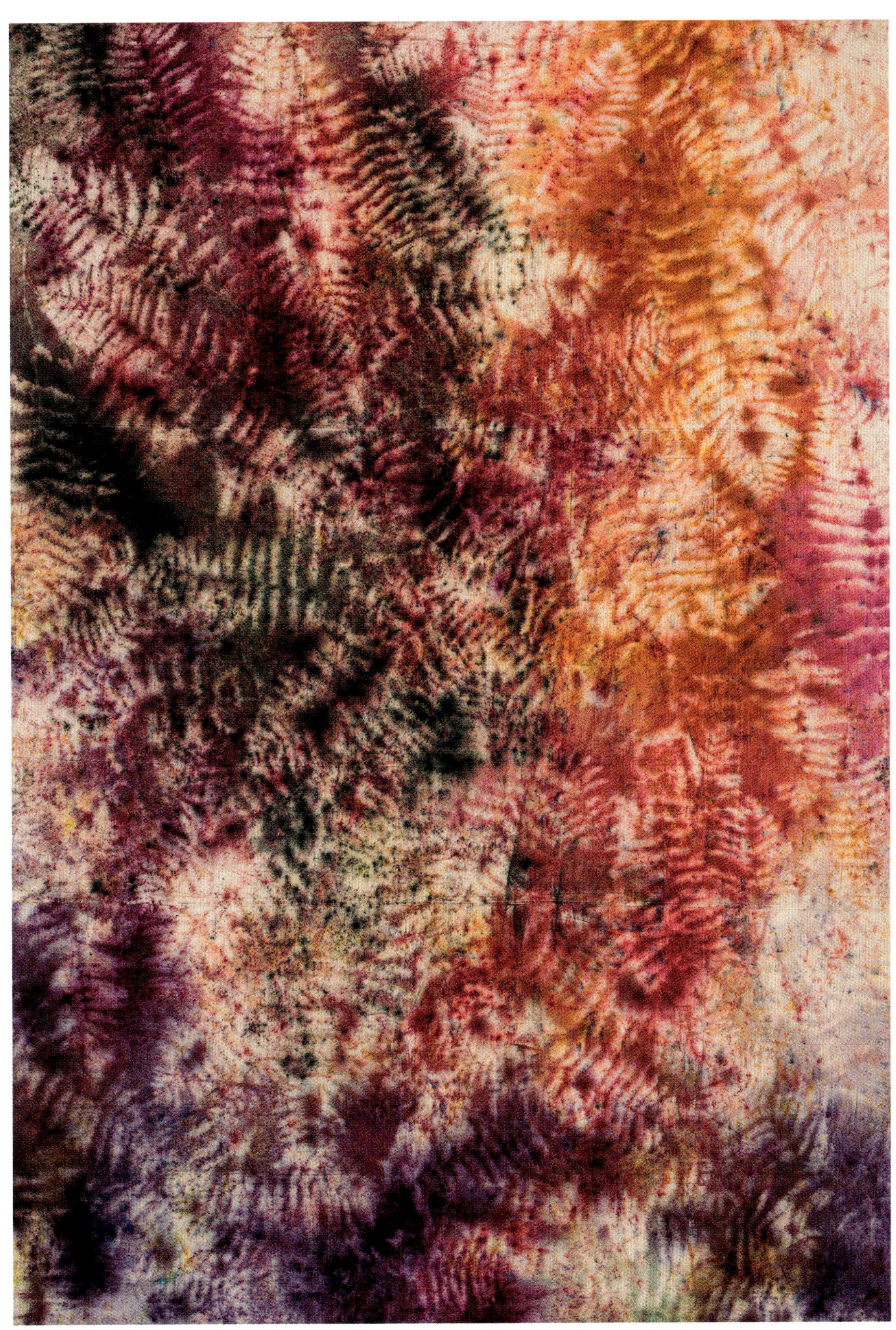

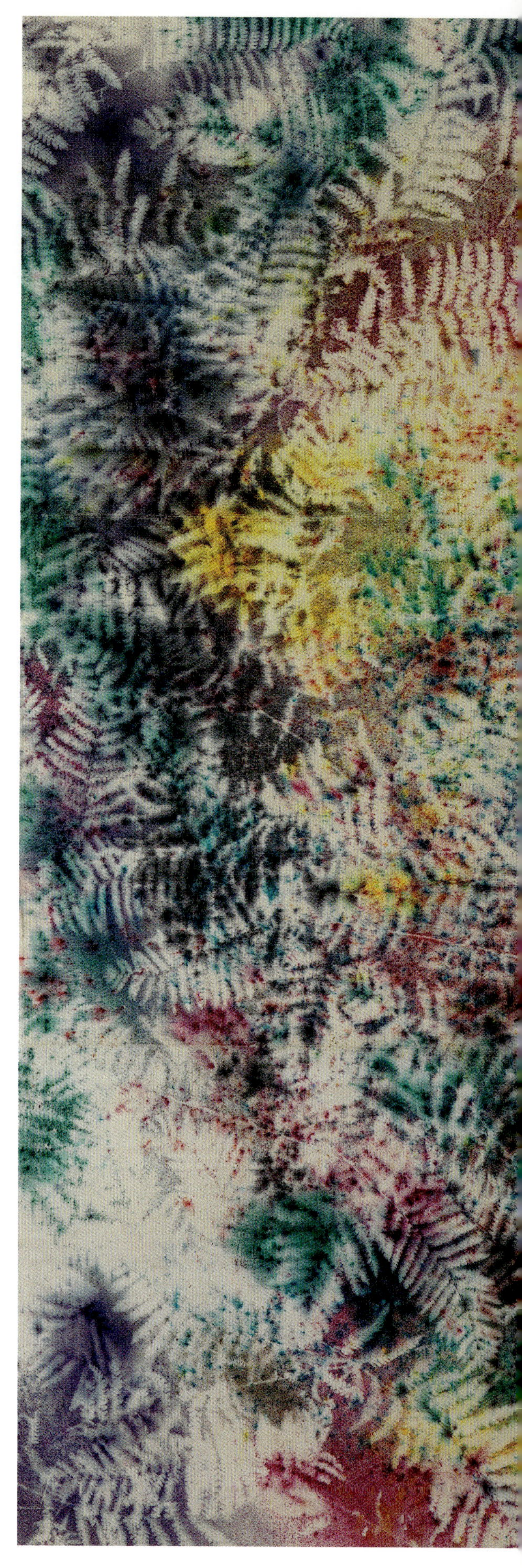

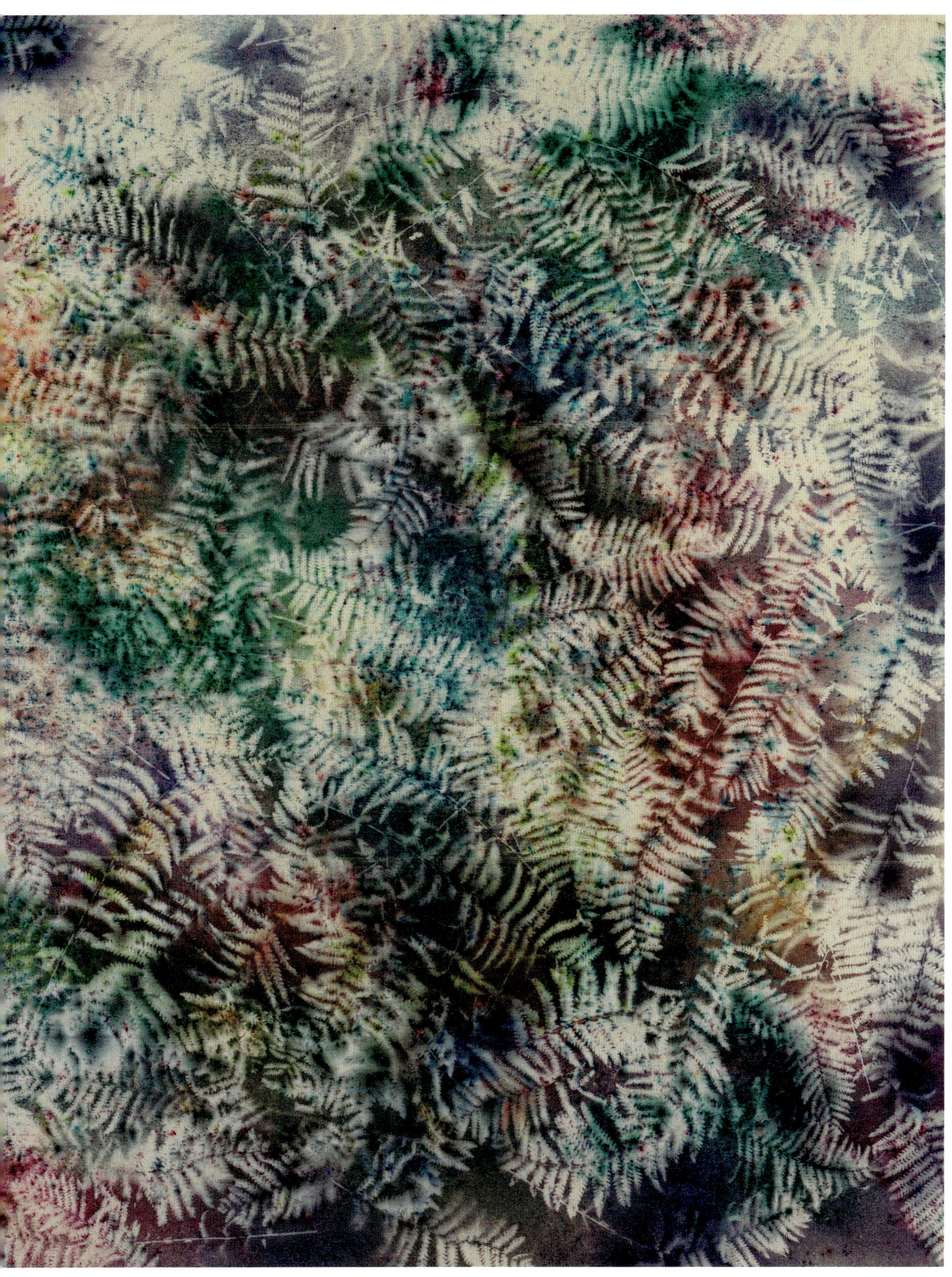

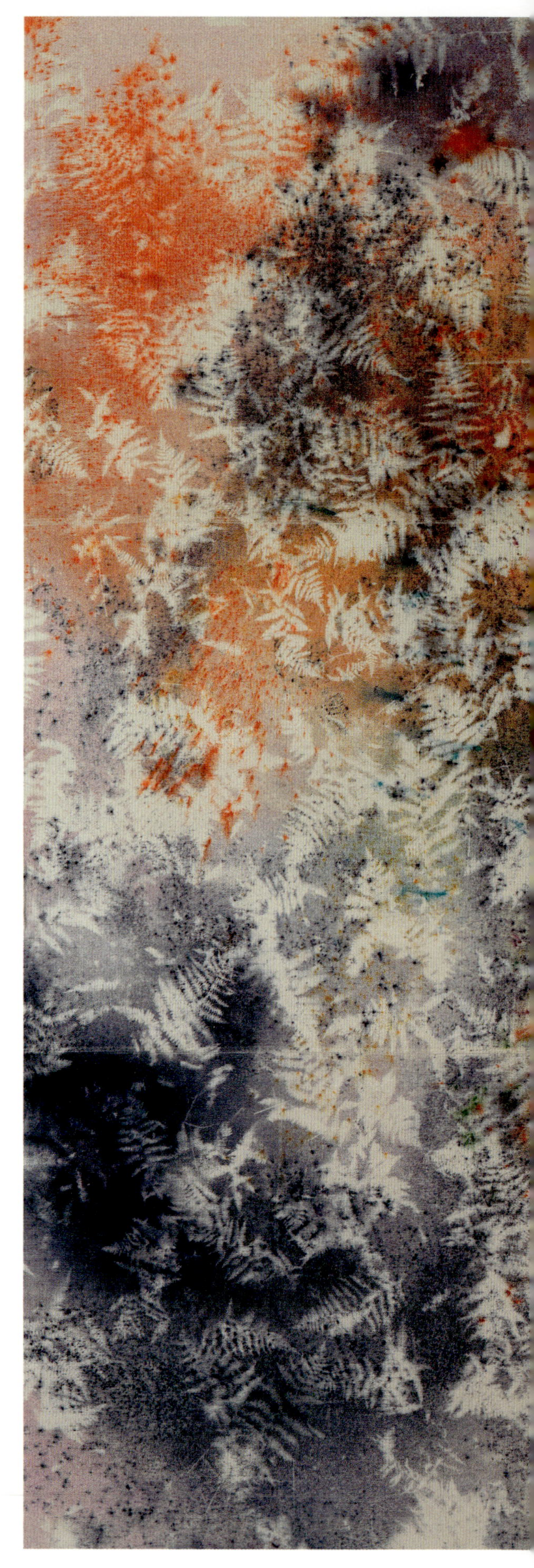

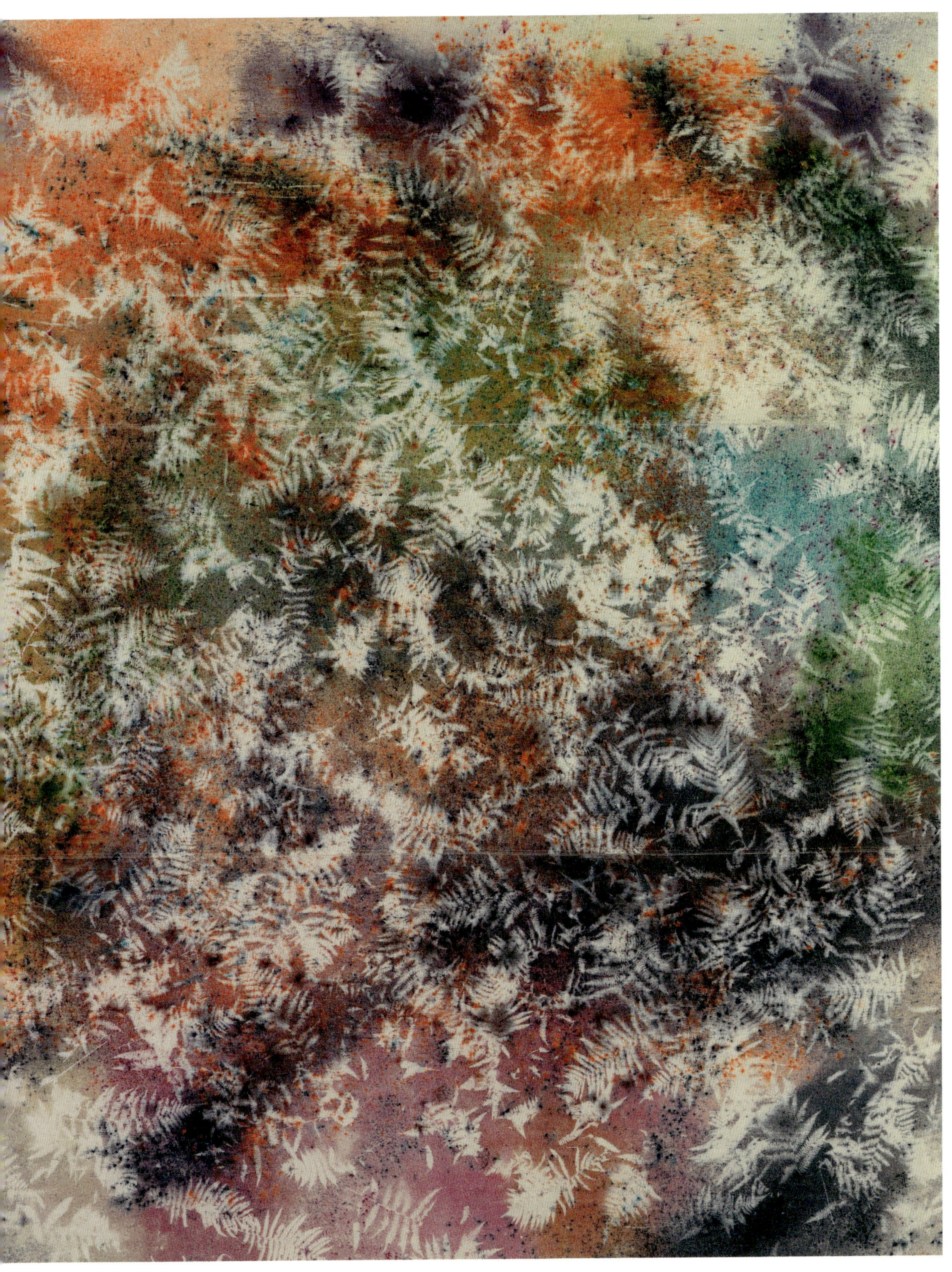

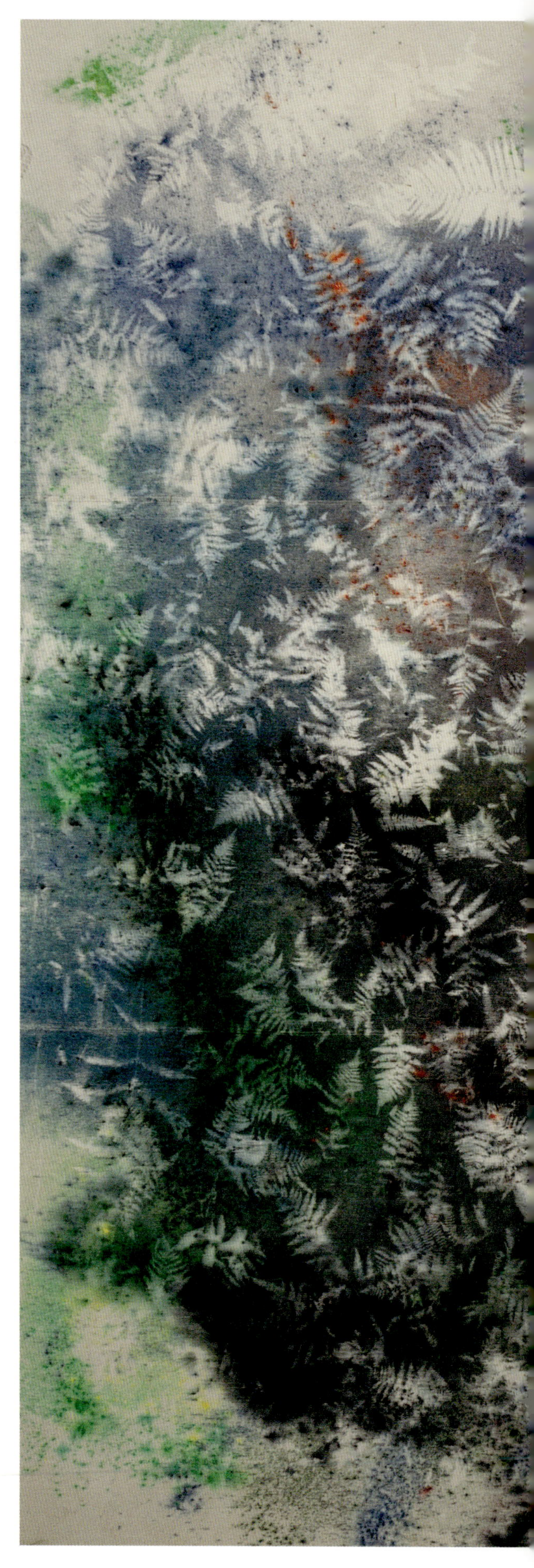

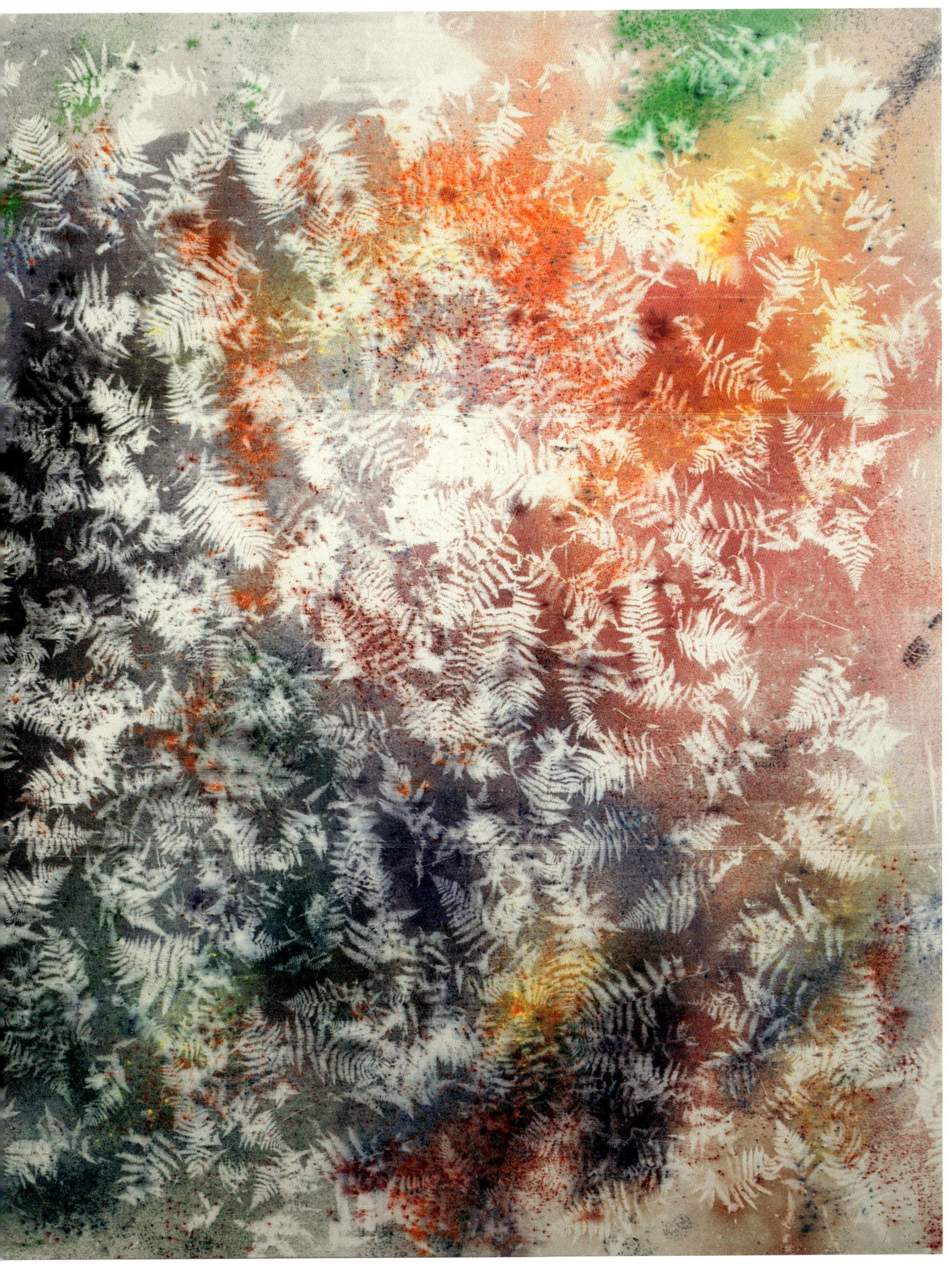

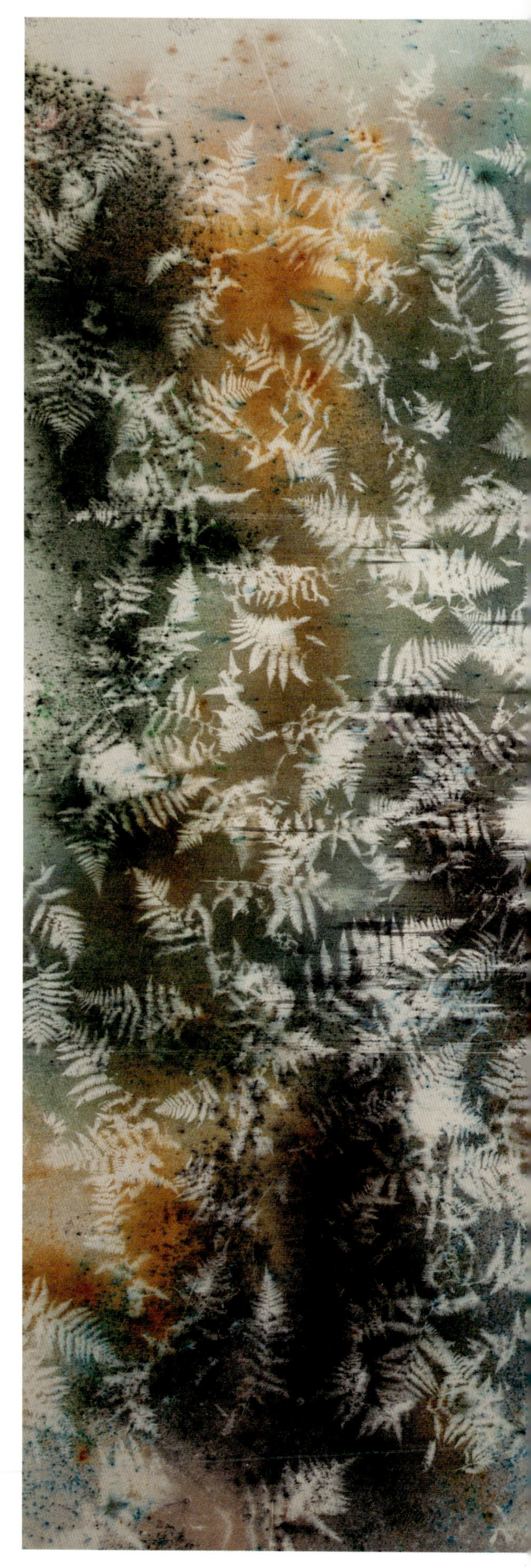

28

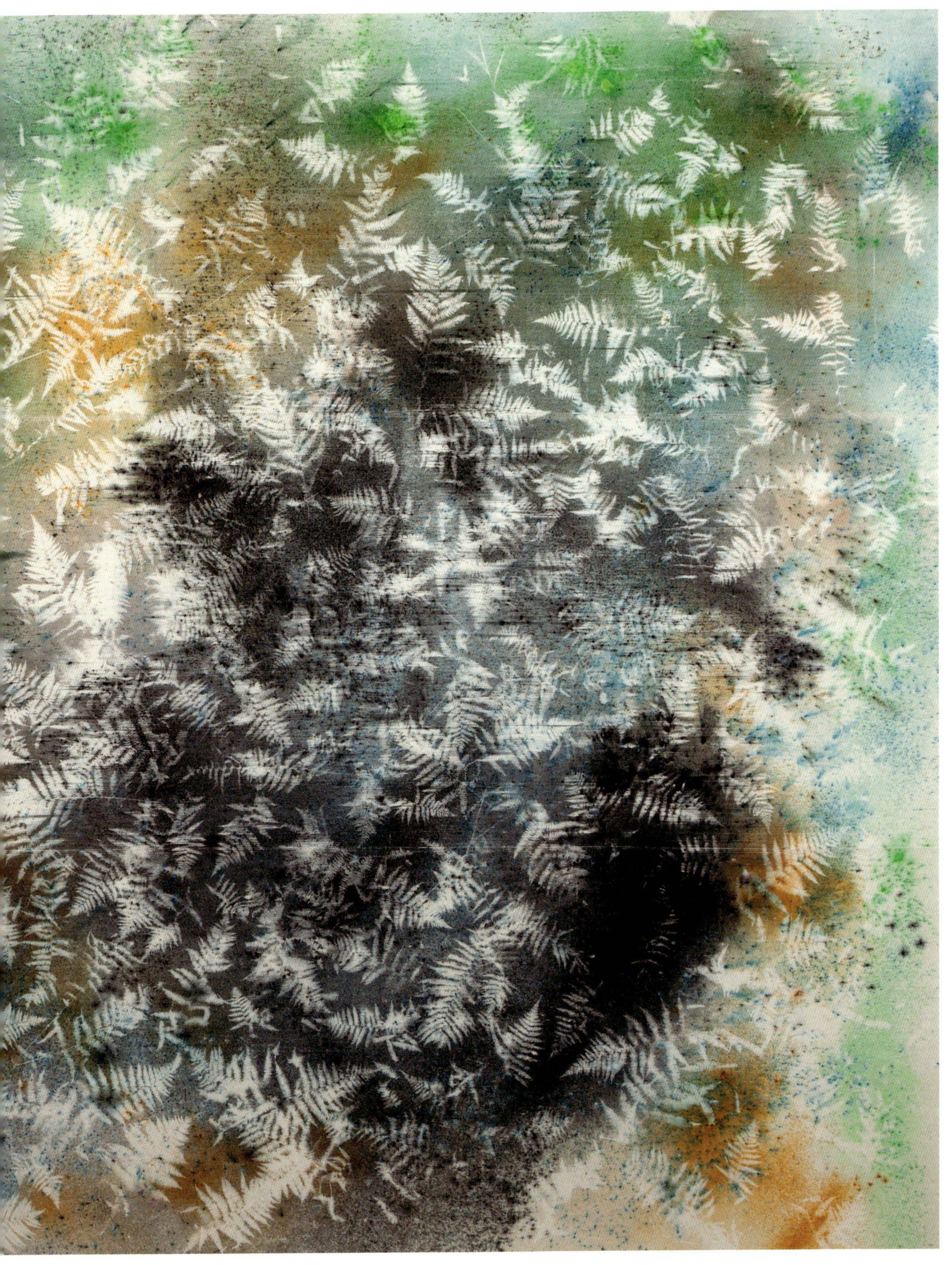

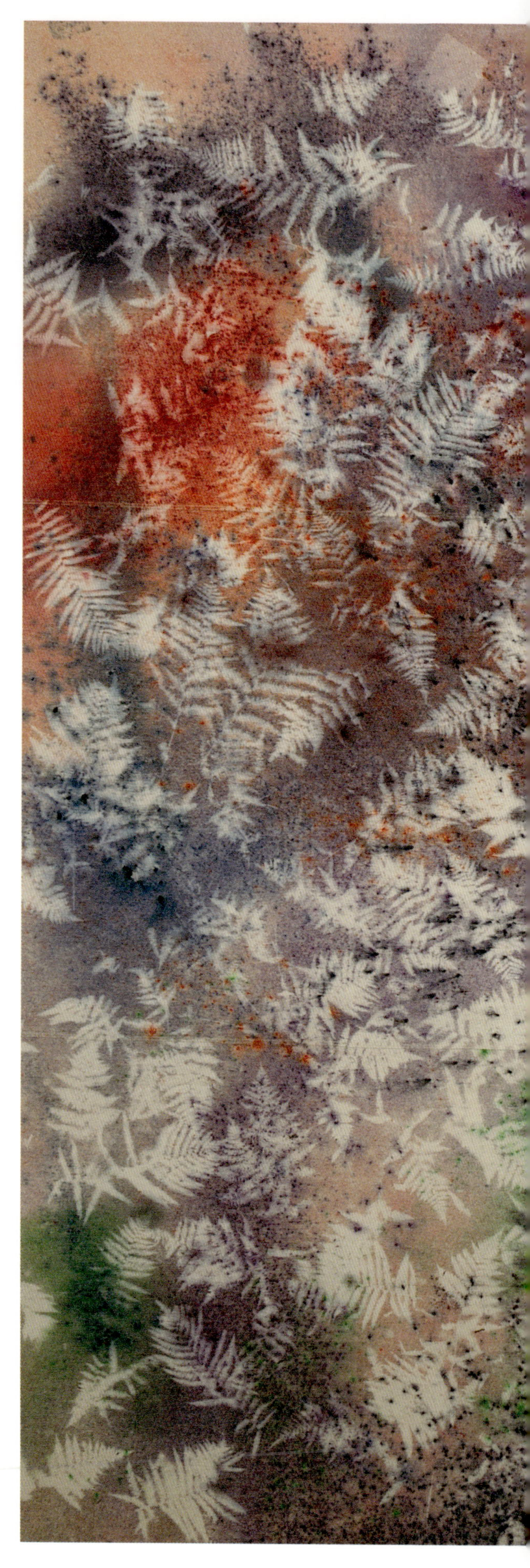

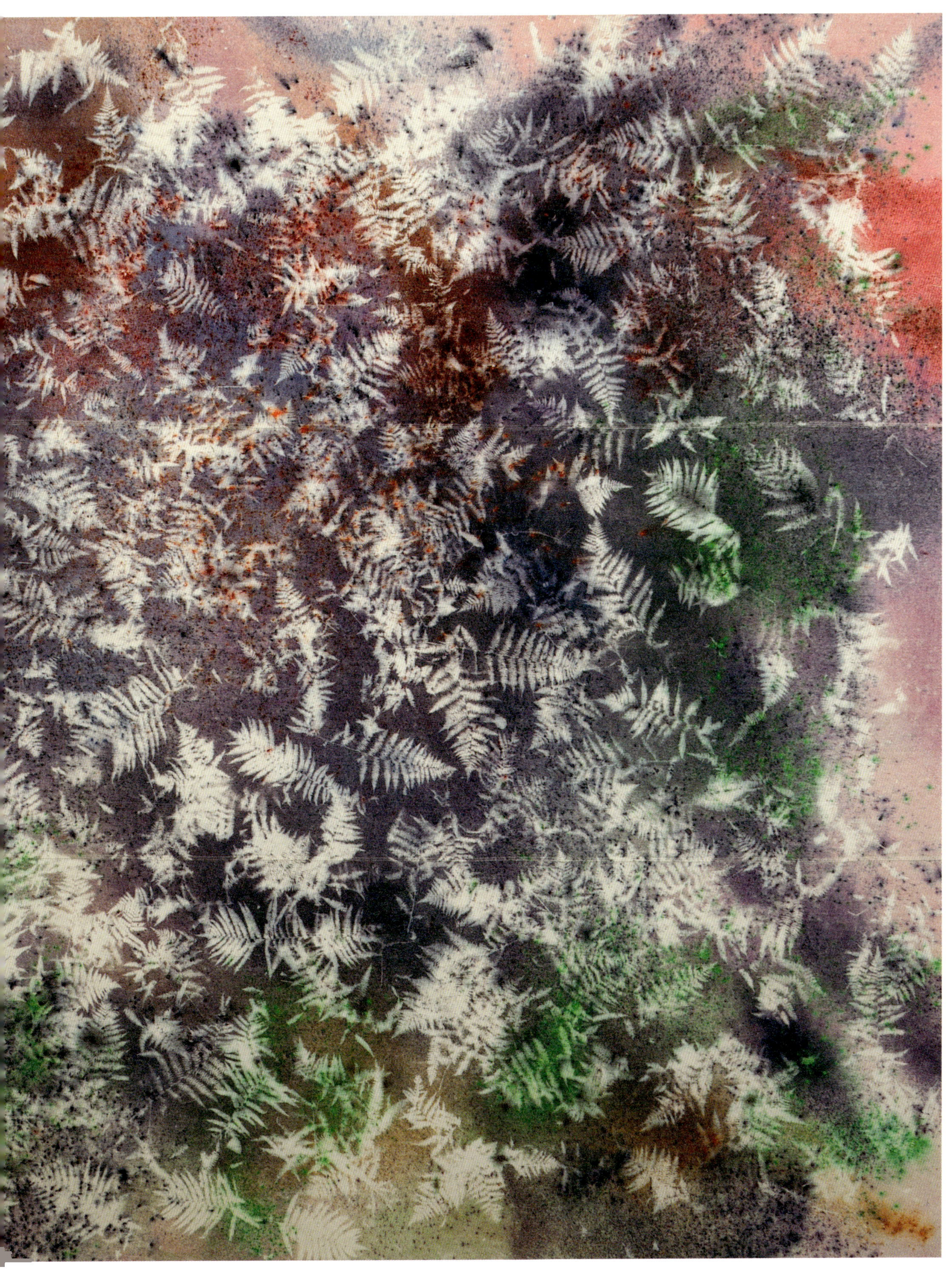

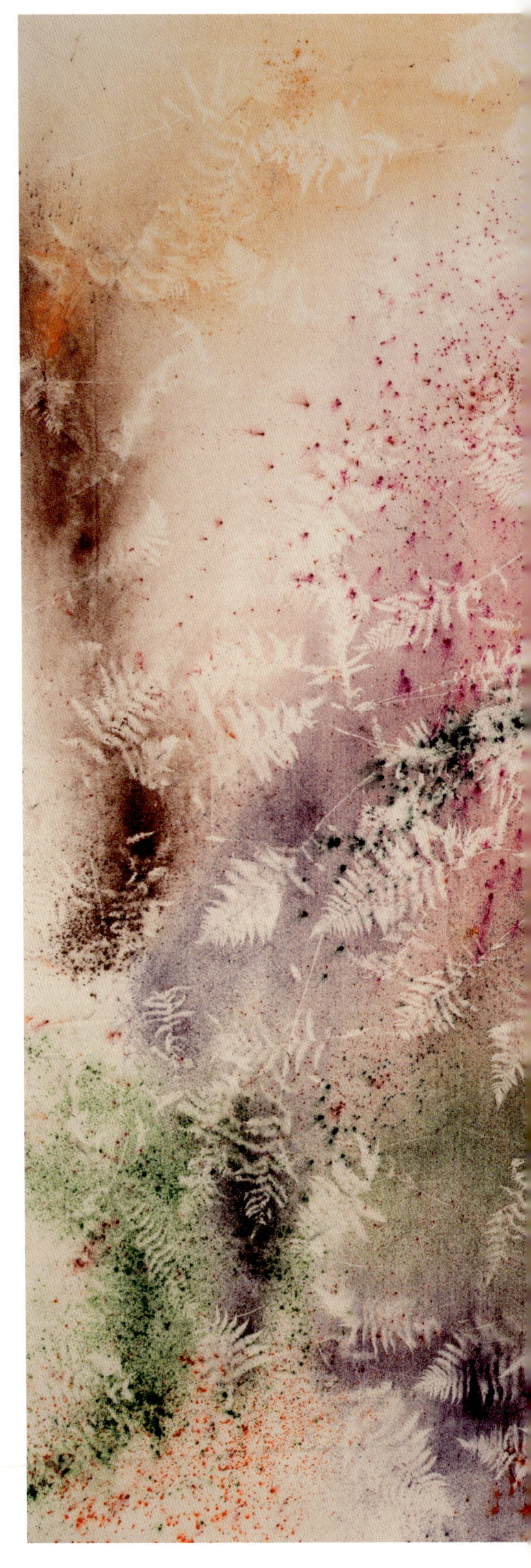

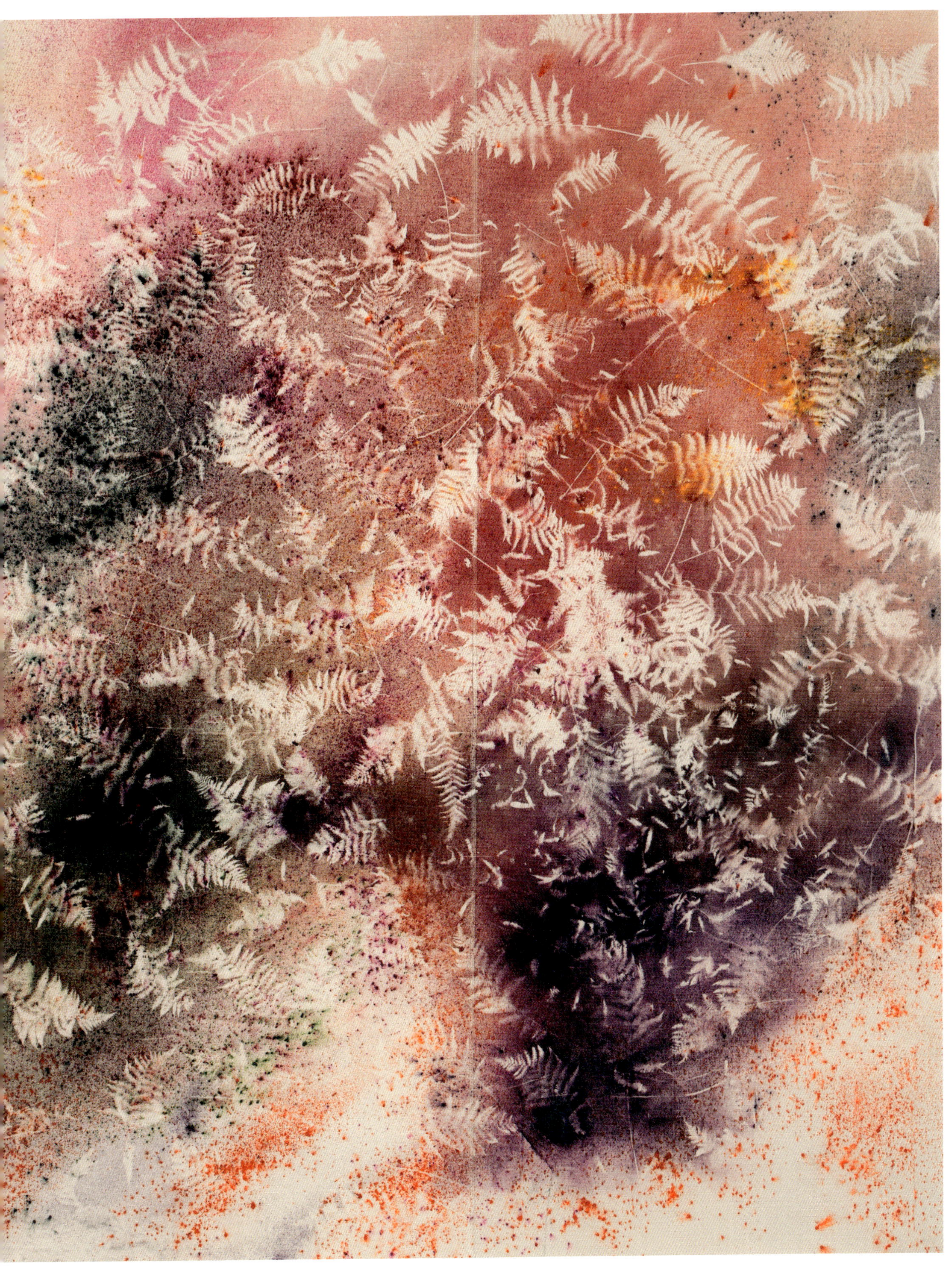

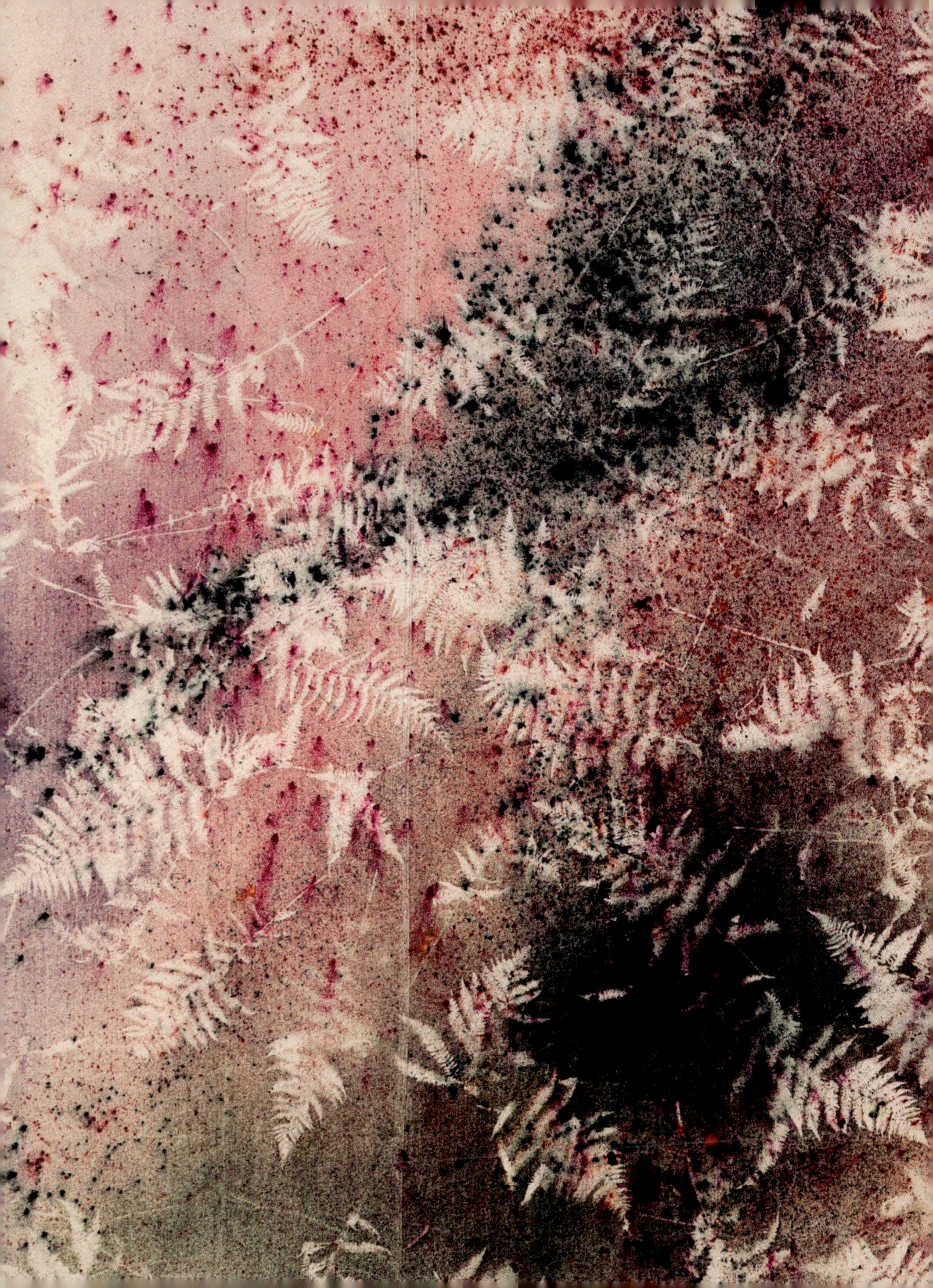

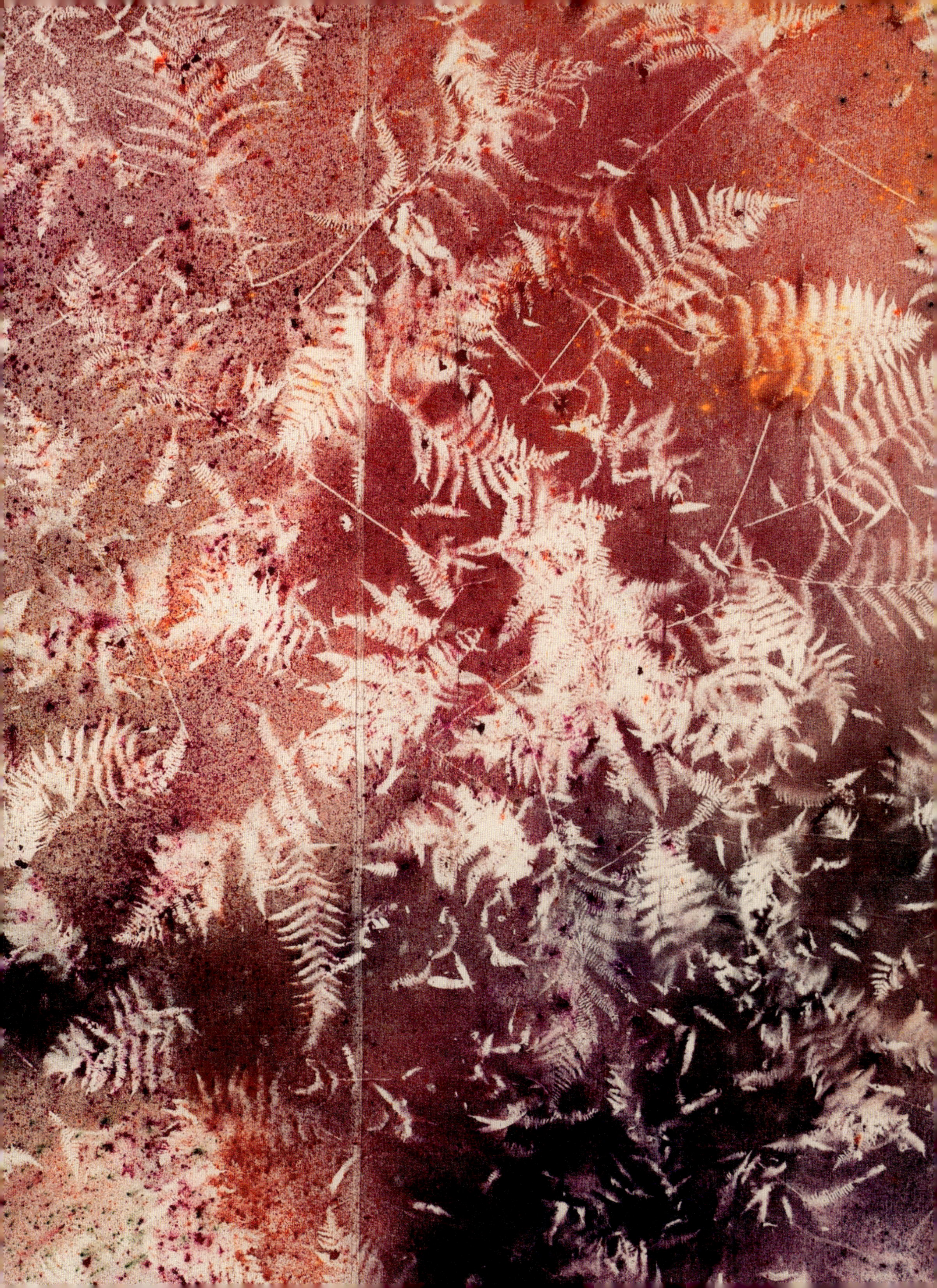

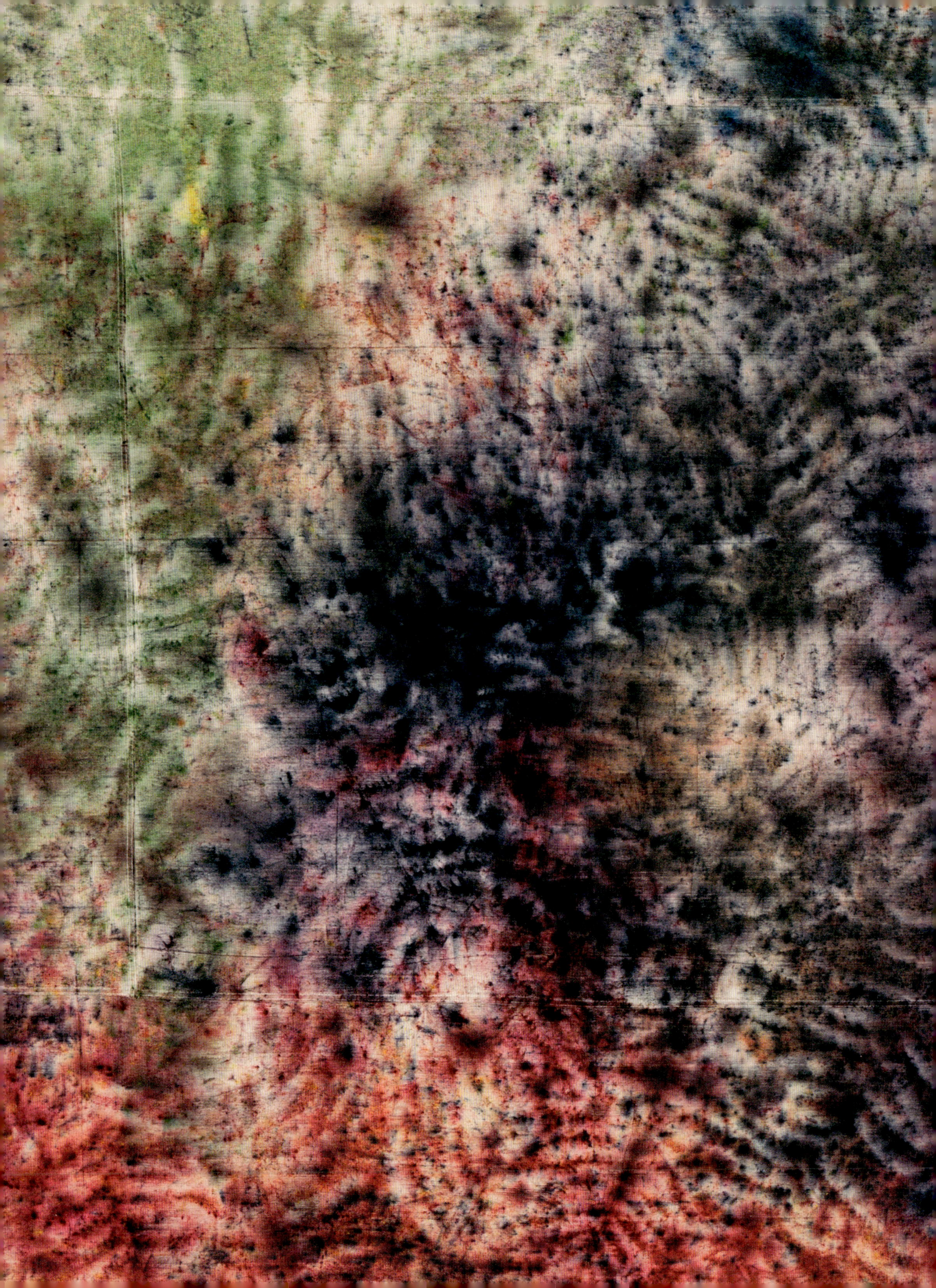

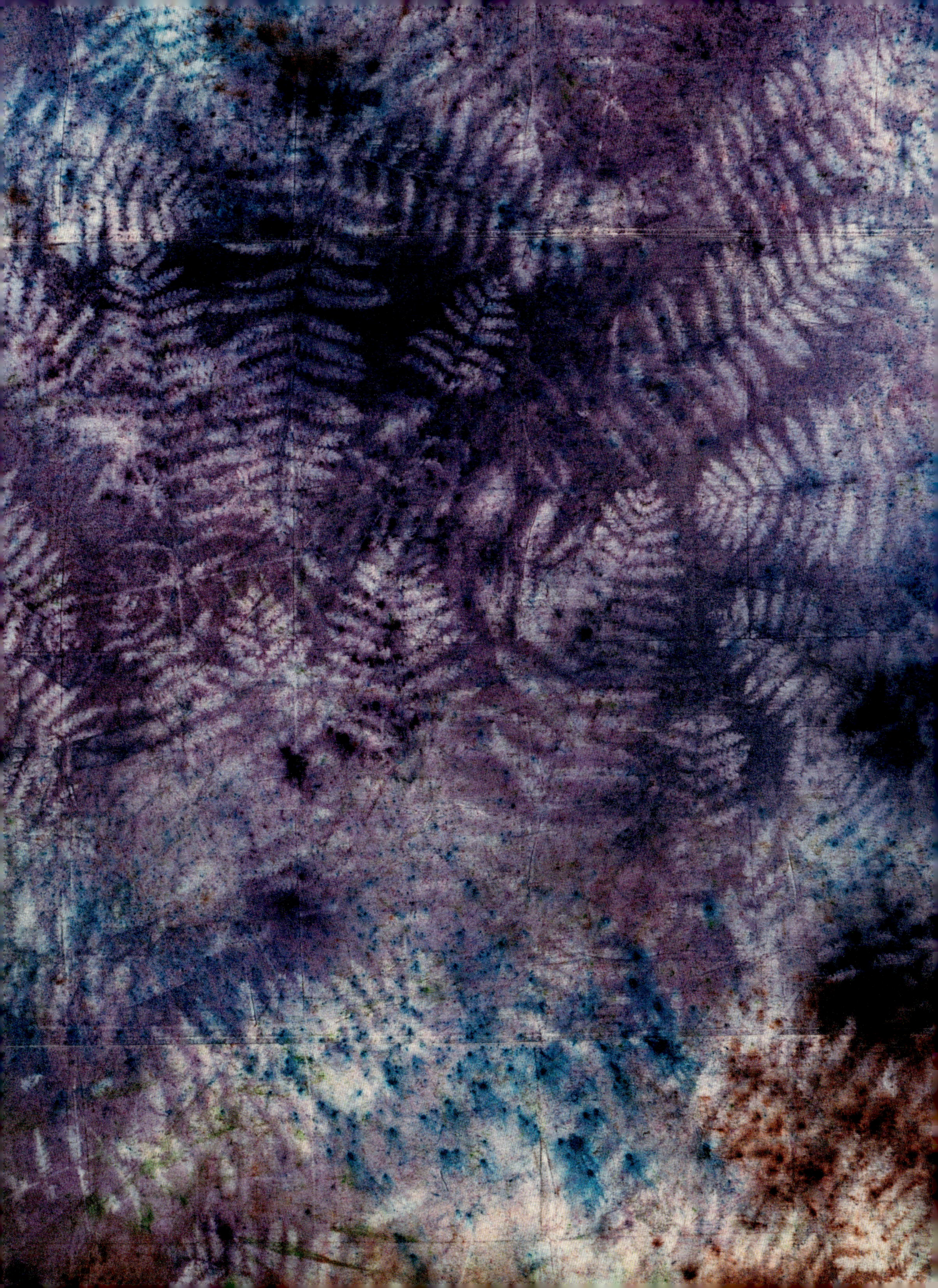

Tony Calderon died on May 17, 2014 in the East Los Angeles neighborhood of Boyle Heights. News of his death came as a shock, not only because he was a father and forty-nine years old at the time, but also because he died at the hand of a one-ton crown of palm fronds. The large mass crushed him mid-sentence while he was having a conversation with his neighbor, but there doesn't seem to be much evidence pointing to the subject of his last words. I've often thought about the warnings I should have offered Calderon prior to that day—warnings about the potential threat of falling palm fronds since their contribution to the number of deaths in the city has steadily inclined. Perhaps these deaths have been the result of the ongoing drought in California, though in a handful of instances residents had used untrained tree-trimmers to rid themselves of the unsightly foliage in order to cut costs and there were consequences. Calderon, it seems, was as much a victim of climate change as he was the economy. Since that day, and every time the "devil winds" come in from the deserts and leave a trail of wreckage and debris in their path, I think about his untimely death and how many people must die each year from falling palm fronds. It was a stockpile of delinquent brush that did him in, but how many others are struck by individual fronds that rip away from impossibly long trunks like projectiles launched from thirty- to forty-foot-high canopies? Los Angeles is littered with palm tree fronds after any significant windstorm, like remnants or fallout from a recent disaster. In the aftermath, residents of particularly tree-lined streets navigate this burden. Car-sized mounds accumulate in parking spaces, towering heaps block sidewalks and roads until the city takes them away. These makeshift mountains are memorials to Calderon, and those like him, whose bodies will be forever interred beneath the crushing weight of the city's most illustrious icon.

VENICE, CA

43.
Untitled (Venice, CA, Palm 17), 2014
Pigment on canvas
48 × 38 inches
(121.9 × 96.5 cm)

45.
Untitled (Venice, CA, Palm 5), 2014
Pigment on canvas
81 × 72 inches
(205.7 × 182.9 cm)

46–47.
Untitled (Venice, CA, Ivy 1), 2014
Pigment on canvas
76 × 288¼ inches
(193 × 732 cm)

48.
Untitled (Venice, CA, Palm drawing 2, diptych), 2014
Pigment on paper
18¼ × 24 inches
(46.5 × 61 cm), each

49.
Untitled (Venice, CA, Palm drawing 3, diptych), 2014
Pigment on paper
18¼ × 24 inches
(46.5 × 61 cm), each

51.
Untitled (Venice, CA, Birds of Paradise drawing 1, diptych), 2014
Pigment on paper
18¼ × 24 inches
(46.5 × 61 cm), each

53.
Untitled (Venice, CA, Palms 18), 2014
Pigment on canvas
97 × 73 inches
(246.4 × 185.4 cm)

54.
Untitled (Venice, CA, Palm drawing 5), 2014
Pigment on paper
24 × 18¼ inches
(61 × 46.5 cm)

55.
Untitled (Venice, CA, Palm drawing 7), 2014
Pigment on paper
24 × 18¼ inches
(61 × 46.5 cm)

57.
Untitled (Venice, CA, Palm drawing 6), 2014
Pigment on paper
24 × 18¼ inches
(61 × 46.5 cm)

59.
Untitled (Venice, CA, Palm drawing 8, diptych), 2014
Pigment on paper
18¼ × 24 inches
(46.5 × 61 cm), each

60.
Untitled (Venice, CA, Birds of Paradise drawing 2), 2014
Pigment on paper
24 × 18 inches
(61 × 45.7 cm)

61.
Untitled (Venice, CA, Birds of Paradise drawing 5), 2014
Pigment on paper
24 × 18 inches
(61 × 45.7 cm)

62.
Untitled (Venice, CA, Birds of Paradise drawing 3), 2014
Pigment on paper
24 × 18 inches
(61 × 45.7 cm)

63.
Untitled (Venice, CA, Birds of Paradise drawing 4), 2014
Pigment on paper
24 × 18 inches
(61 × 45.7 cm)

65.
Untitled (Venice, CA, Birds of Paradise 2), 2014
Pigment on canvas
101 × 73 inches
(256.5 × 185.4 cm)

66.
Untitled (Venice, CA, Palms 13), 2014
Pigment on canvas
116 × 76 inches
(294.5 × 193 cm)

67.
Untitled (Venice, CA, Palms 8), 2014
Pigment on canvas
116 × 76 inches
(294.5 × 193 cm)

69.
Untitled (Venice, CA, Palm 1), 2014
Pigment on canvas
120 × 76 inches
(304.8 × 193 cm)

71.
Untitled (Venice, CA, Palm 12), 2014
Pigment on canvas
100 × 76 inches
(254 × 193 cm)

73.
Untitled (Venice, CA, Palm 10), 2014
Pigment on canvas
106 × 76 inches
(269 × 193 cm)

75.
Untitled (Venice, CA, Palm 11), 2014
Pigment on canvas
97 × 76 inches
(246.4 × 193 cm)

77.
Untitled (Venice, CA, Palm 9), 2014
Pigment on canvas
98 × 74 inches
(249 × 188 cm)

79.
Untitled (Venice, CA, Palm 2), 2014
Pigment on canvas
94 × 65 inches
(238.6 × 165.1 cm)

80.
Untitled (Venice, CA, Palm 6), 2014
Pigment on canvas
87 × 63 inches
(221 × 160 cm)

81.
Untitled (Venice, CA, Palm 3), 2014
Pigment on canvas
94 × 65 inches
(238.6 × 165.1 cm)

83.
Untitled (Venice, CA, Palm 7), 2014
Pigment on canvas
96 × 76 inches
(244 × 193 cm)

85.
Untitled (Venice, CA, Palm 14), 2014
Pigment on canvas
96 × 73 inches
(244 × 185.4 cm)

86–89.
Details of *Untitled (Venice, CA, Palms 18)*

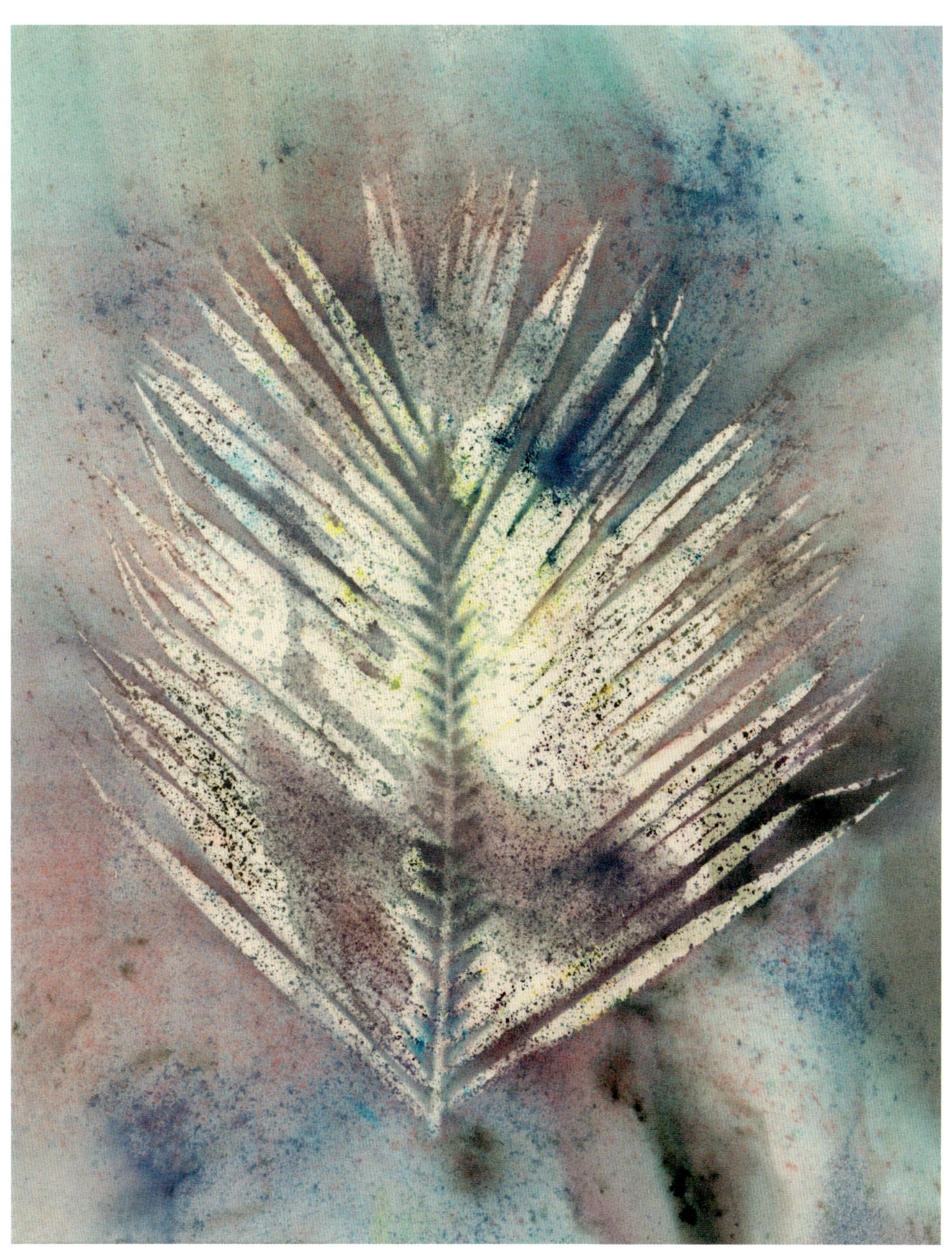

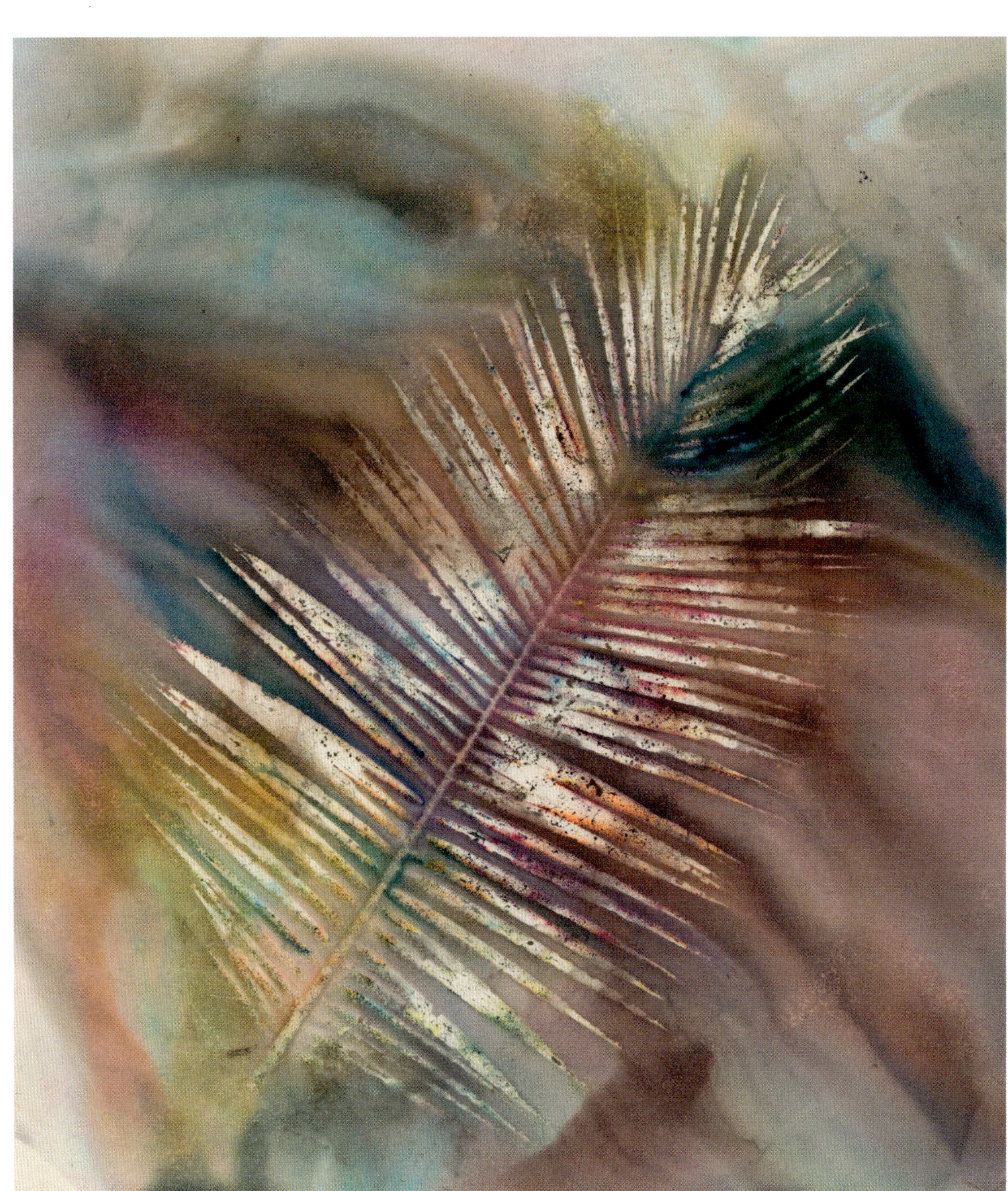

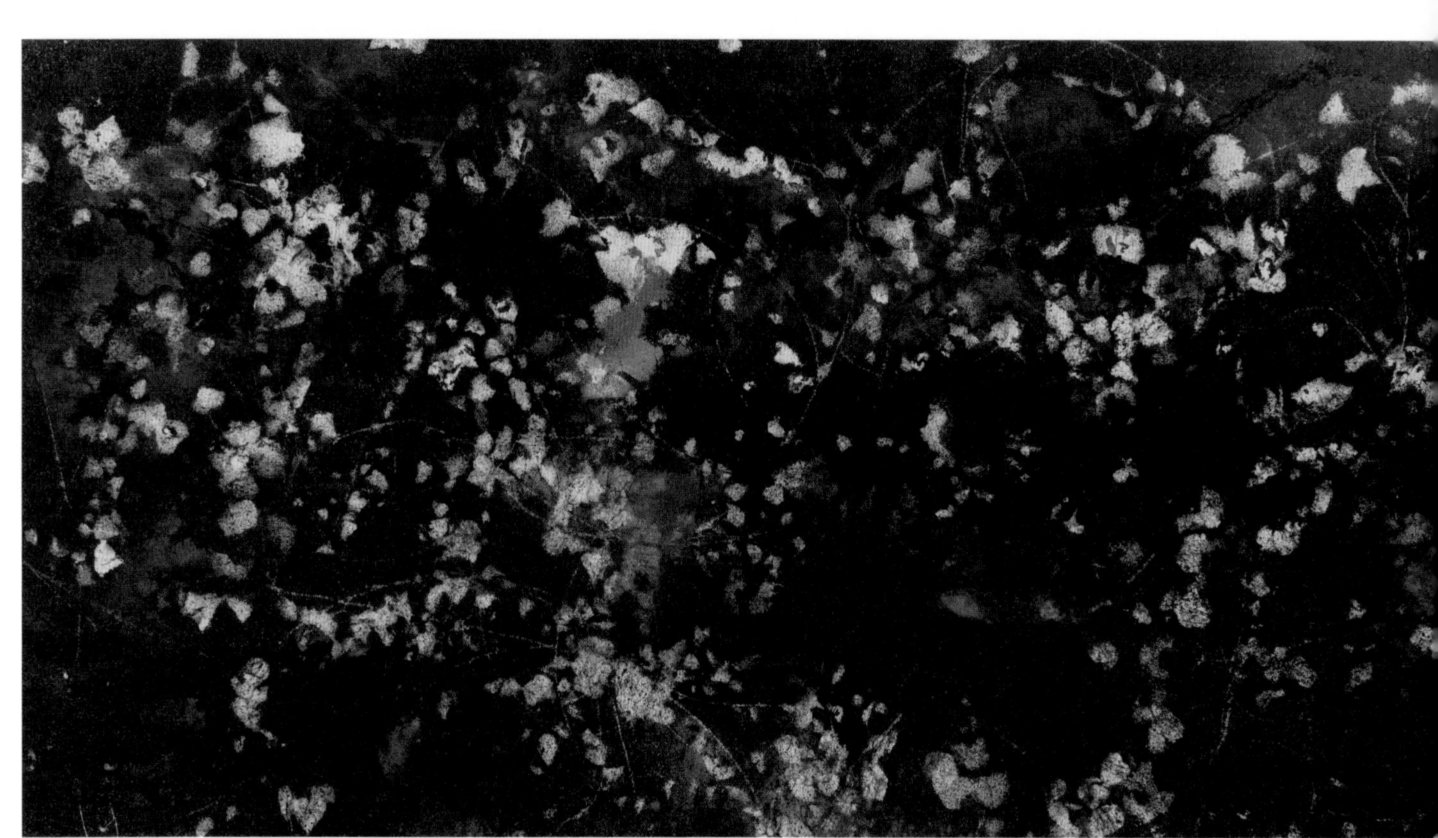

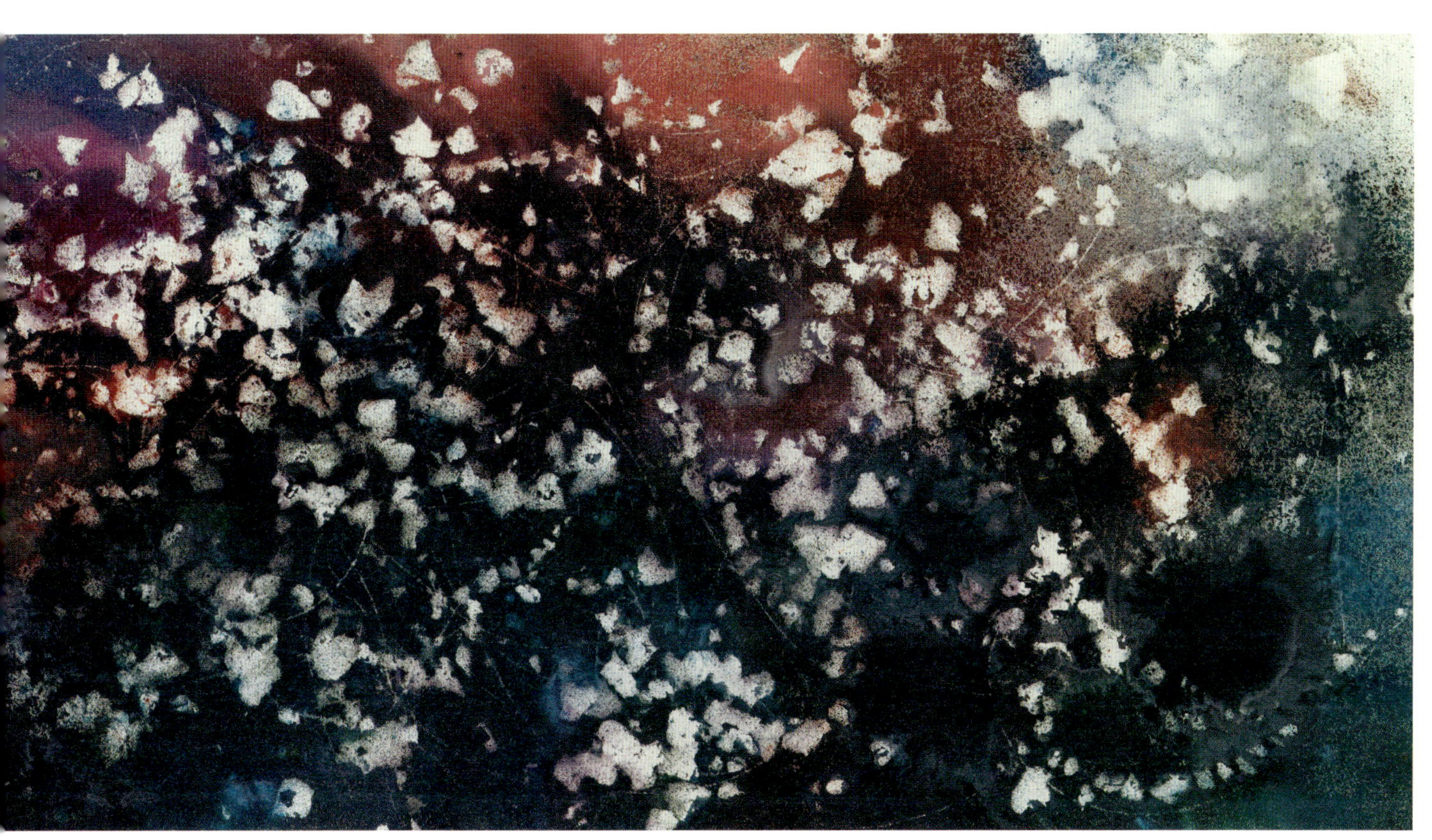

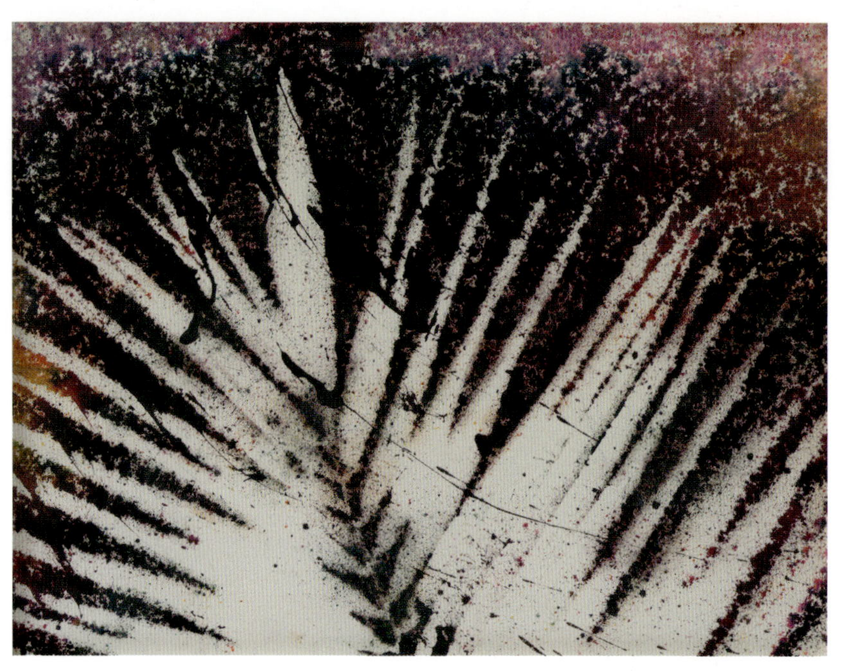

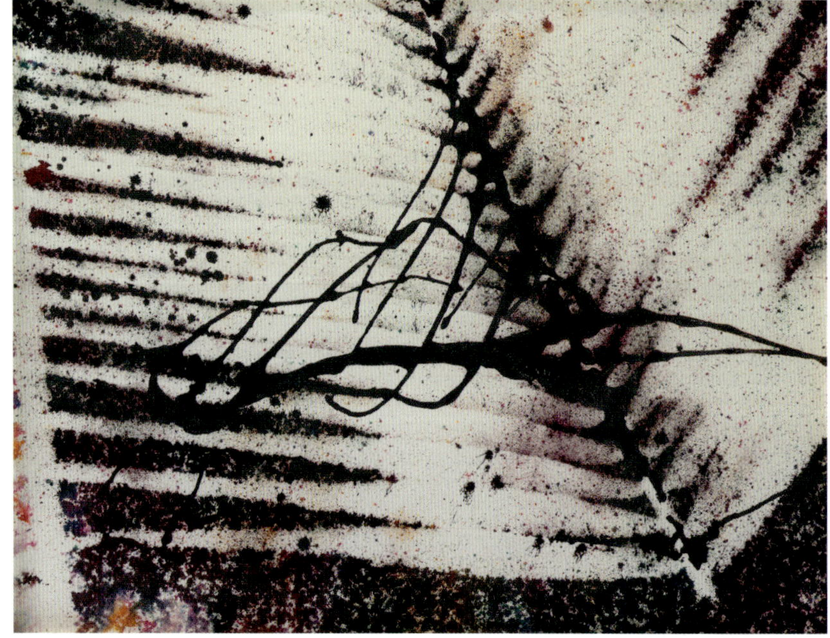

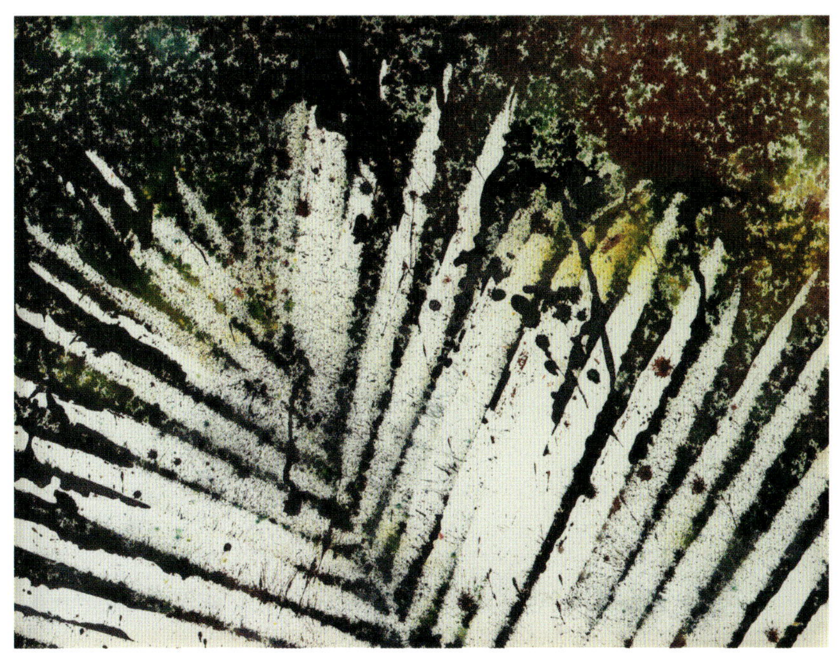

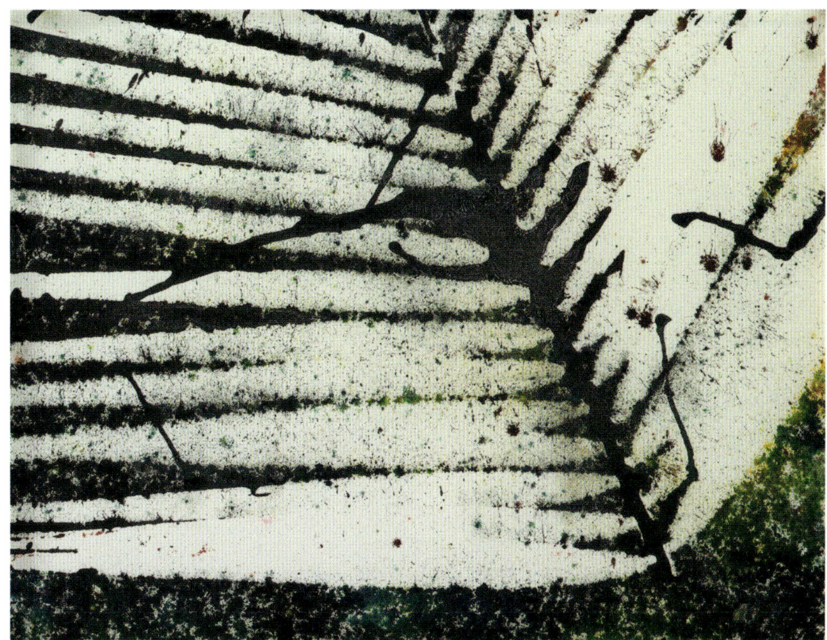

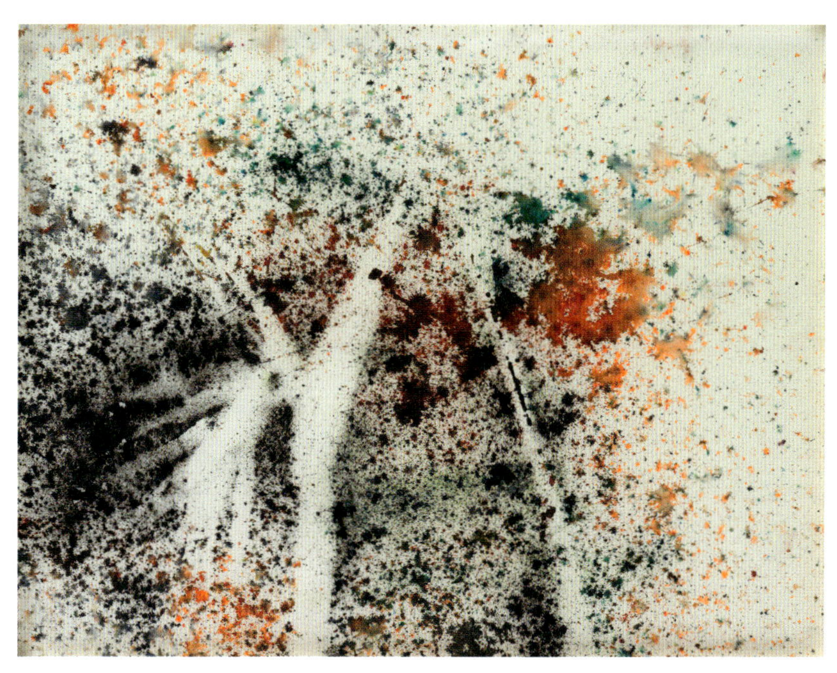

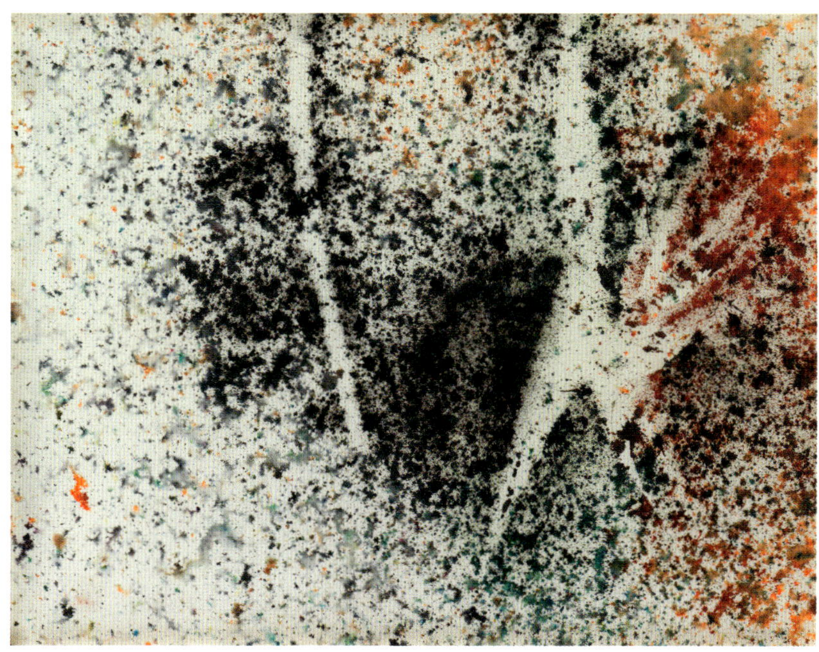

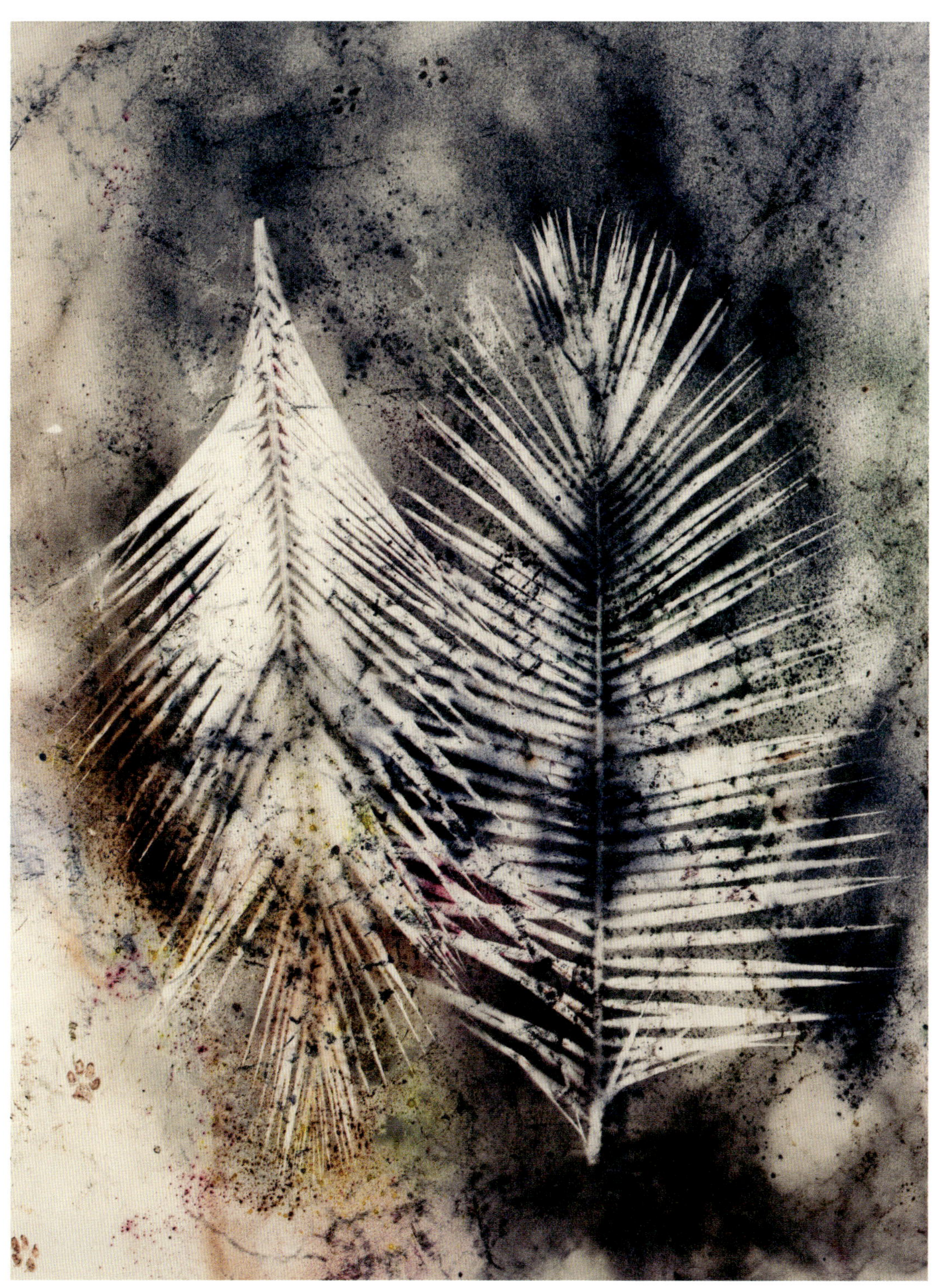

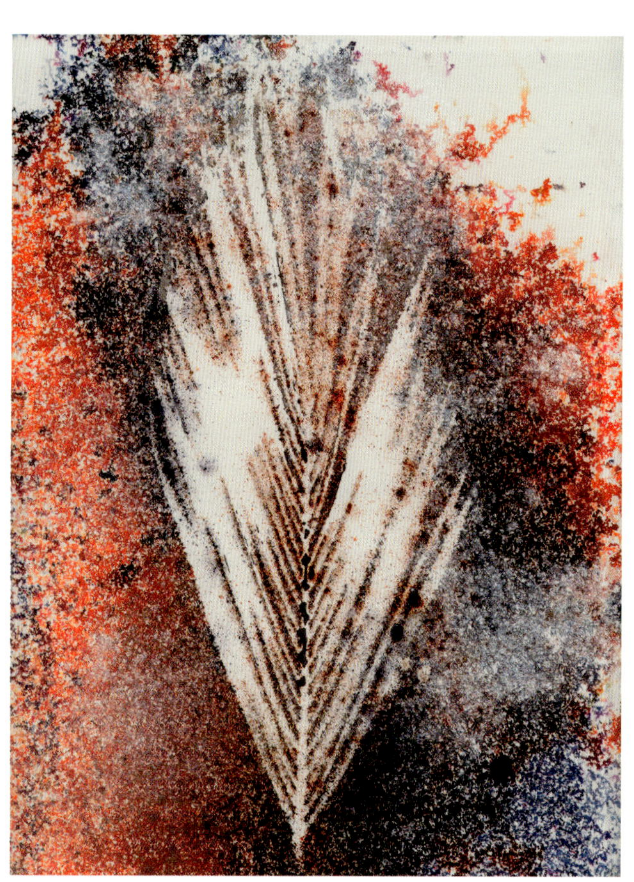

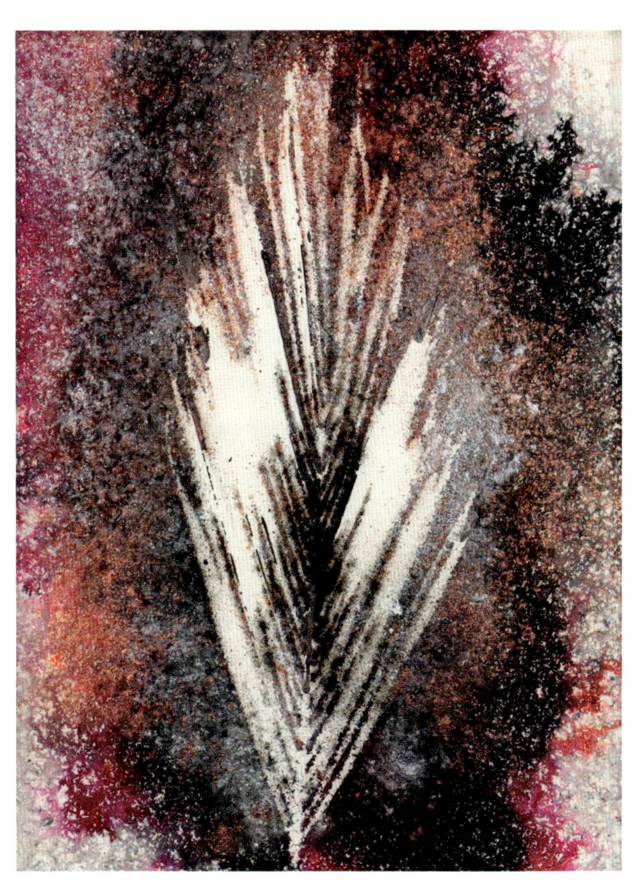

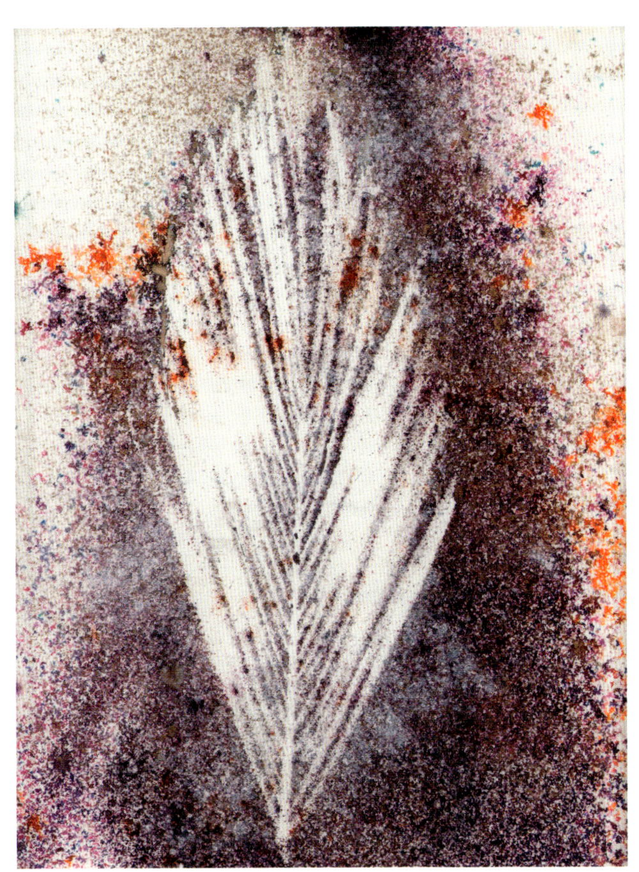

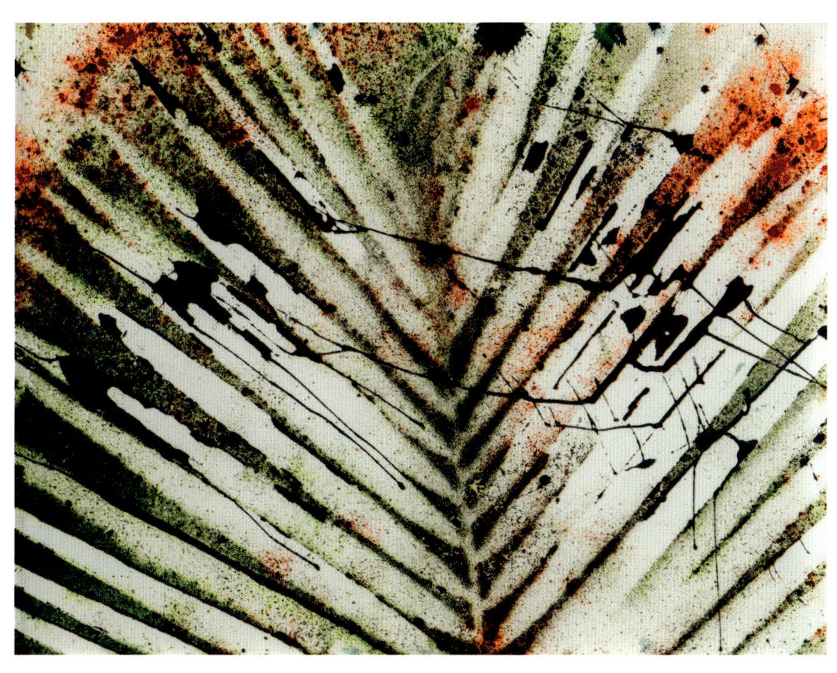

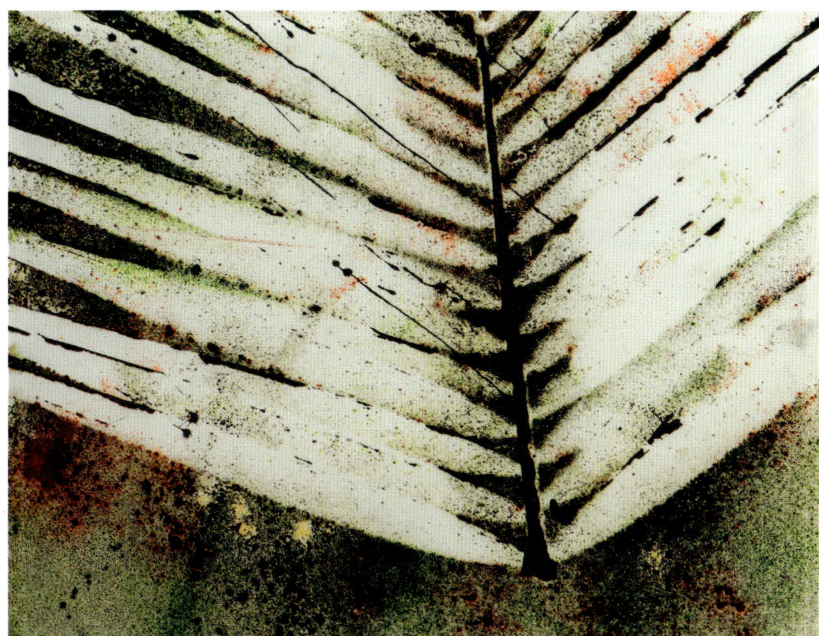

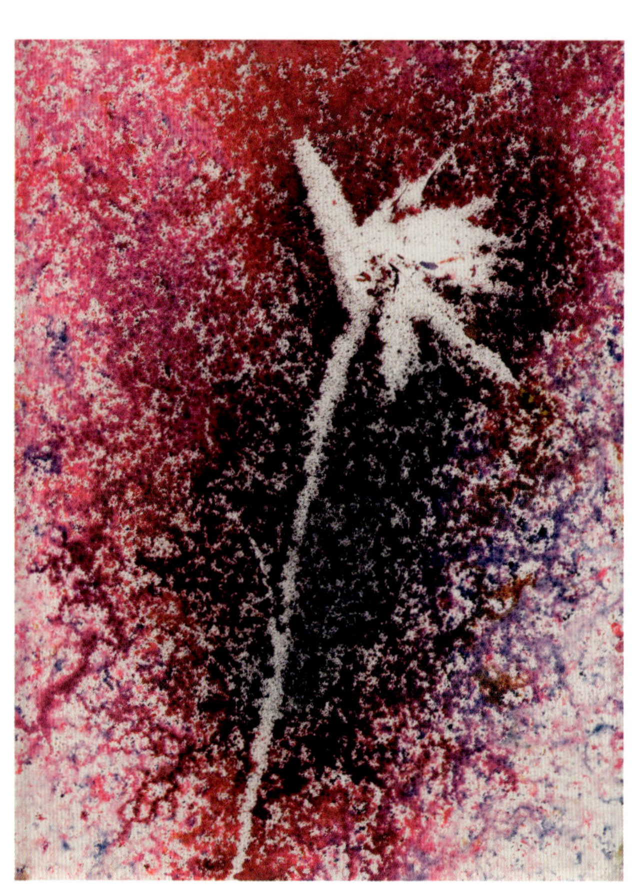

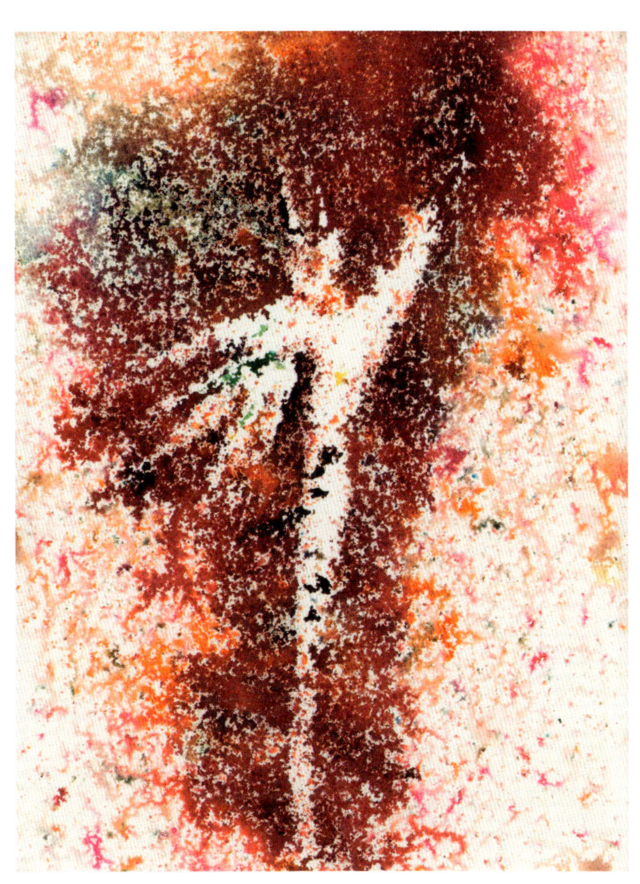

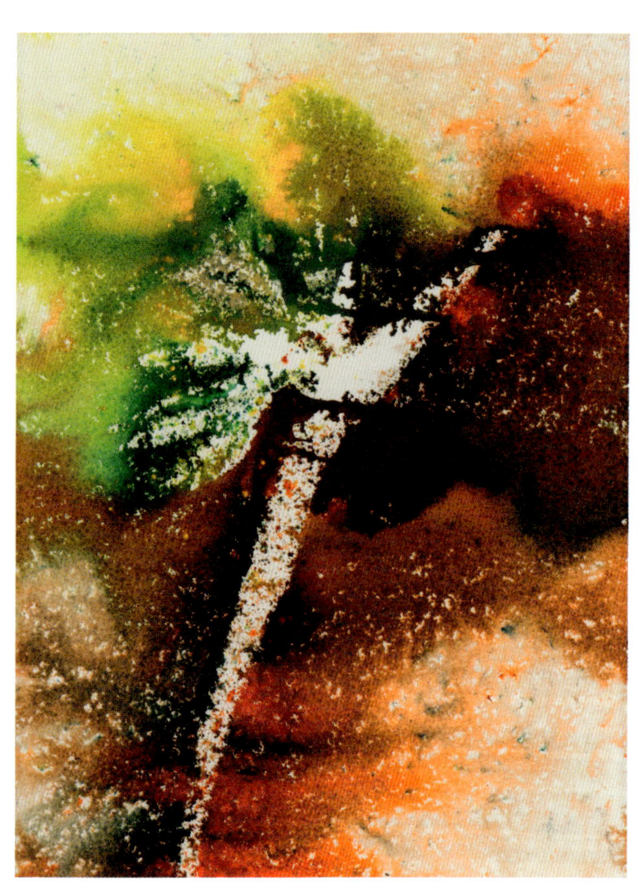

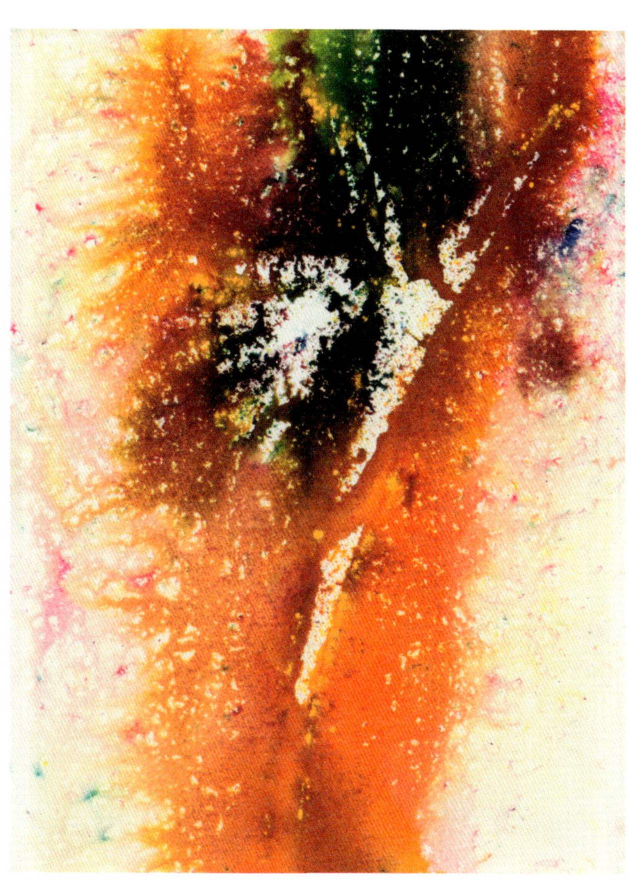

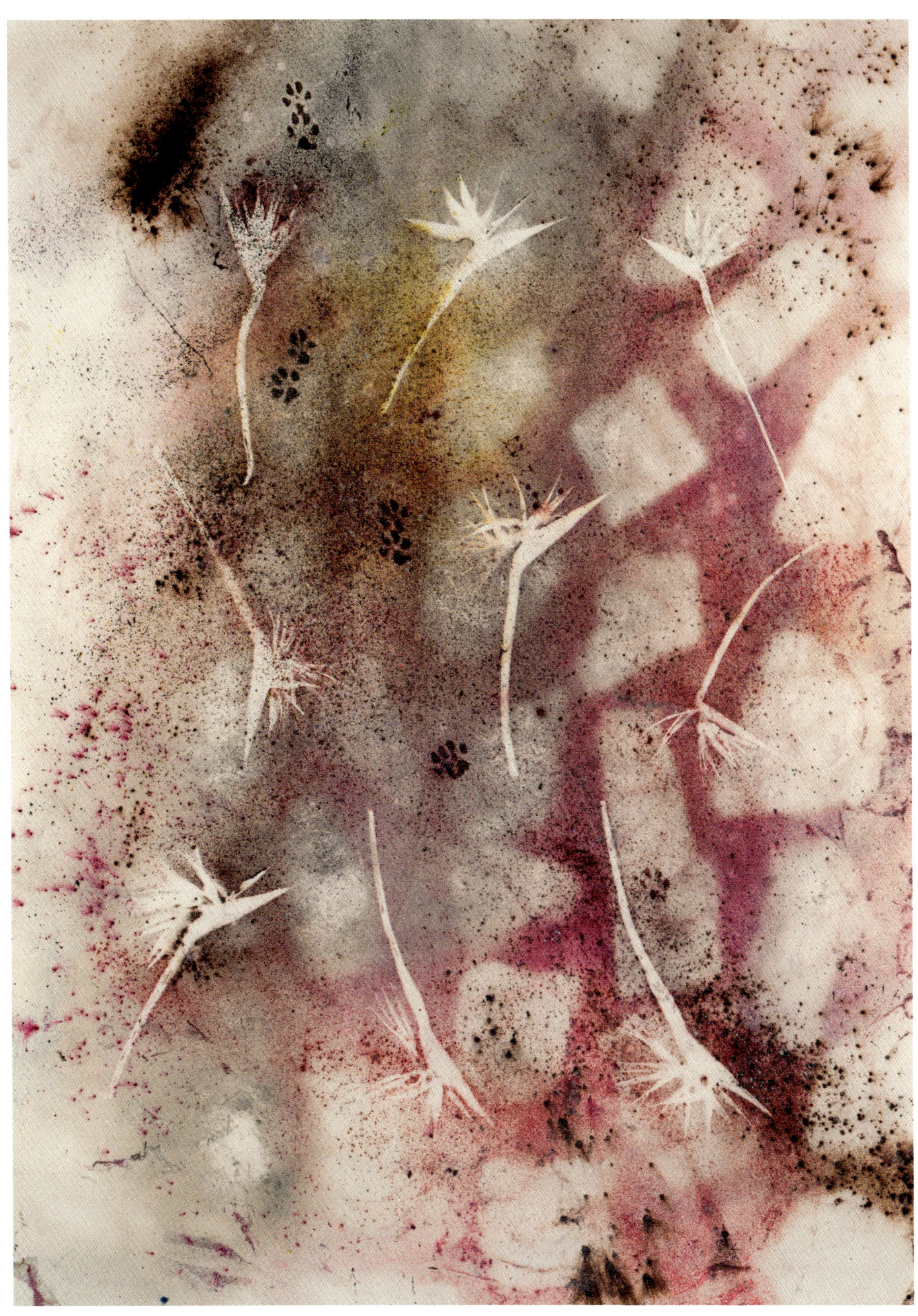

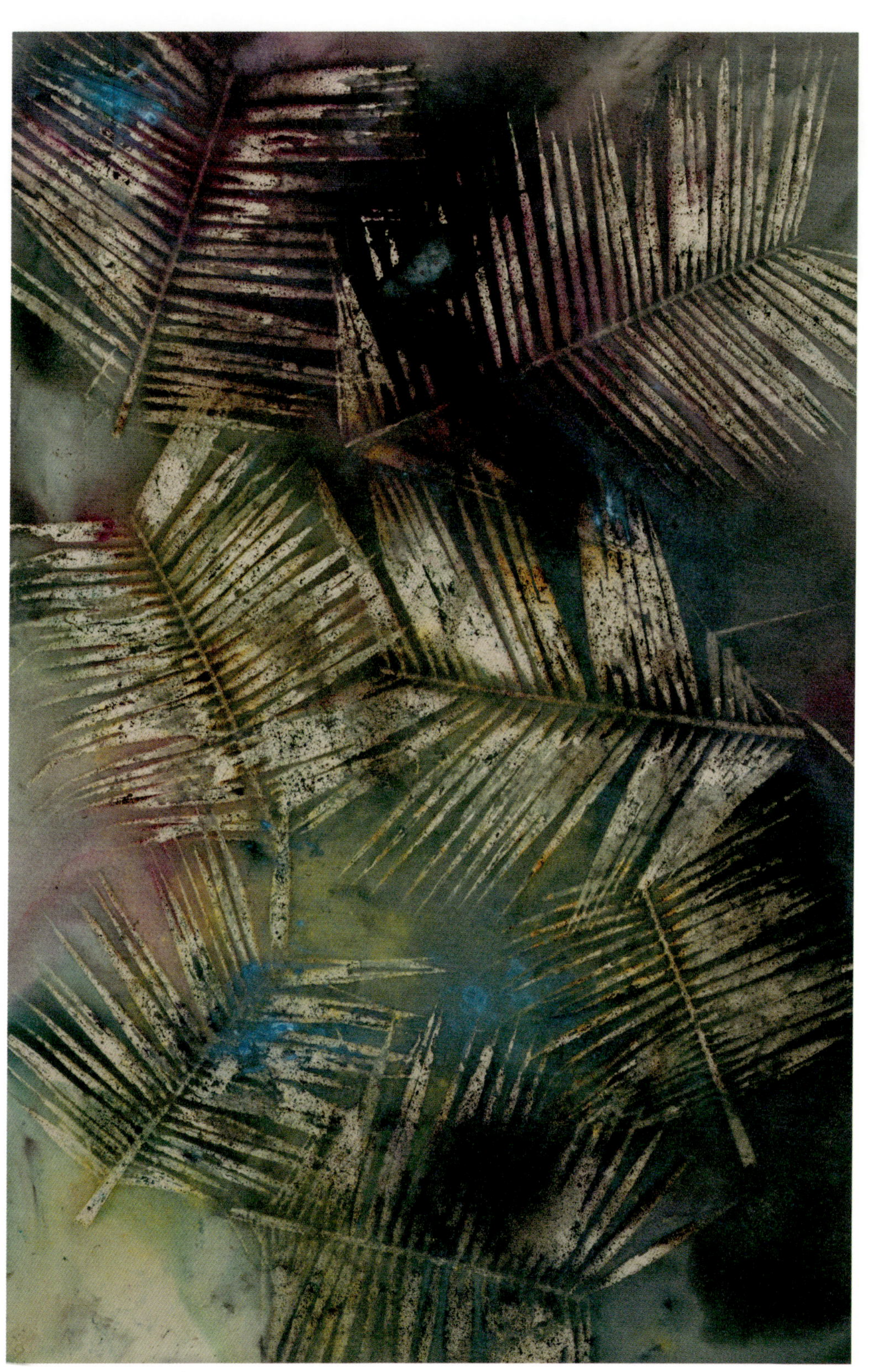

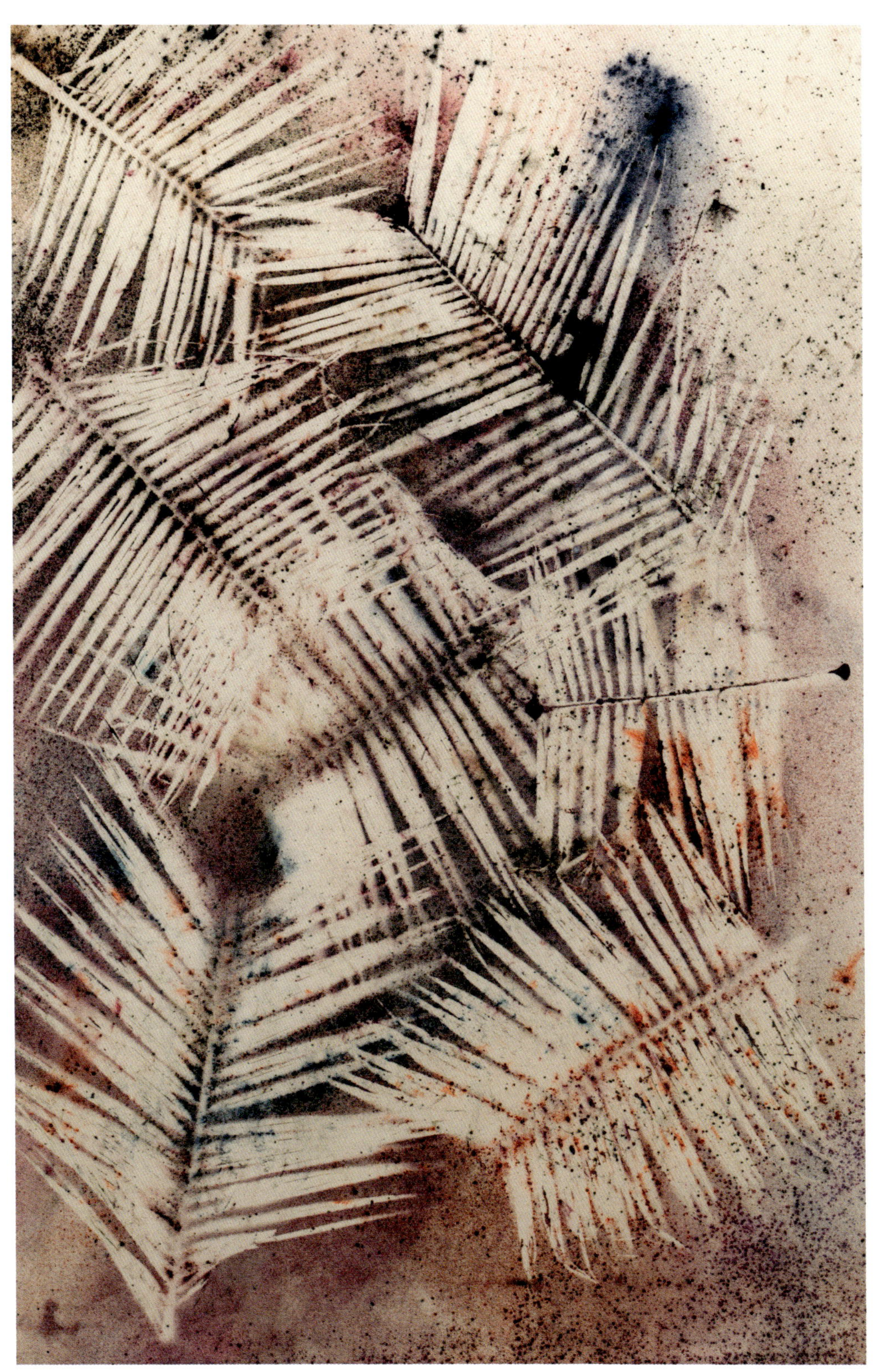

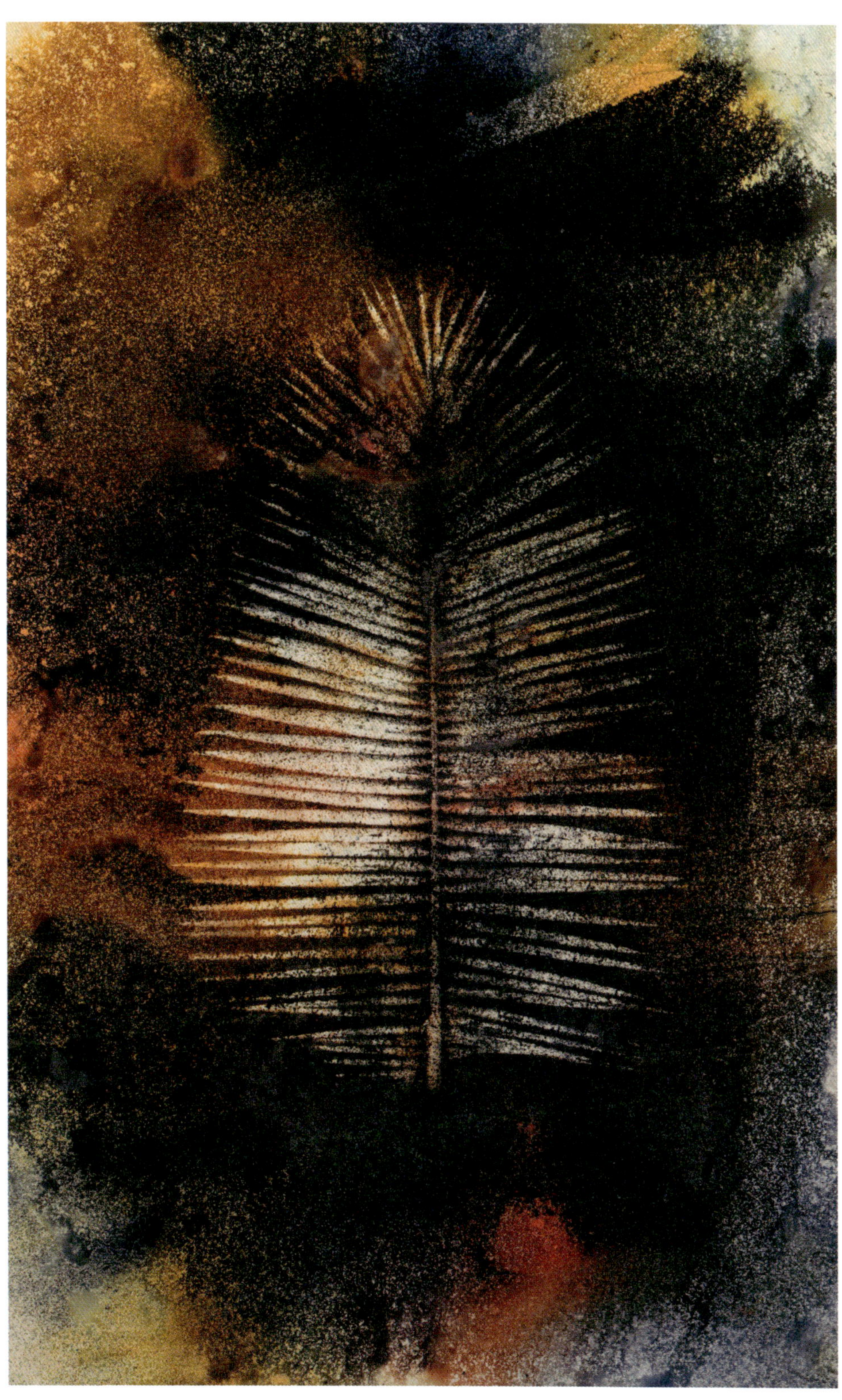

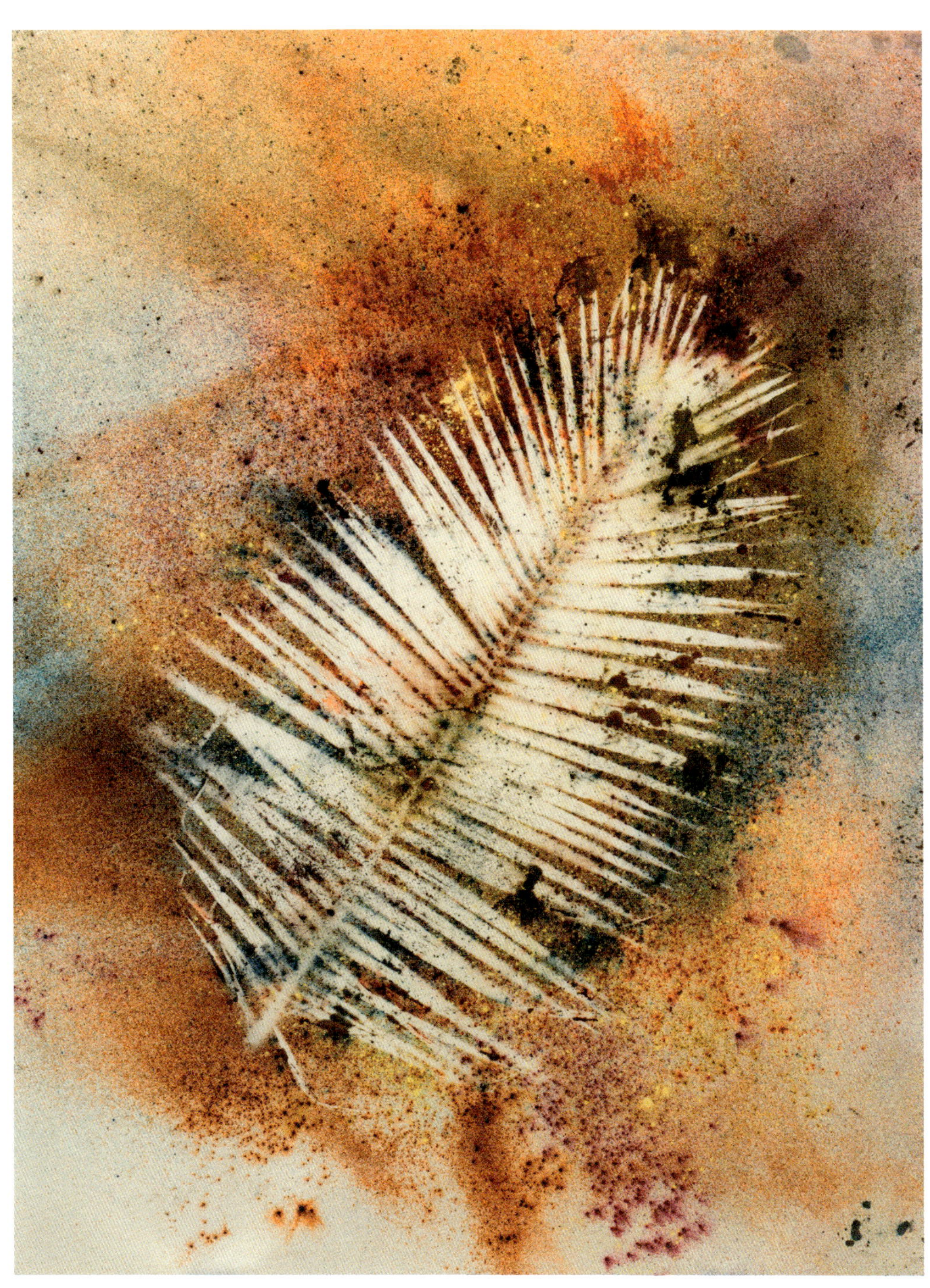

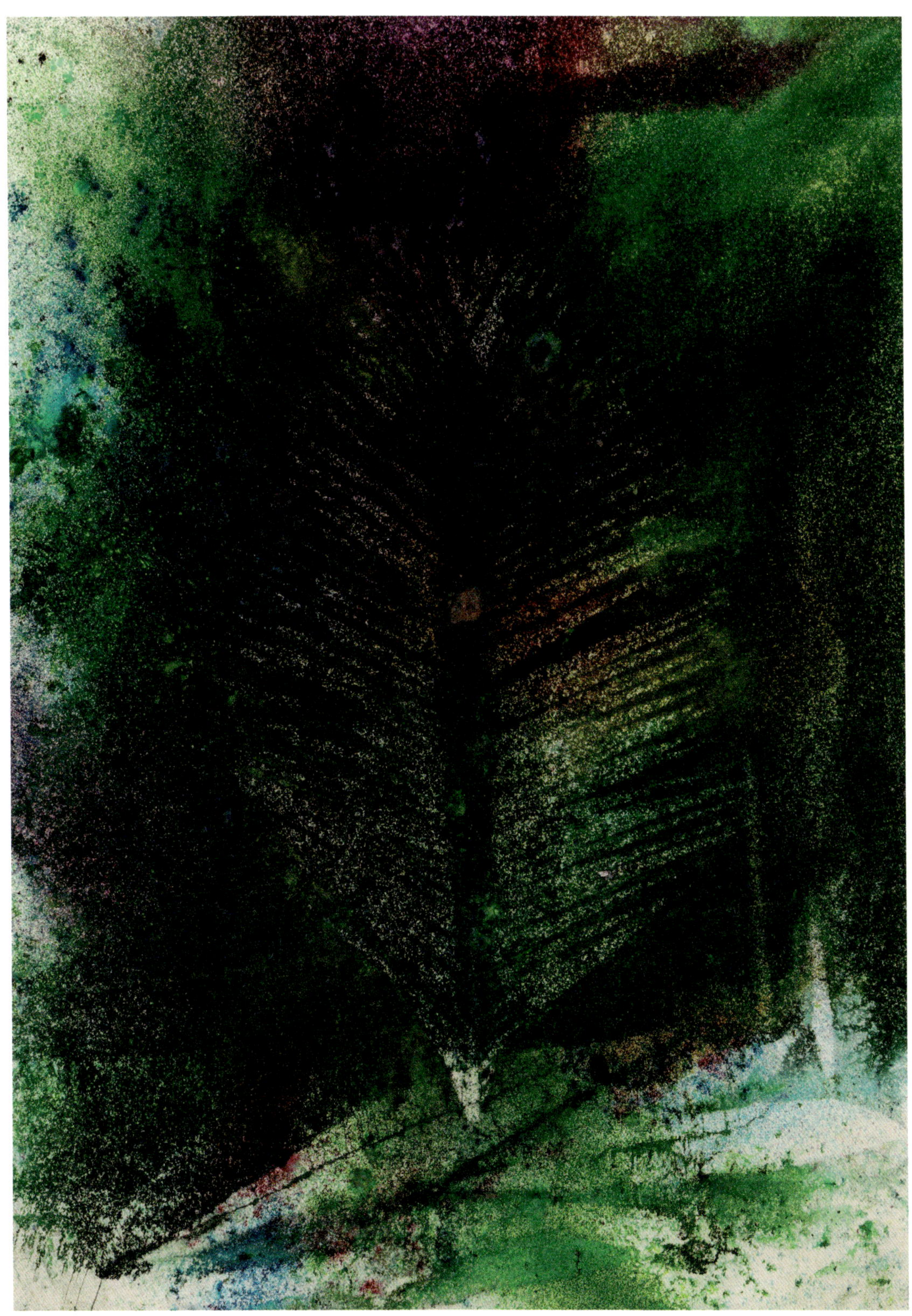

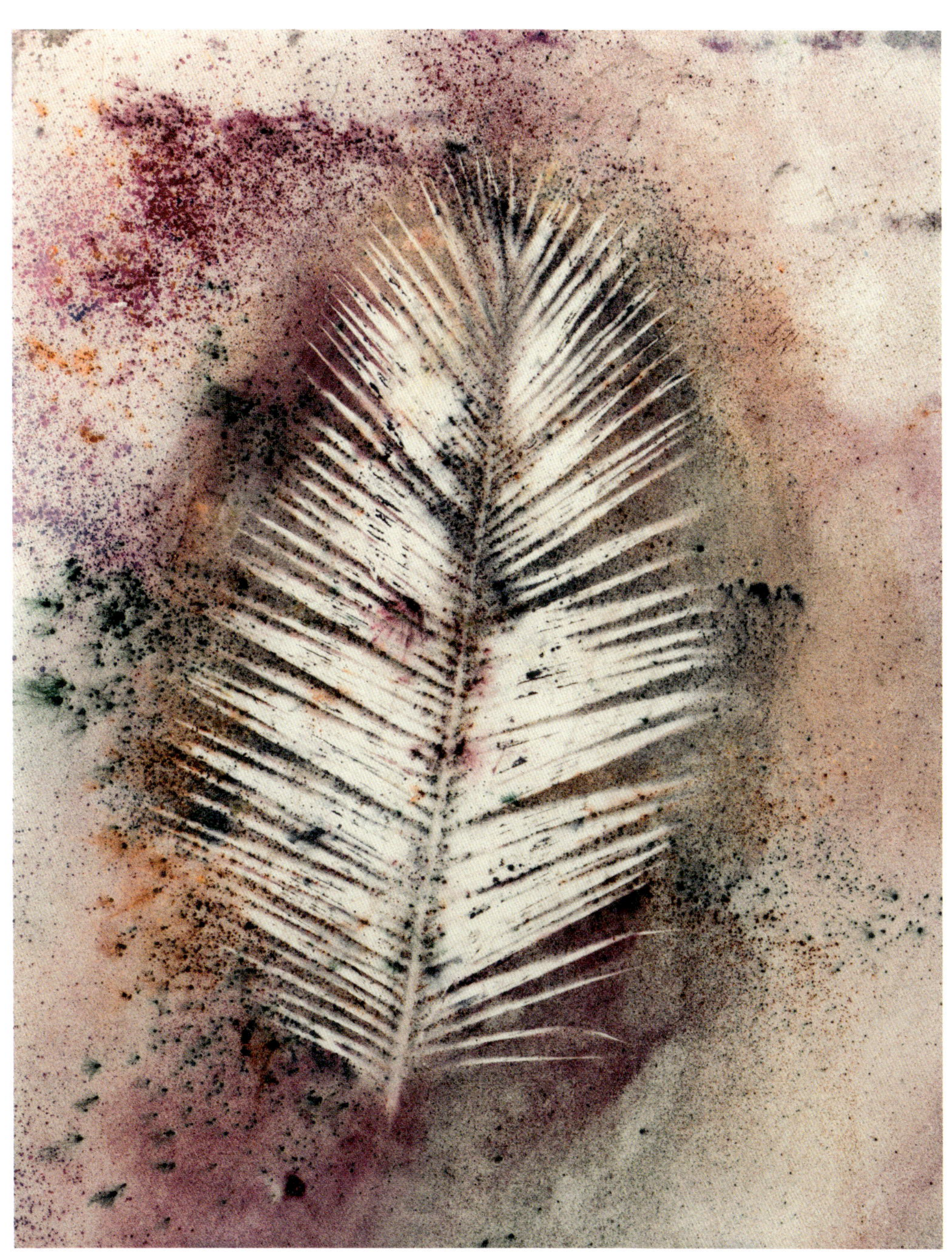

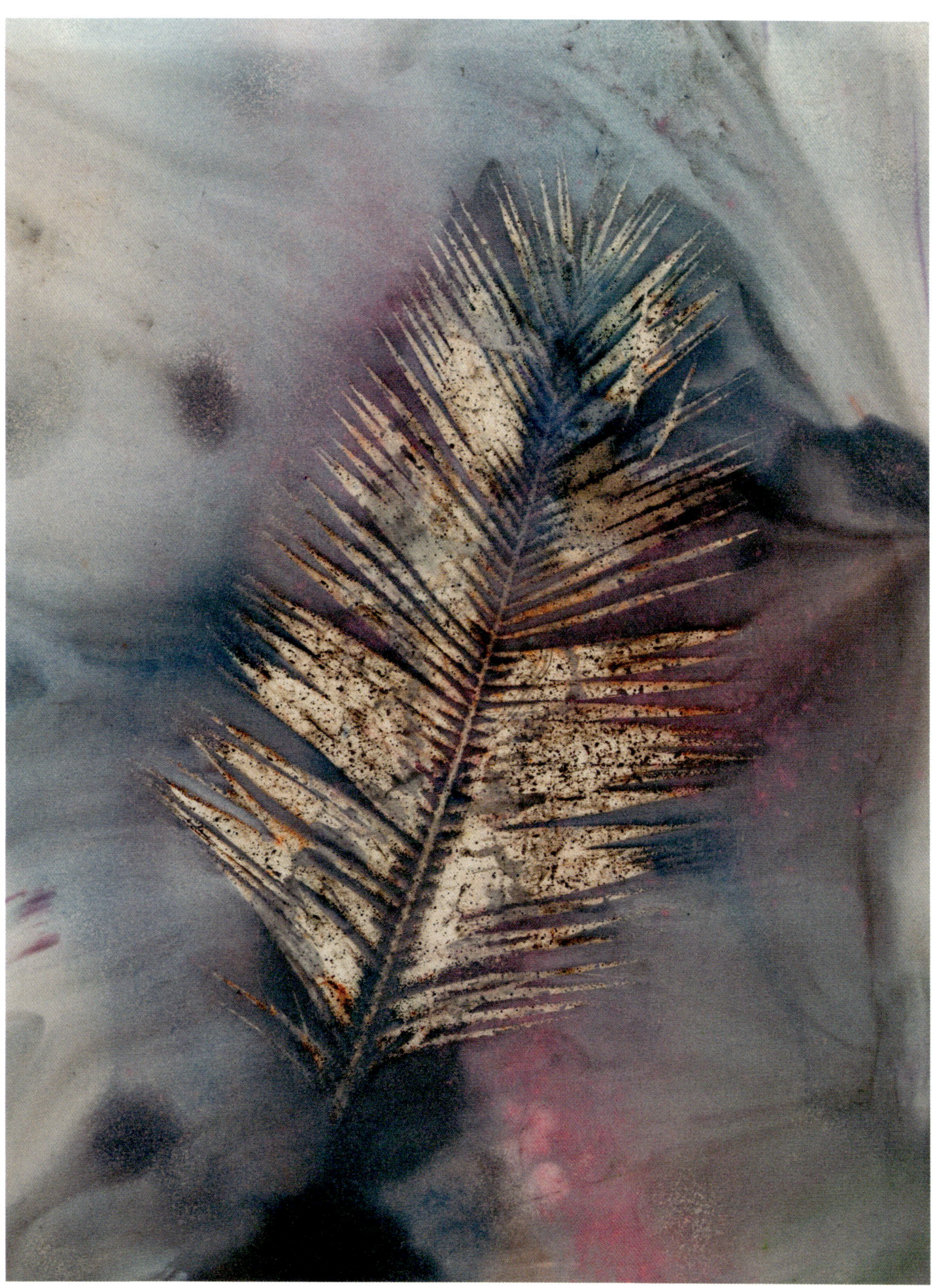

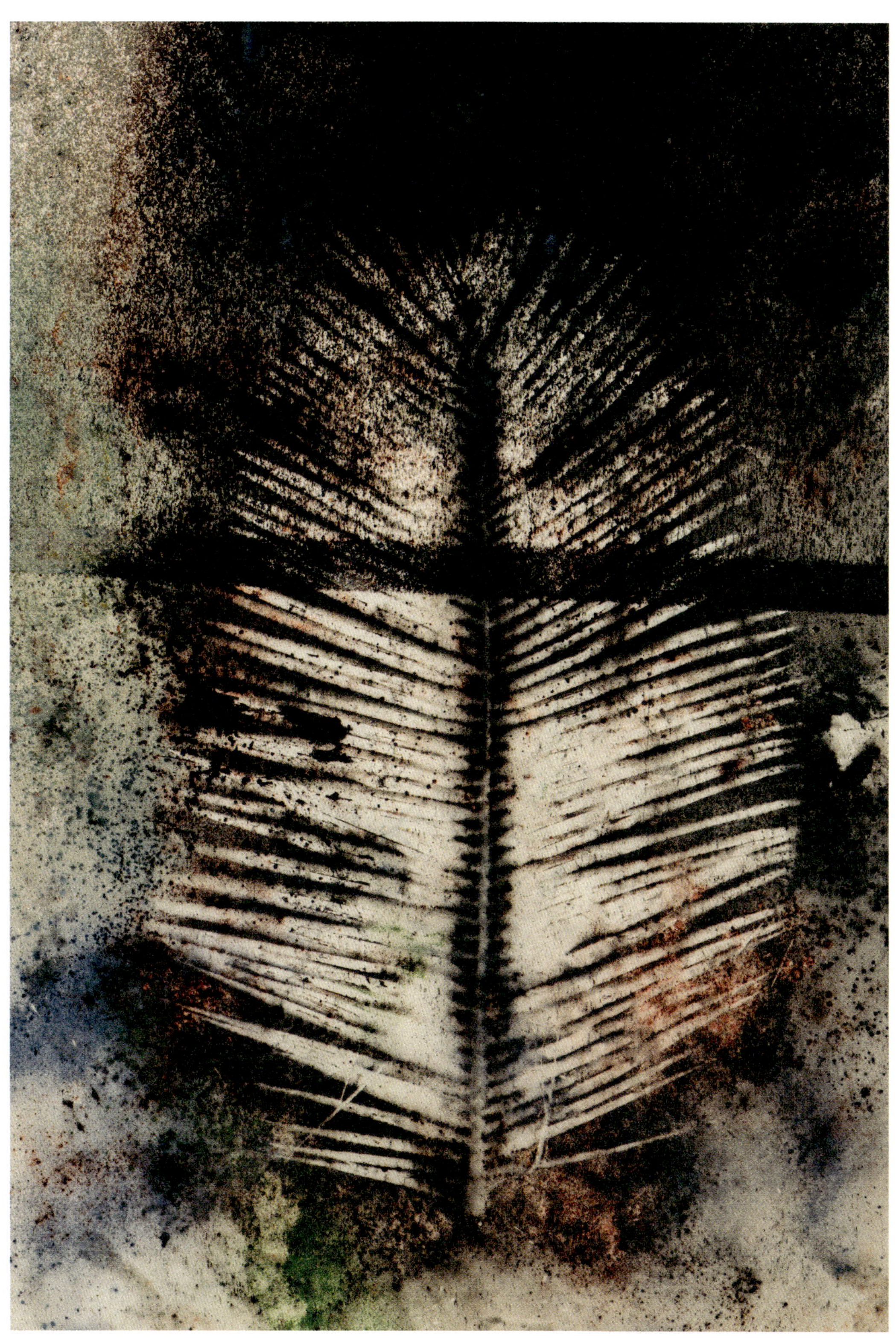

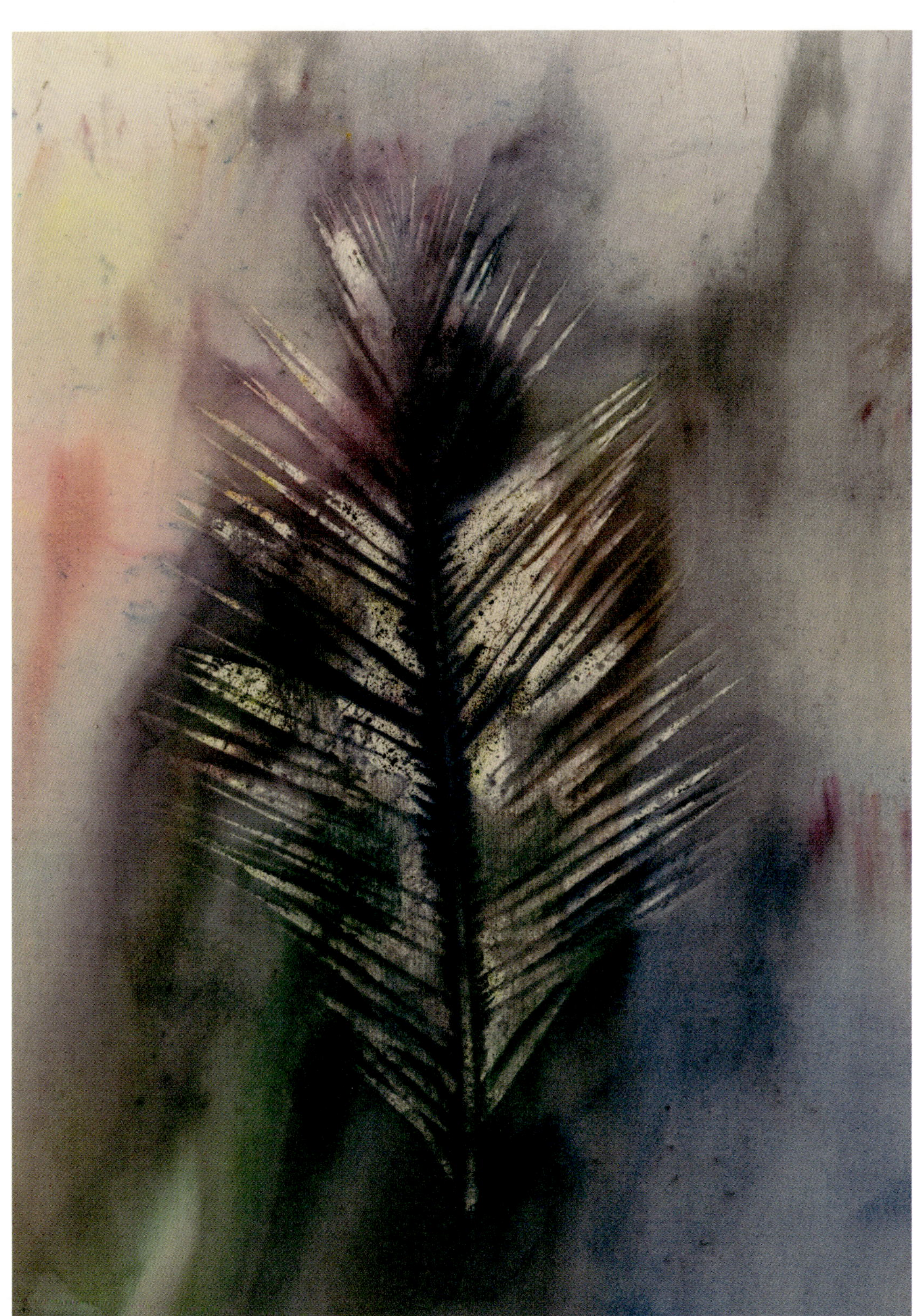

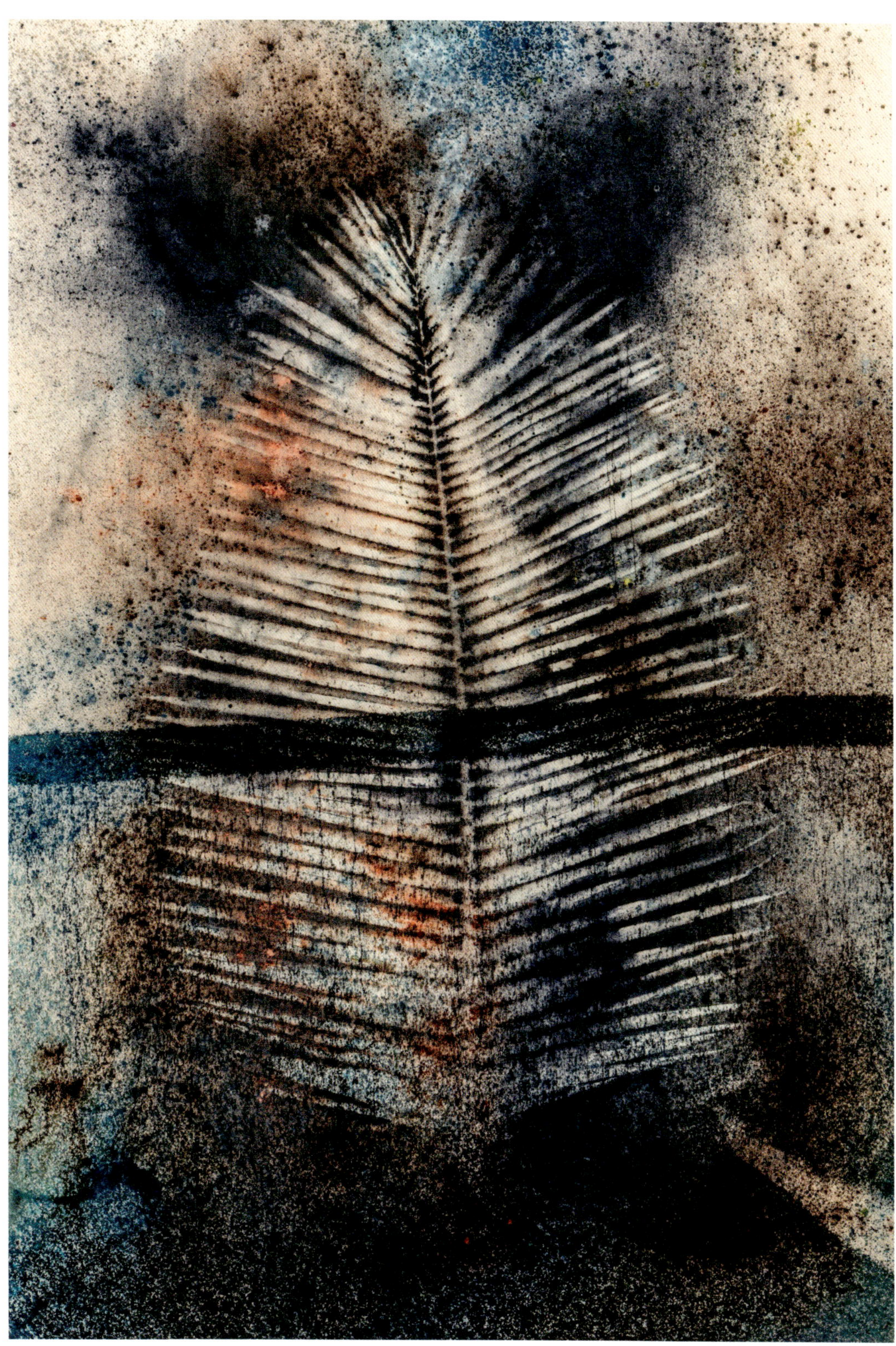

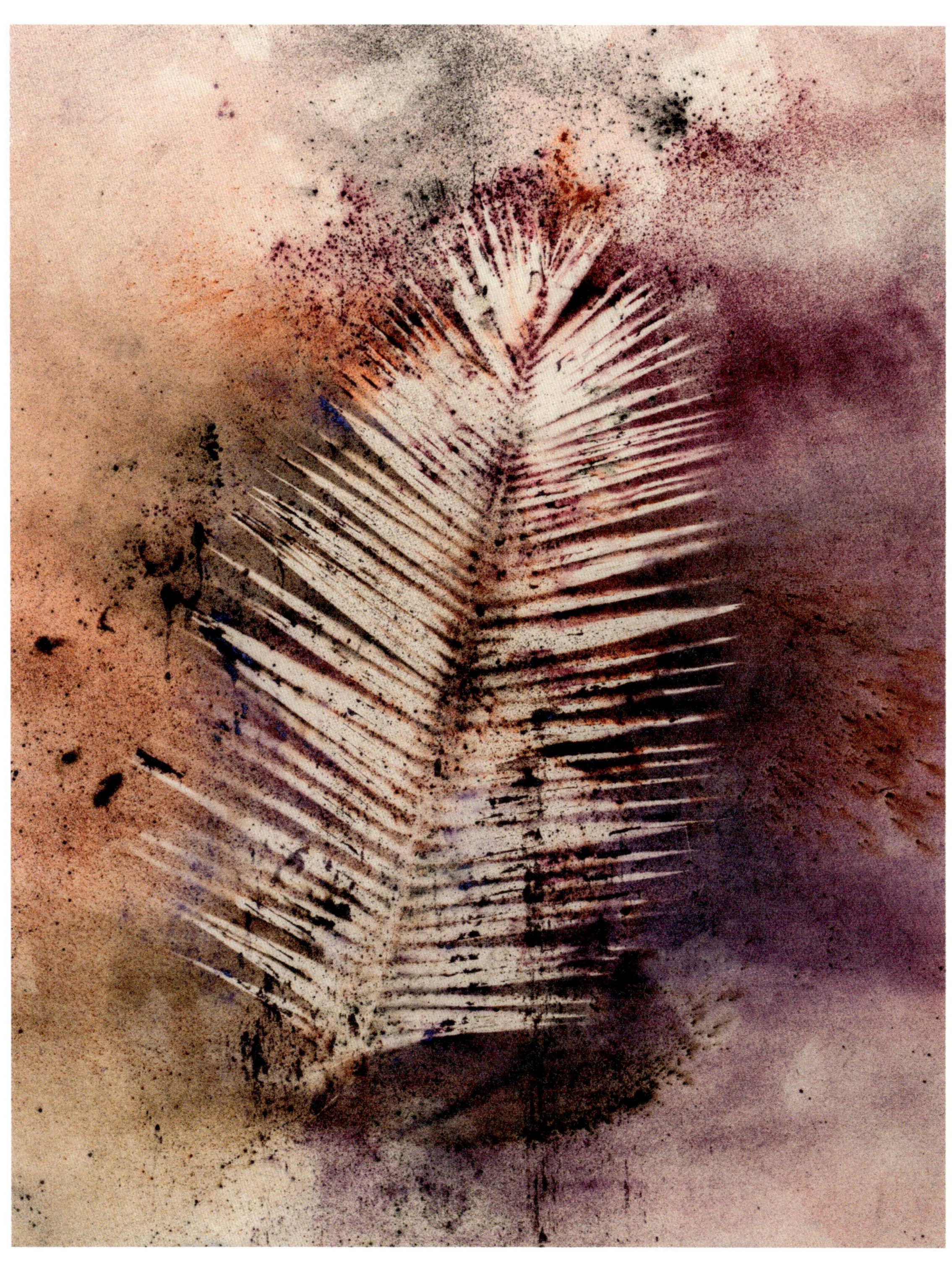

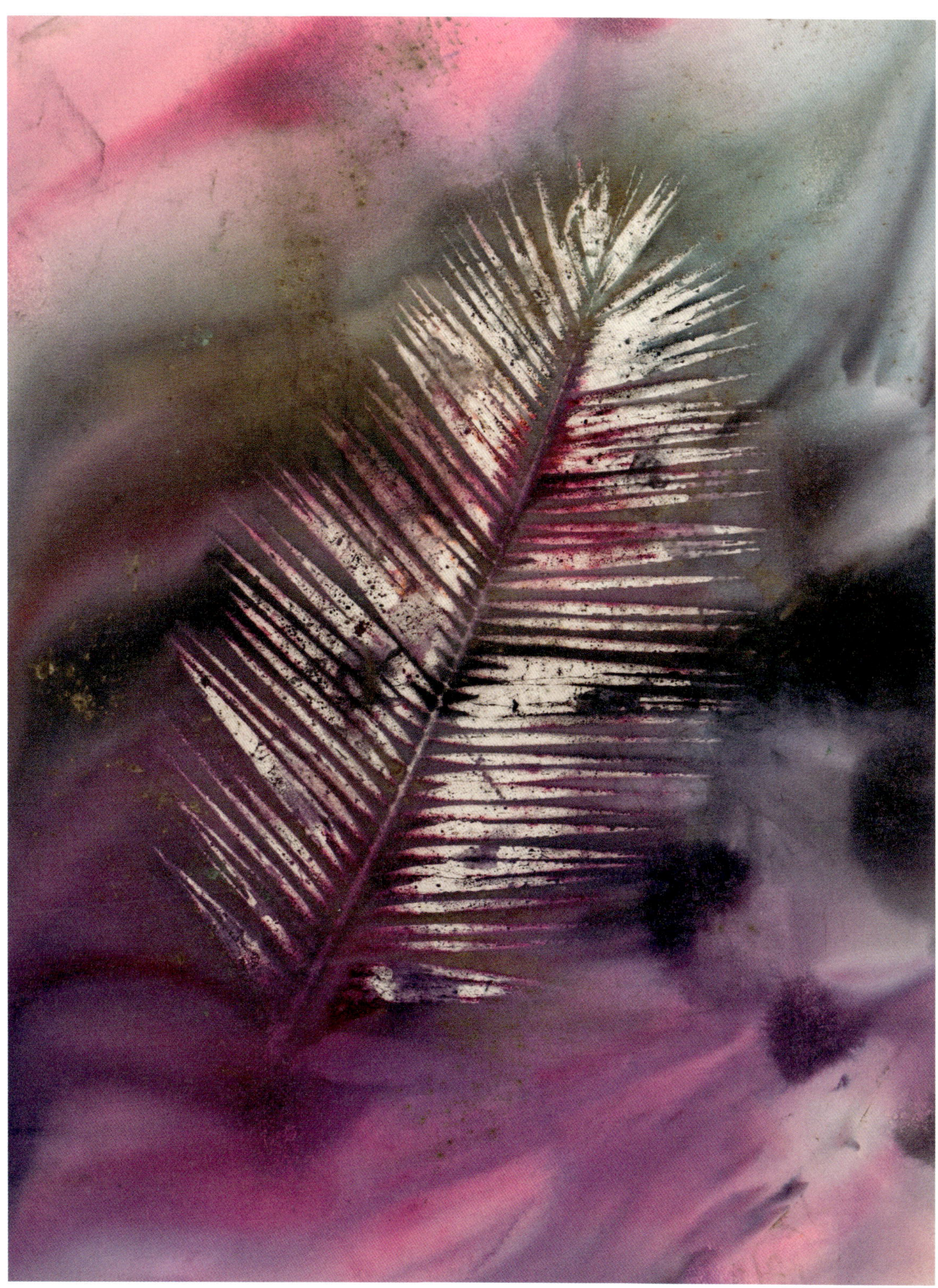

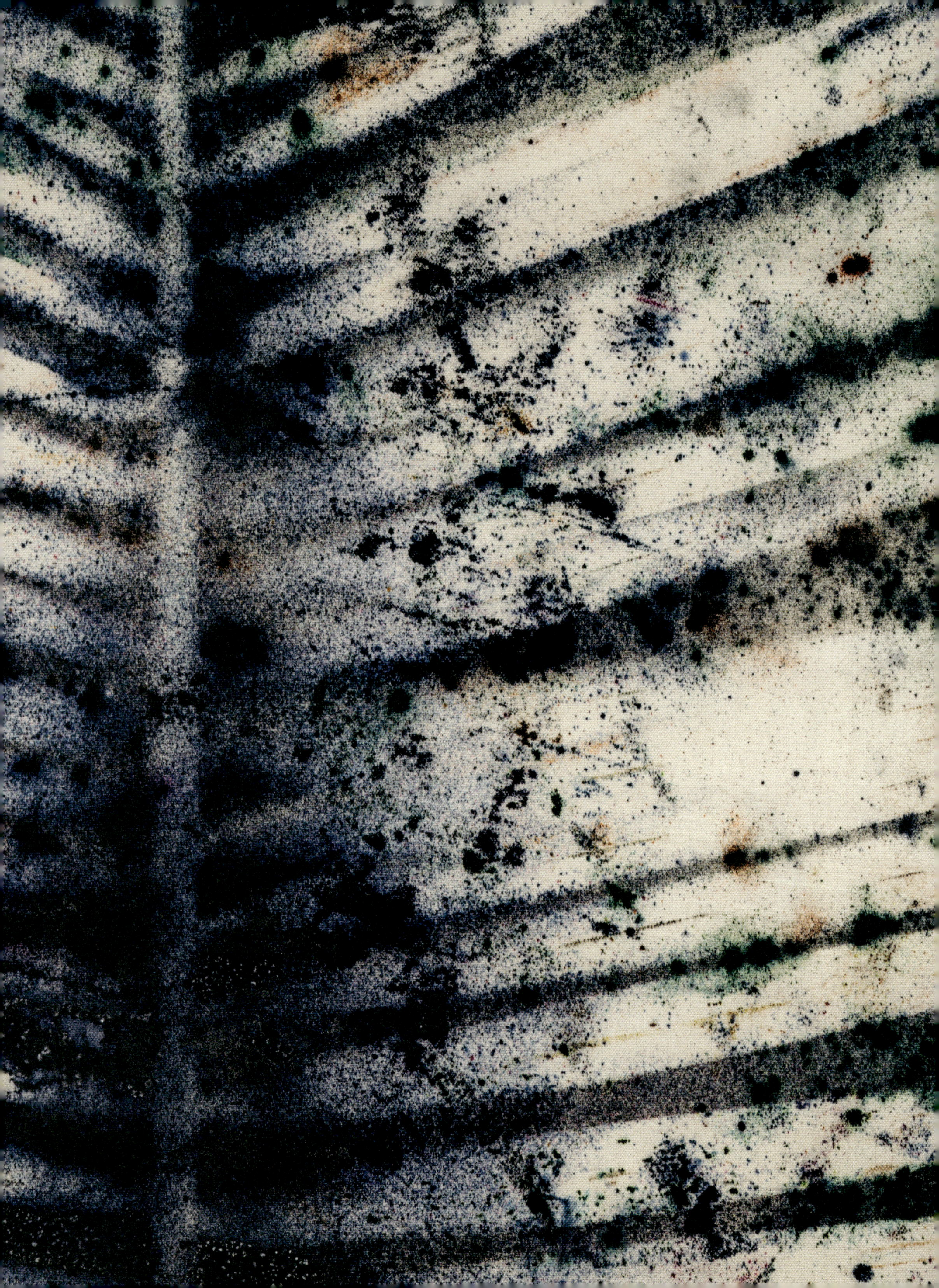

Hudson is a city located along the west border of Columbia County, New York. It receives 40 inches of rain annually. The number of days with any measurable precipitation is 109. On average, there are 181 sunny days per year in Hudson. The July high is around 85 degrees. The January low is 15 degrees. High-pressure systems often move just off the Atlantic coast, become more or less stagnant for several days, and then a persistent airflow from the southwest or south affects the region where Hudson is located. This circulation brings on the very warm, often humid, weather of the summer seas and the mild, more pleasant temperatures during the fall, winter, and spring seasons. Moisture or precipitation throughout the state is transported primarily from the Gulf of Mexico and Atlantic Ocean through circulation patterns and storm systems of the atmosphere. Distribution of precipitation within the state is greatly influenced by topography and proximity to the Great Lakes and Atlantic Ocean. There exists a fairly uniform distribution of precipitation during the year. There are no distinctly dry or wet seasons, which are regularly repeated on an annual basis. Minimum precipitation occurs in the winter season. The climate contributes greatly to the agricultural, industrial, commercial, and recreational economy of the area where Hudson is located. Plant growth is thereby retarded, allowing a great variety of freeze-sensitive crops, especially tree and vine fruits, to reach critical early stages of development when the risk of freeze injury is minimized or greatly reduced.

HUDSON, NY

95.
*Untitled (Hudson, NY,
Black Eyed Susans 1)*, 2014
Pigment on canvas
96 × 72 inches
(243.8 × 183 cm)

97.
*Untitled (Hudson, NY,
Black Eyed Susans 2)*, 2014
Pigment on canvas
96 × 72 inches
(243.8 × 183 cm)

98–99.
*Untitled (Hudson, NY,
Hickory Tree)*, 2014
Pigment on canvas
138 × 162 inches
(350.5 × 411.5 cm)

100–01.
*Untitled (Hudson, NY,
Birch Tree)*, 2014
Pigment on canvas
138 × 162 inches
(350.5 × 411.5 cm)

102–03.
*Untitled (Hudson, NY,
Sumac Tree 1)*, 2014
Pigment on canvas
138 × 162 inches
(350.5 × 411.5 cm)

104–05.
*Untitled (Hudson, NY,
3 Baby Maple Trees)*, 2014
Pigment on canvas
93 × 132 inches
(236.2 × 335.3 cm)

106–07.
*Untitled (Hudson, NY,
3 Baby Ash Trees)*, 2014
Pigment on canvas
93 × 132 inches
(236.2 × 335.3 cm)

108–09.
Detail of *Untitled
(Hudson, NY,
Black Eyed Susans 1)*

110–11.
Detail of *Untitled
(Hudson, NY,
Black Eyed Susans 2)*

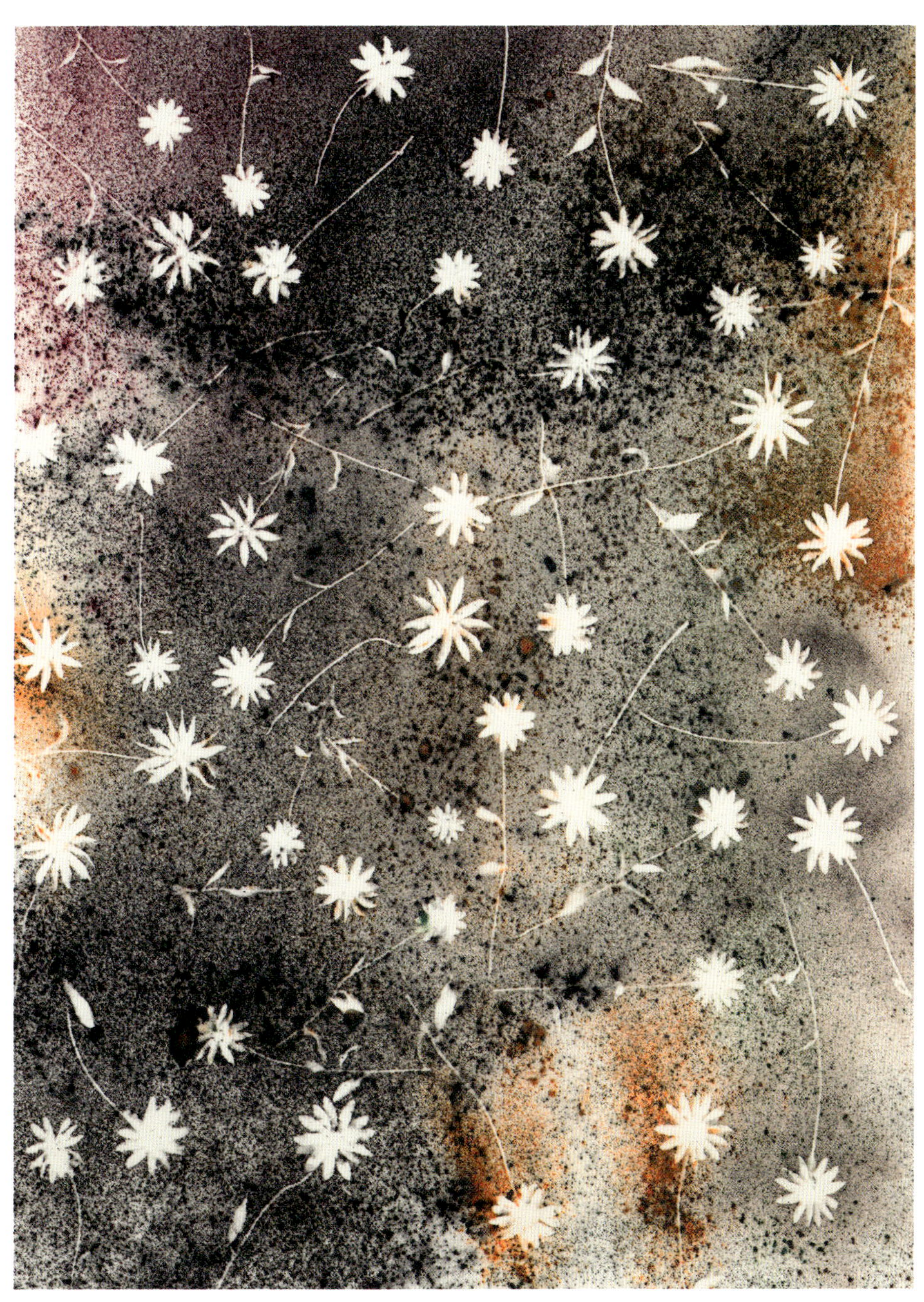

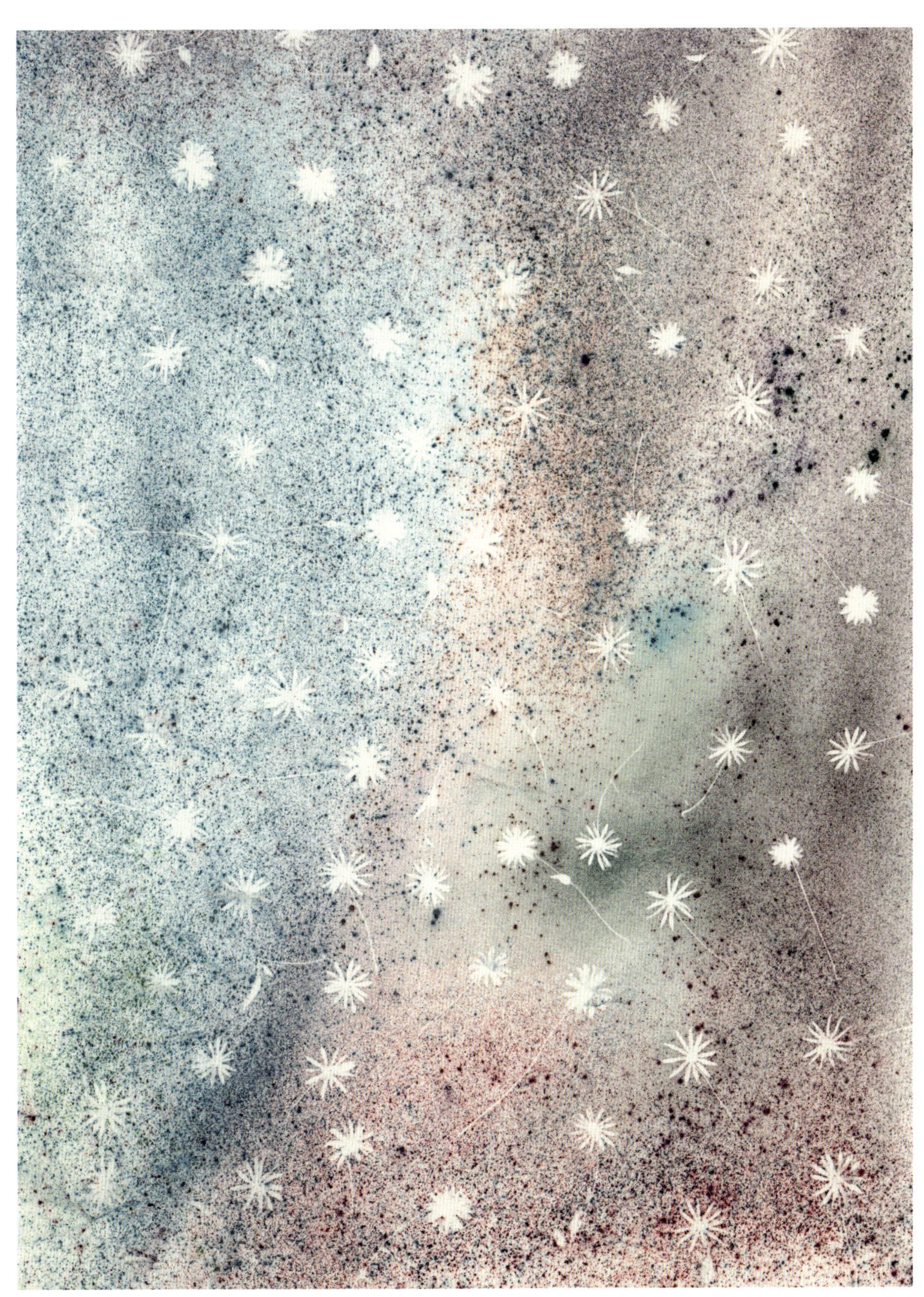

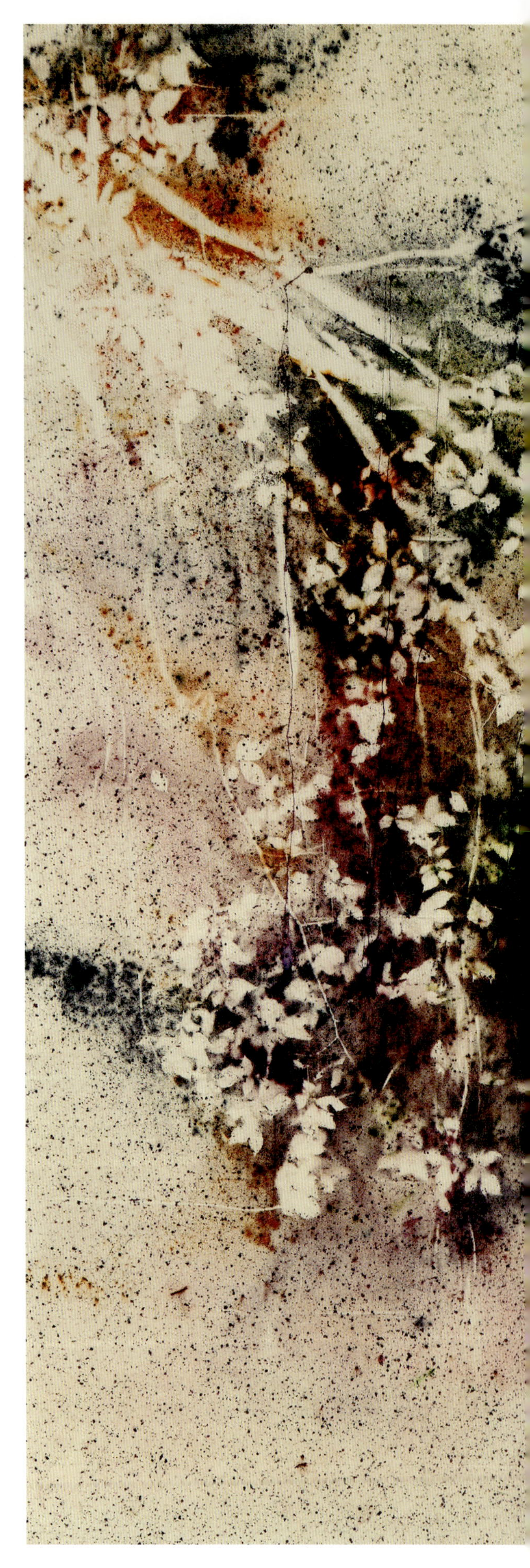

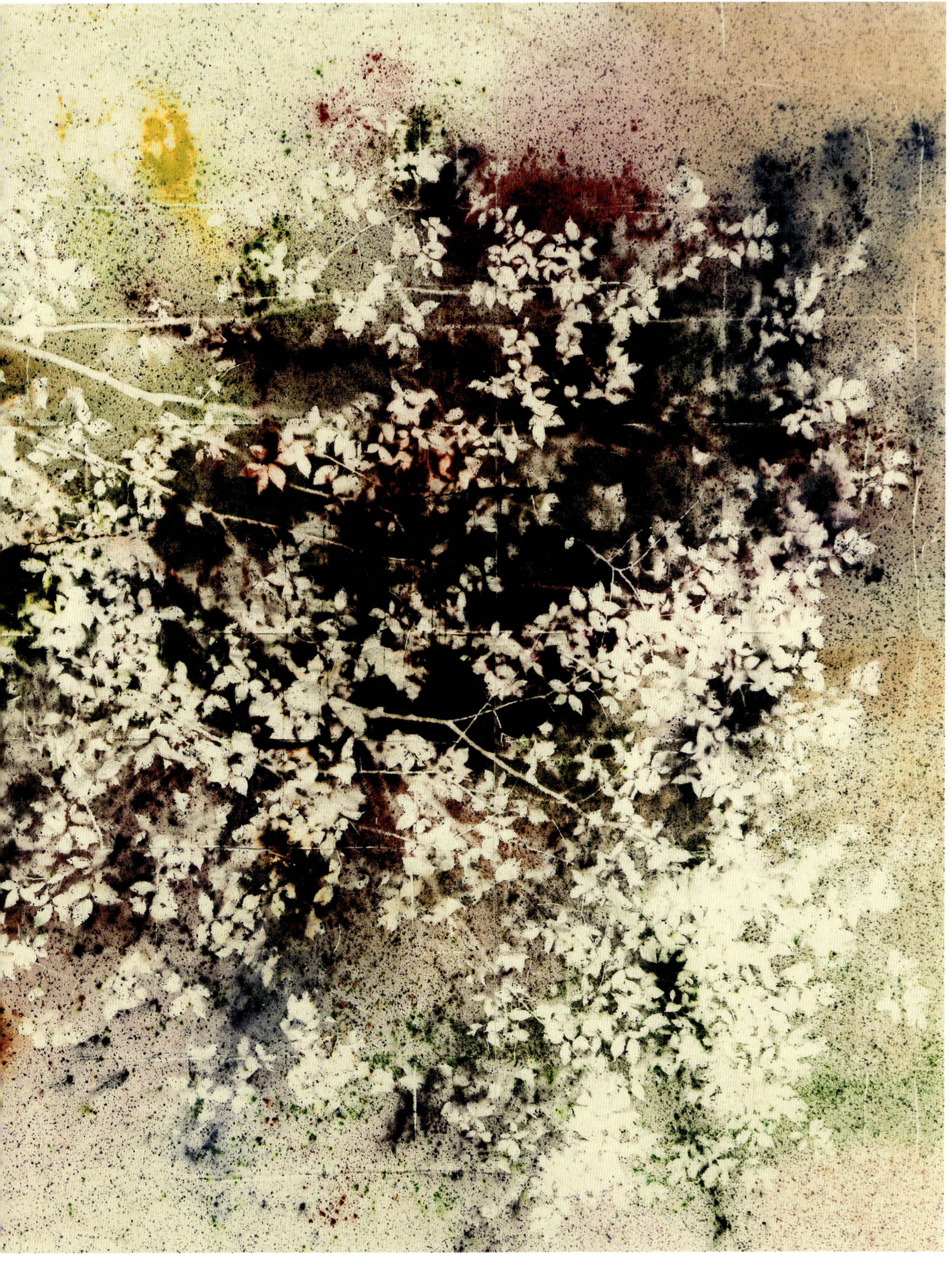

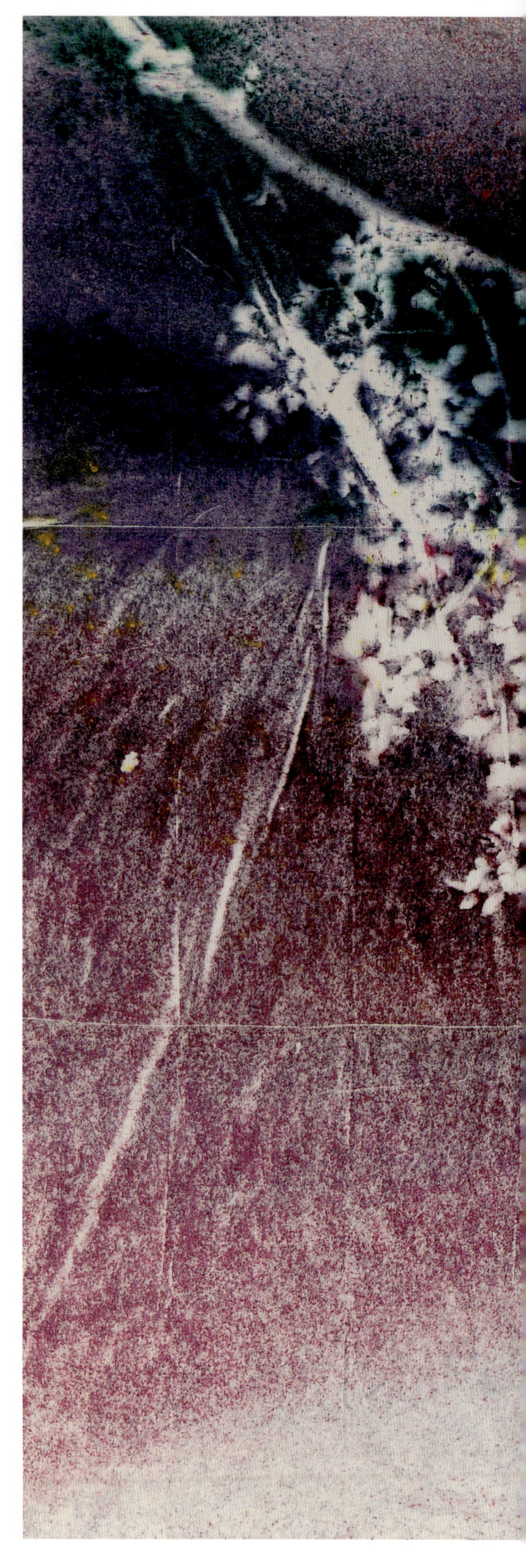

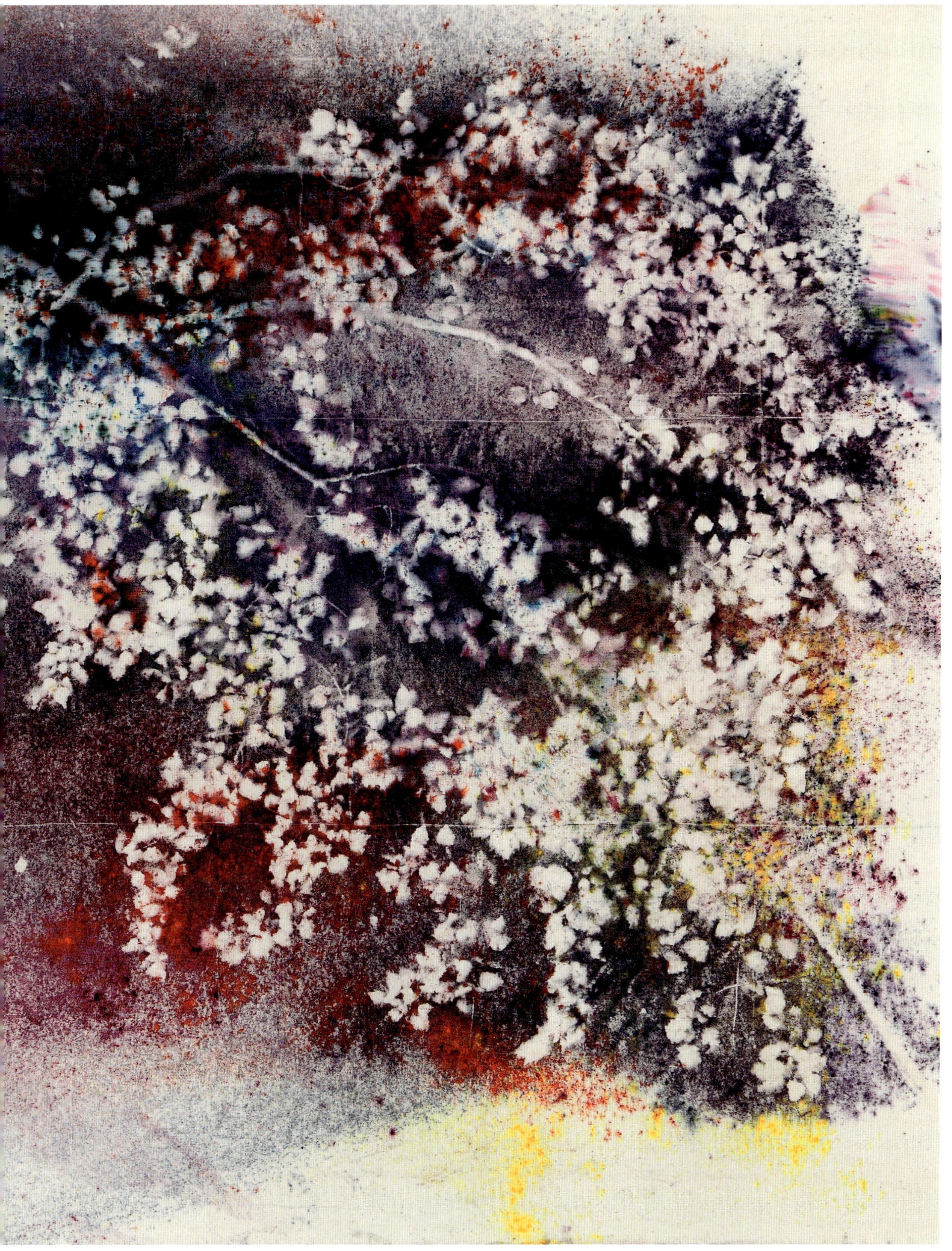

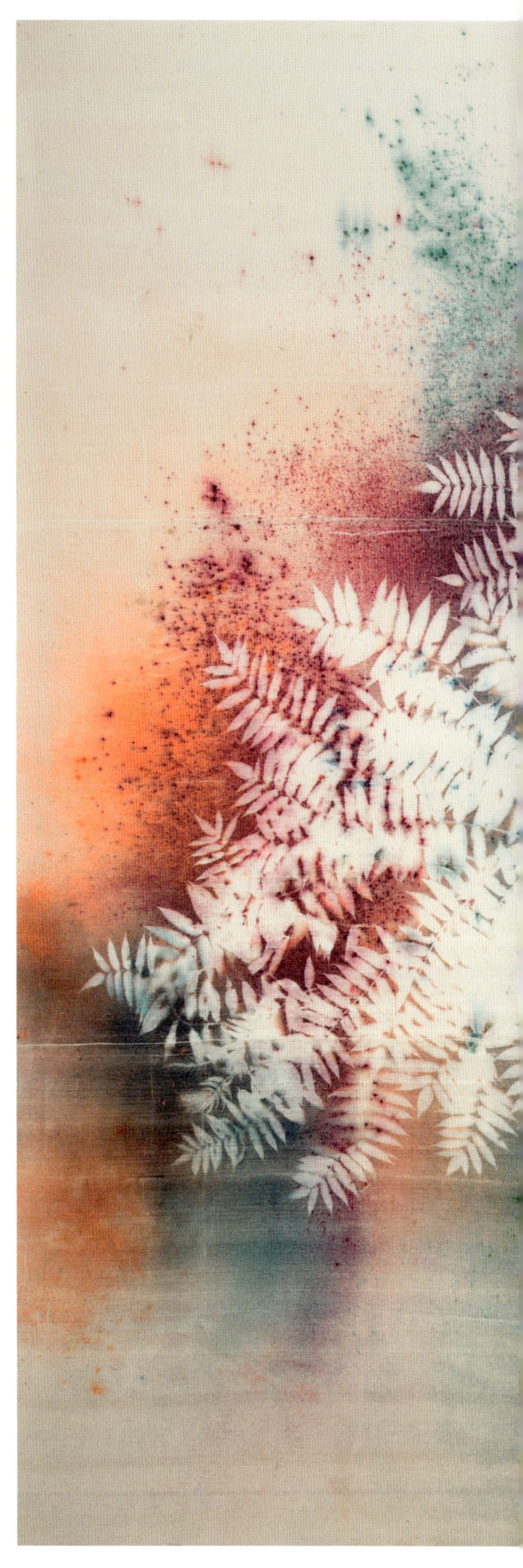

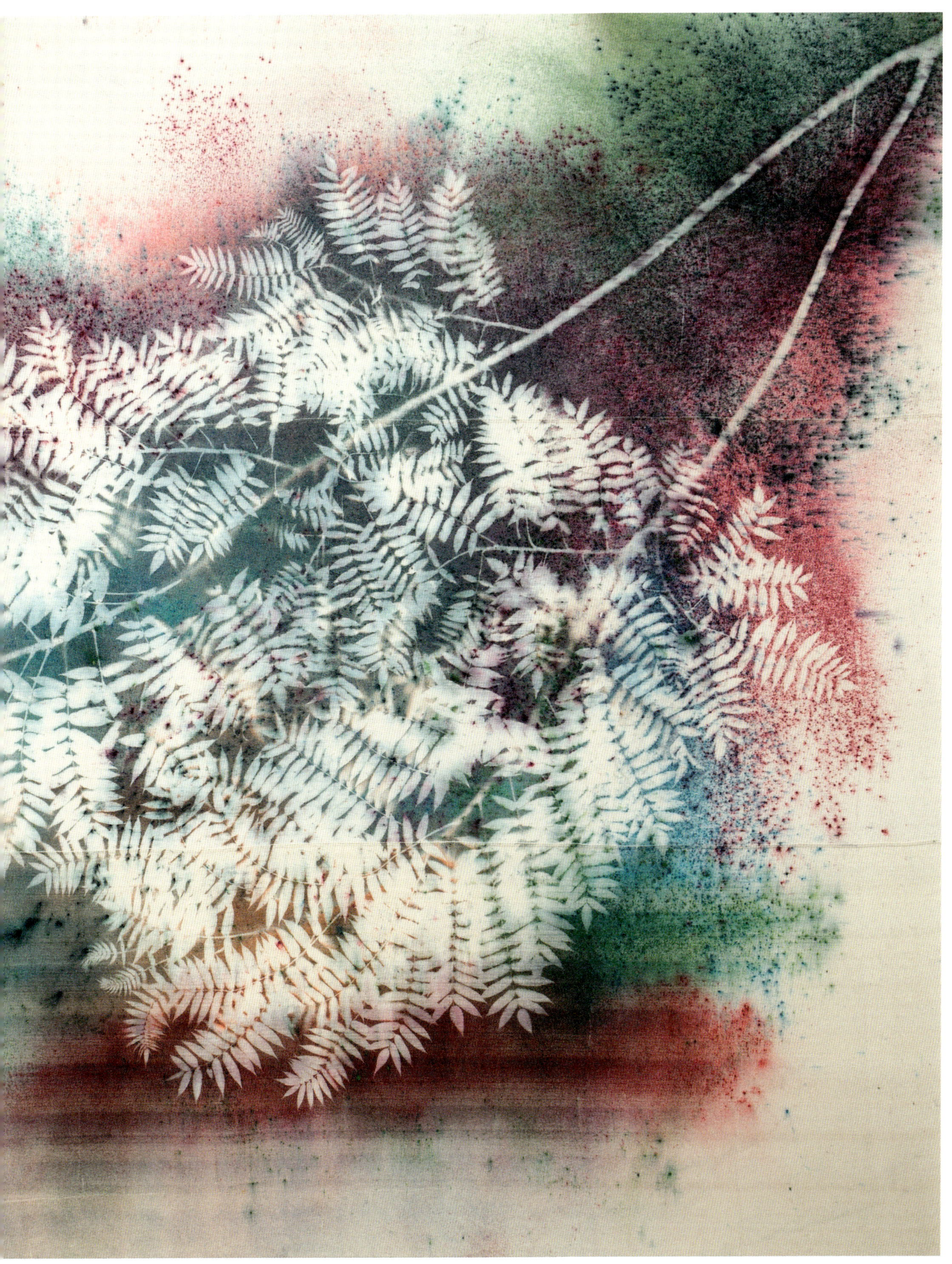

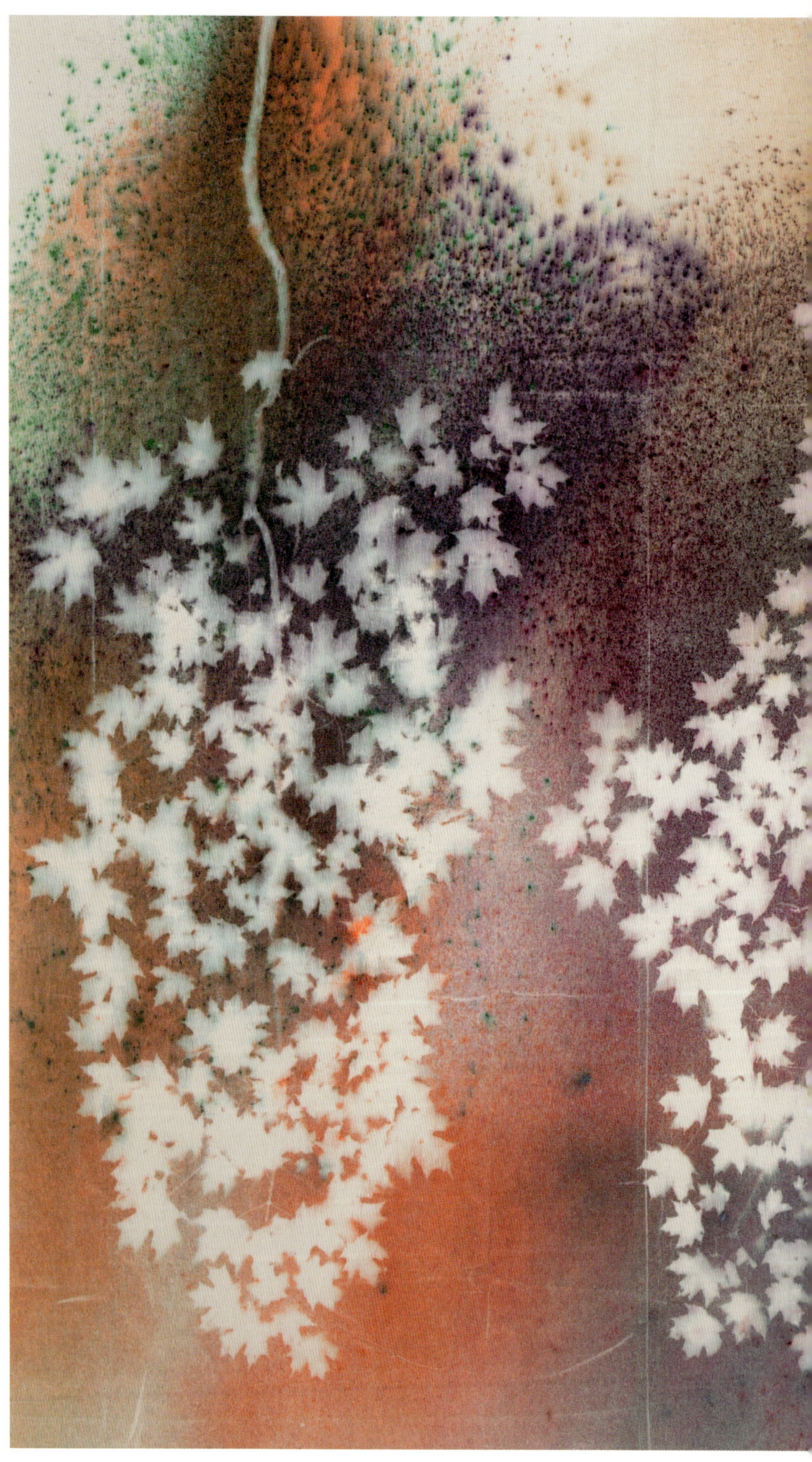

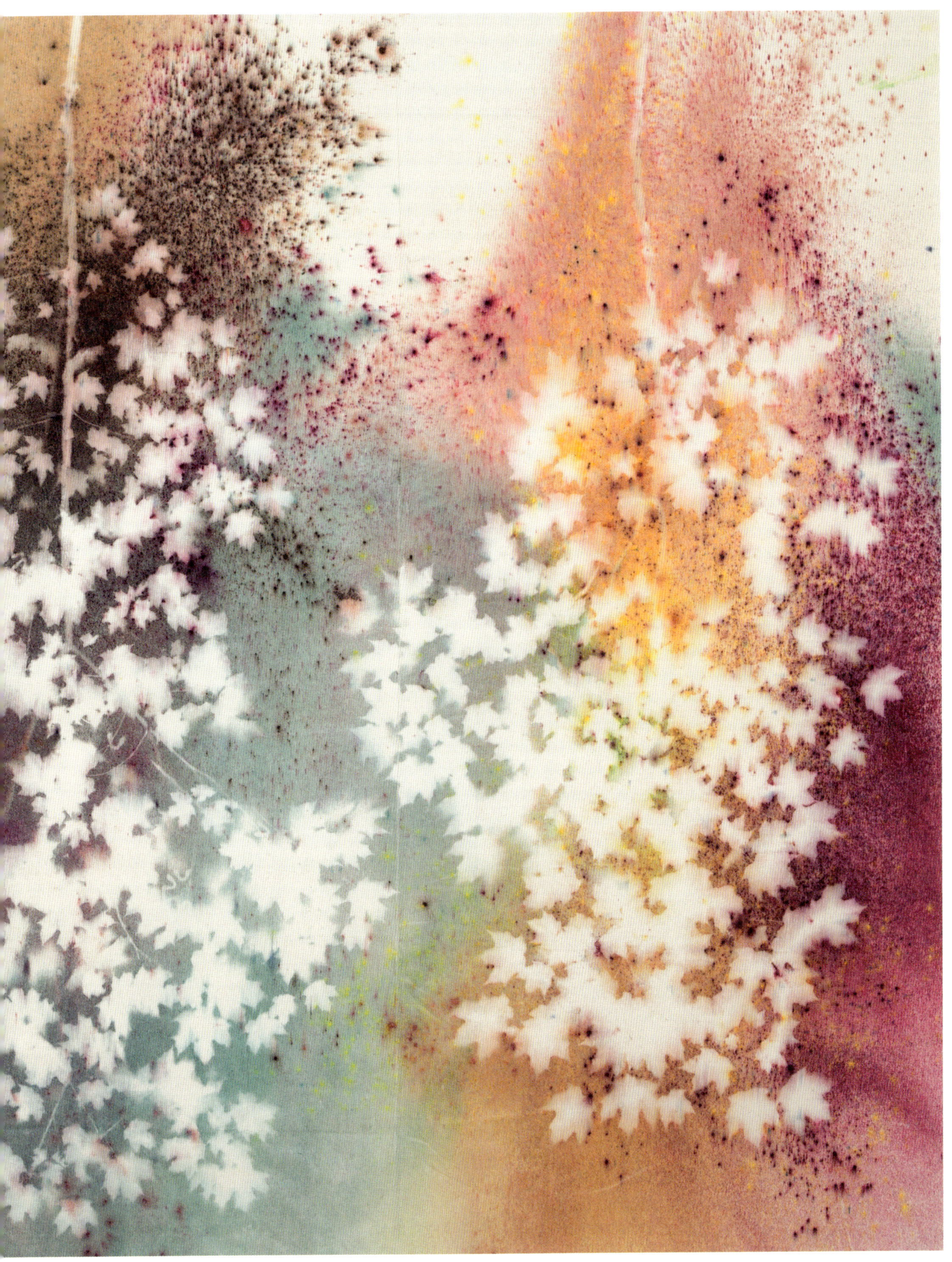

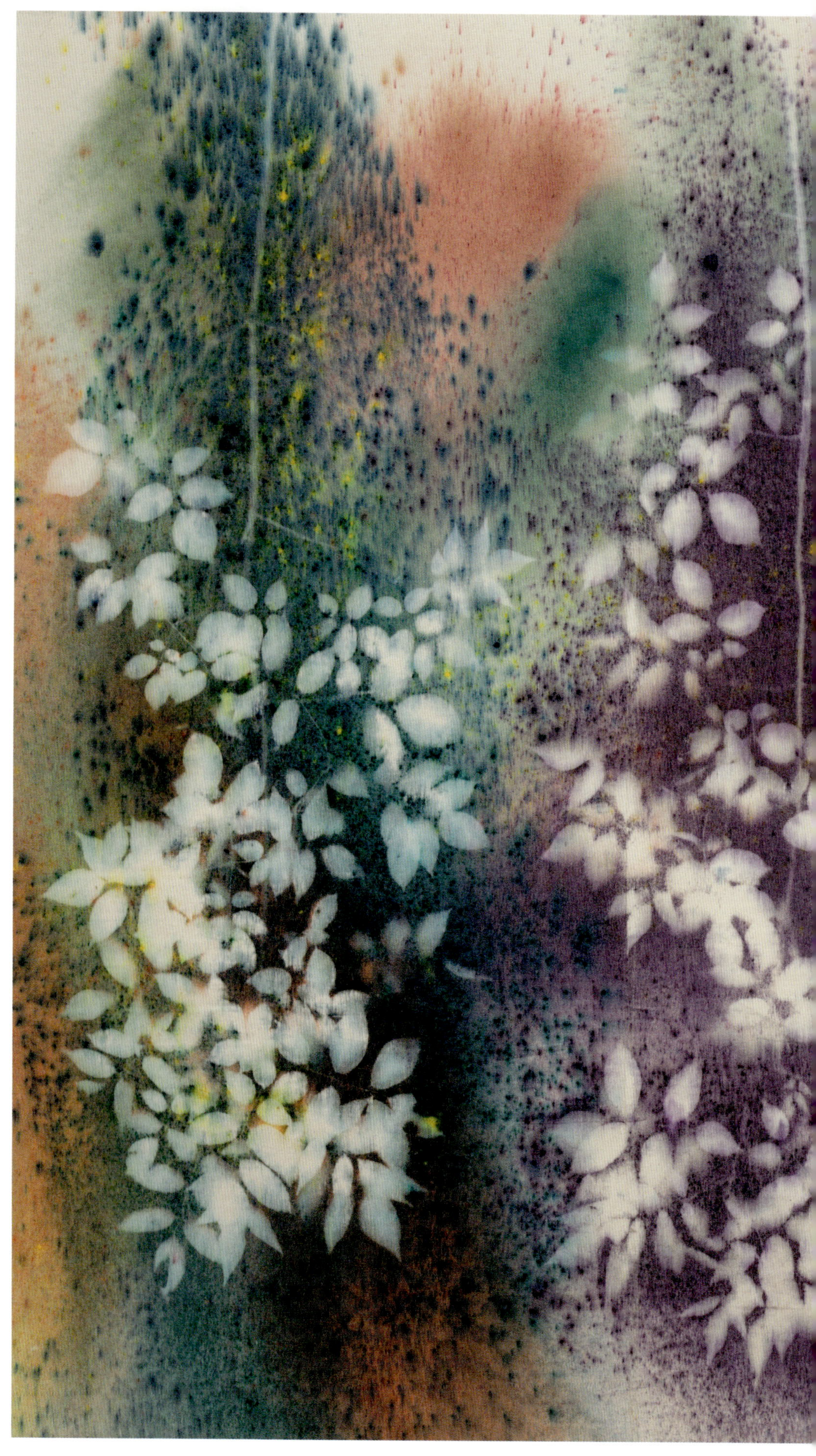

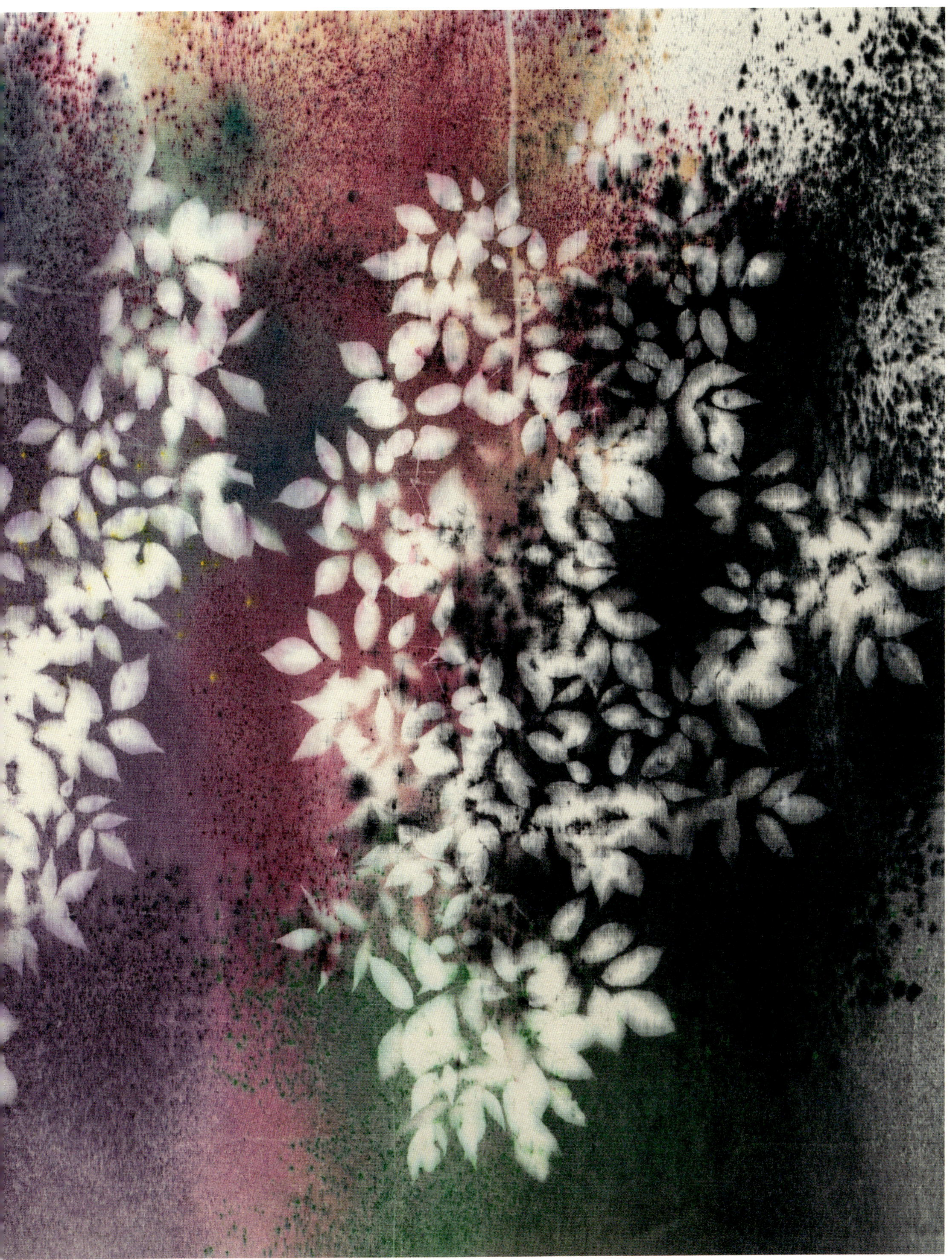

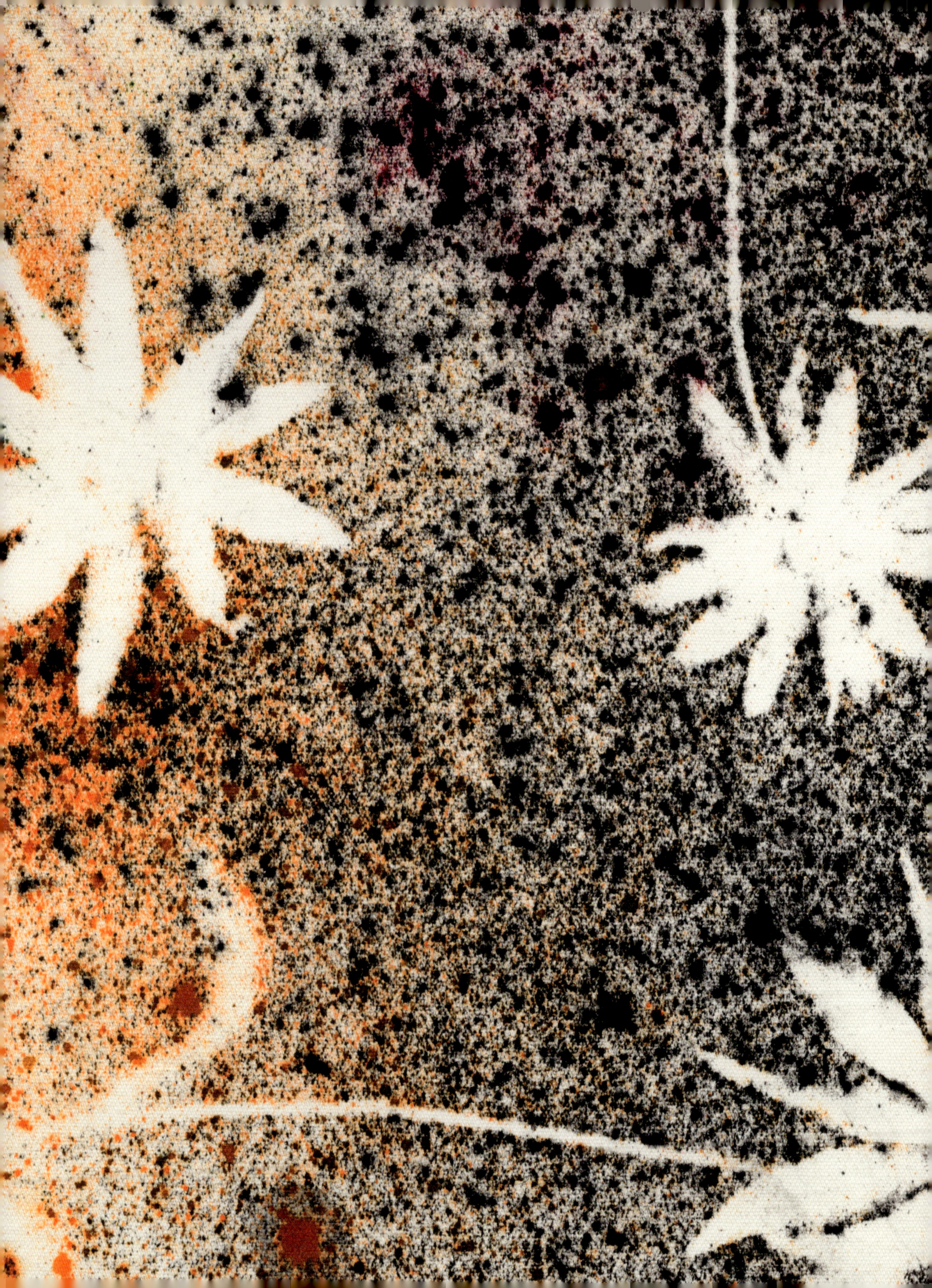

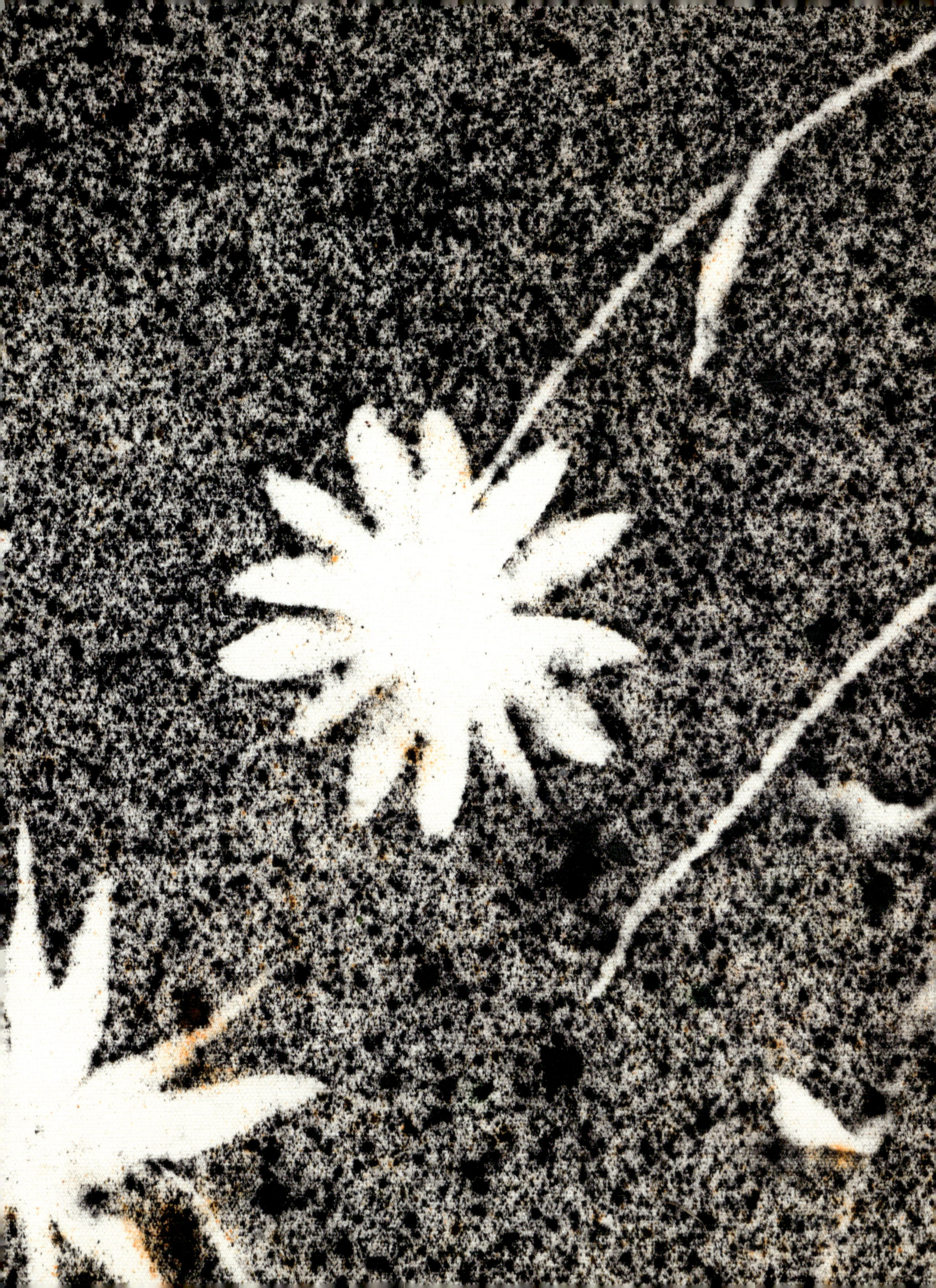

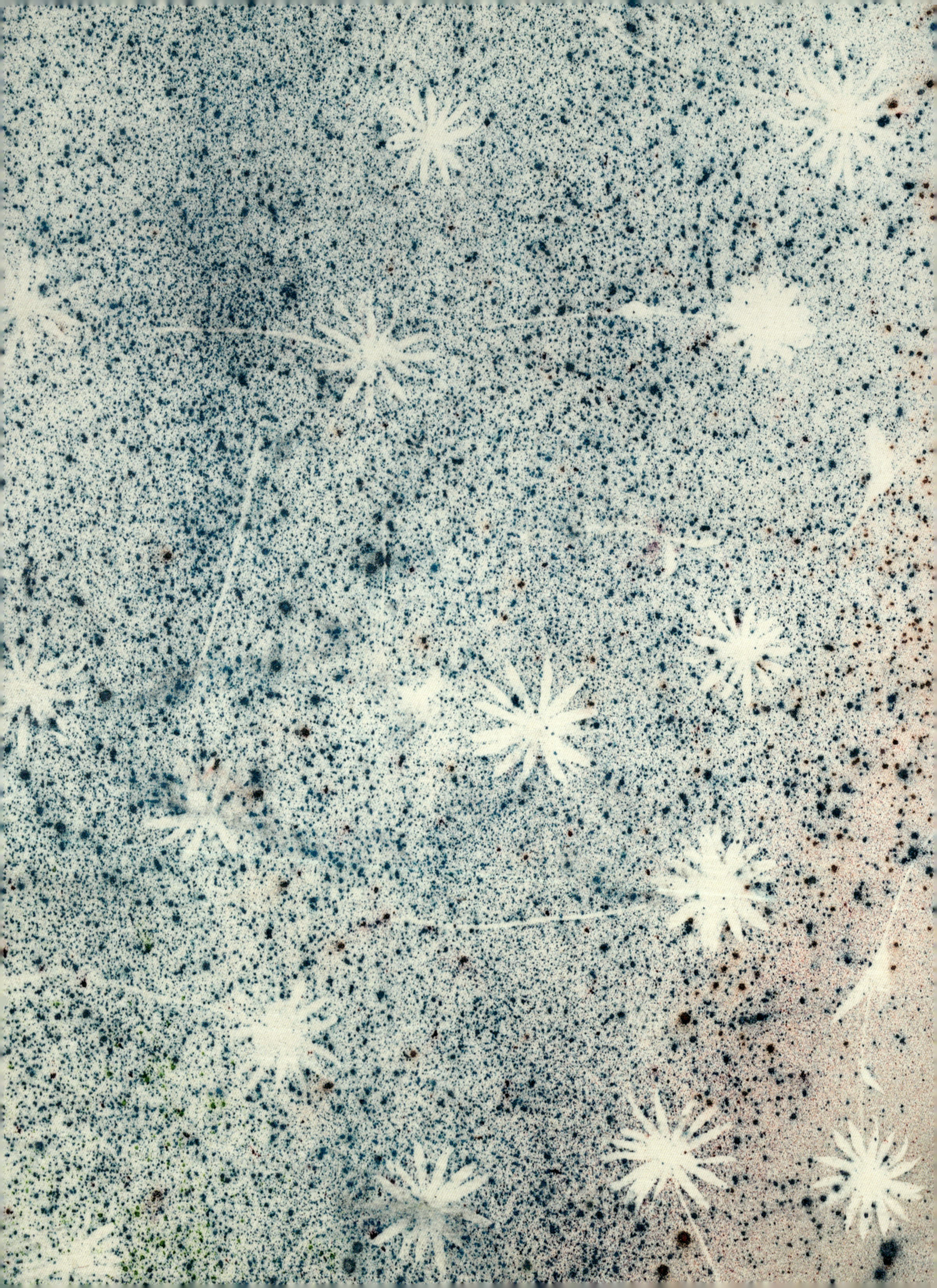

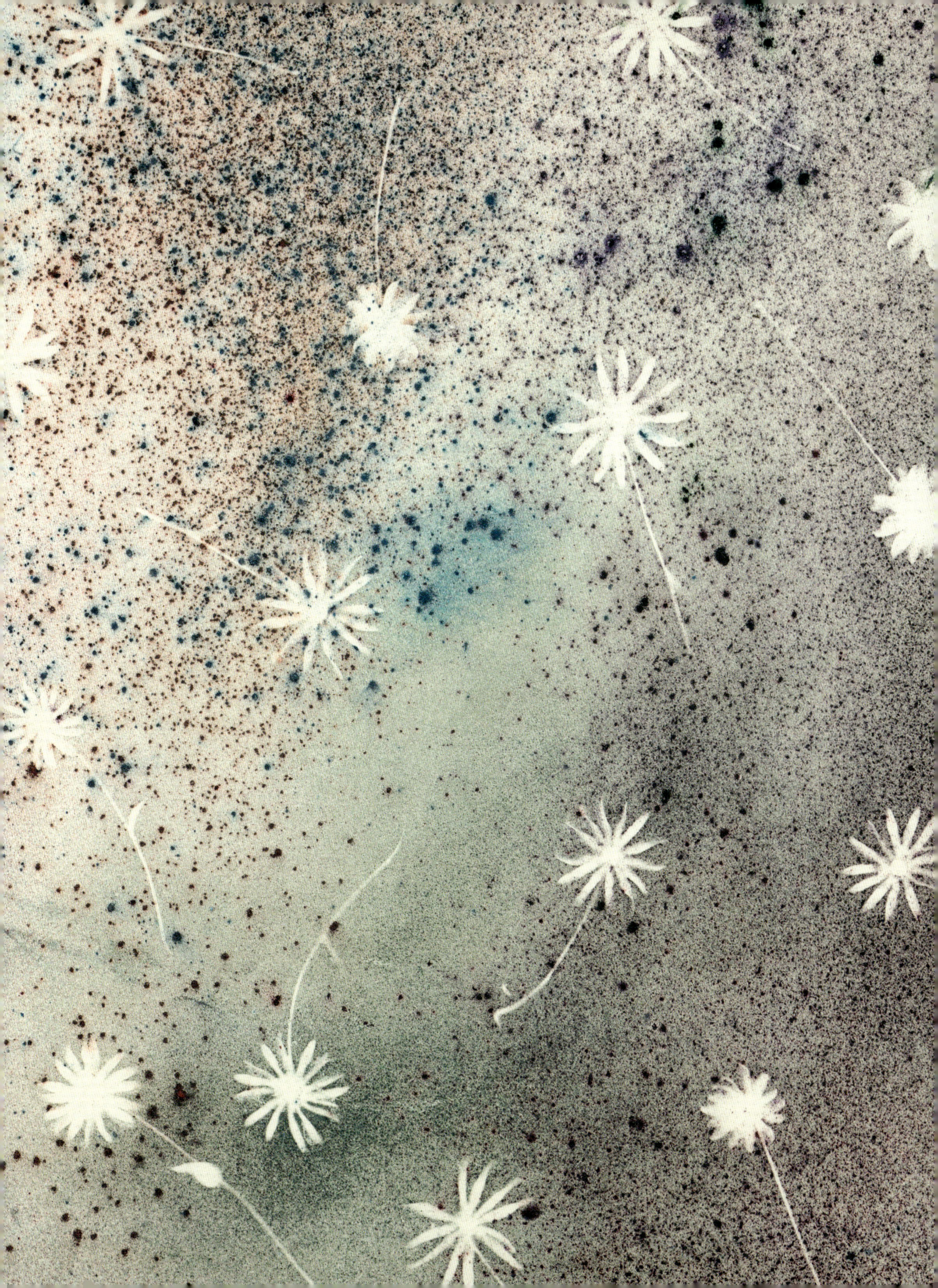

For the series outlined in *Plein Air*, Sam Falls empowered the natural and environmental conditions of four distinct locations to assist in the completion of individual works on canvas. As part of a larger practice concerned with removing or reducing his own role in the processes of making, Falls outlined a set of guidelines at the outset of the project that determined how the specific locations would impress themselves onto the works and lend their unique qualities to the overall production, as indexes of material presence rather than representations of place as such. Initiated in Hartland, Vermont, where the artist was raised, and concluding at a residency in Sarvisalo, Finland, the series also unfolded in Venice, California, and Hudson, New York, where Falls maintains a studio between Los Angeles. While the parameters at each location included raw, untreated canvas and random selections of three-ounce containers of powdered pigment, the variations in the series depended upon the abundant local plant life and the conditions of the readymade environment, namely the percentage of precipitation found at each place.

Palm fronds, birds of paradise, ferns, Black-eyed Susans, apple blossom petals, birch and sumac trees, tiger lilies, buttercups, and the like are outlined on the canvases, their shapes determined by the swaths of color that inventory where they once rested in an open field, a yard, or a lawn. In each instance, Falls subjected the materials to the natural elements over the course of a day or a night, producing various effects that are themselves markers of time and the abundance or lack of rainfall over a given period. These variations account for the different relationships to place and duration throughout the works in the series. Approximating the gestural impact and dense accumulations of splatter paint or the washy wispiness of color-field abstraction, the canvases are united by their deferment to nature, to the processes by which the conditions at a particular site can be employed in the service of production. This approach is bred out of certain sensitivities to the world and its inherent ways of working and shaping matter, as much as it is from a desire to console the difficult task of creating things, ideas, and images.

SARVISALO, FIN

116.
*Untitled
(Sarvisalo, Finland,
Buttercups 1)*, 2014
Pigment on canvas
50 × 40 inches
(127 × 101.6 cm)

117.
*Untitled
(Sarvisalo, Finland,
Ash 1)*, 2014
Pigment on canvas
96 × 80 inches
(243.8 × 203.2 cm)

119.
*Untitled
(Sarvisalo, Finland,
Apple Blossom
Petals 5)*, 2014
Pigment on canvas
66⅞ × 52⅜ inches
(170 × 133 cm)

121.
*Untitled
(Sarvisalo, Finland,
Apple Blossom
Petals 1)*, 2014
Pigment on canvas
52⅜ × 45¼ inches
(133 × 115 cm)

122.
*Untitled
(Sarvisalo, Finland,
Apple Blossom
Petals 2)*, 2014
Pigment on canvas
52⅜ × 46⅛ inches
(133 × 117 cm)

123.
*Untitled
(Sarvisalo, Finland,
Apple Blossom
Petals 3)*, 2014
Pigment on canvas
52⅜ × 46½ inches
(133 × 118 cm)

125.
*Untitled
(Sarvisalo, Finland,
Apple Blossom
Petals 4)*, 2014
Pigment on canvas
66 × 51⅝ inches
(167.5 × 131 cm)

127.
*Untitled
(Sarvisalo, Finland,
Apple Blossom
Petals 7)*, 2014
Pigment on canvas
111⅜ × 65¾ inches
(283 × 167 cm)

129.
*Untitled
(Sarvisalo, Finland,
Apple Blossom
Petals 8)*, 2014
Pigment on canvas
111⅜ × 78¾ inches
(283 × 200 cm)

131.
*Untitled
(Sarvisalo, Finland,
Apple Blossom
Petals 9)*, 2014
Pigment on canvas
111⅜ × 75¼ inches
(283 × 191 cm)

133.
*Untitled
(Sarvisalo, Finland,
Apple Blossom
Petals 10)*, 2014
Pigment on canvas
111⅜ × 83½ inches
(283 × 212 cm)

135.
*Untitled
(Sarvisalo, Finland,
Sumac Tree 1)*, 2014
Pigment on canvas
111⅜ × 102 inches
(283 × 259 cm)

137.
*Untitled
(Sarvisalo, Finland,
Sumac Tree 2)*, 2014
Pigment on canvas
153¾ × 111⅜ inches
(390.5 × 283 cm)

139.
*Untitled
(Sarvisalo, Finland,
Birch Tree 1)*, 2014
Pigment on canvas
149⅝ × 111⅜ inches
(380 × 283 cm)

140–41.
Detail of *Untitled
(Sarvisalo, Finland,
Sumac Tree 1)*

142–43.
Detail of *Untitled
(Sarvisalo, Finland,
Apple Blossom Petals 10)*

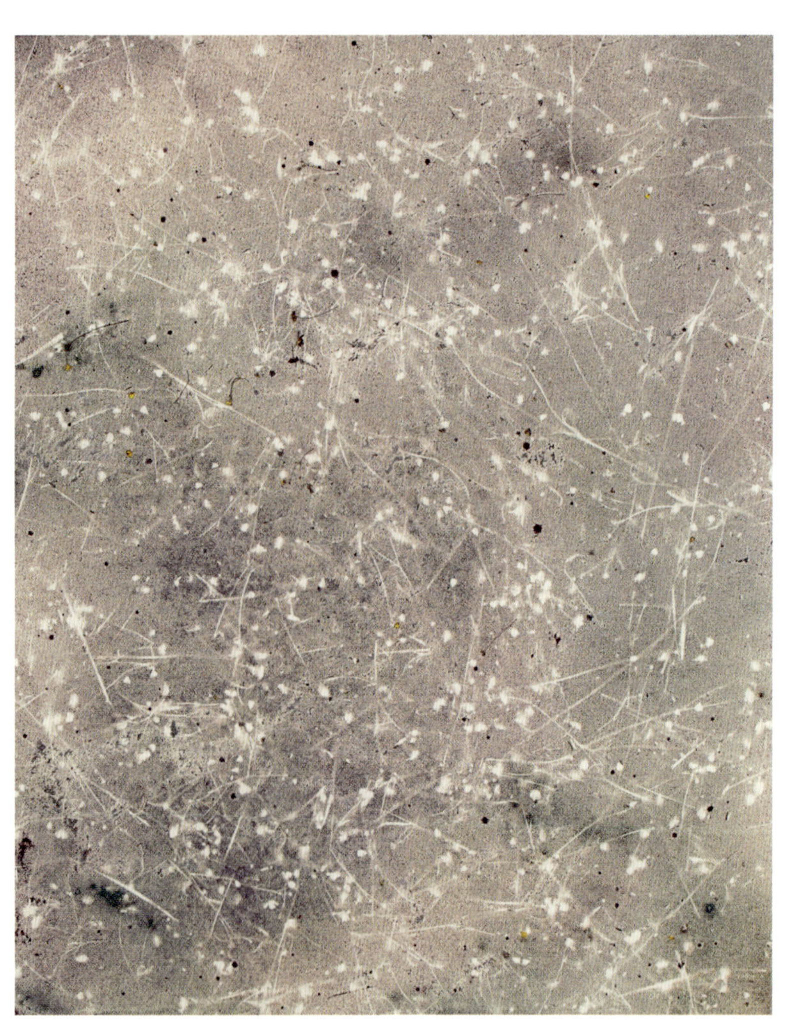

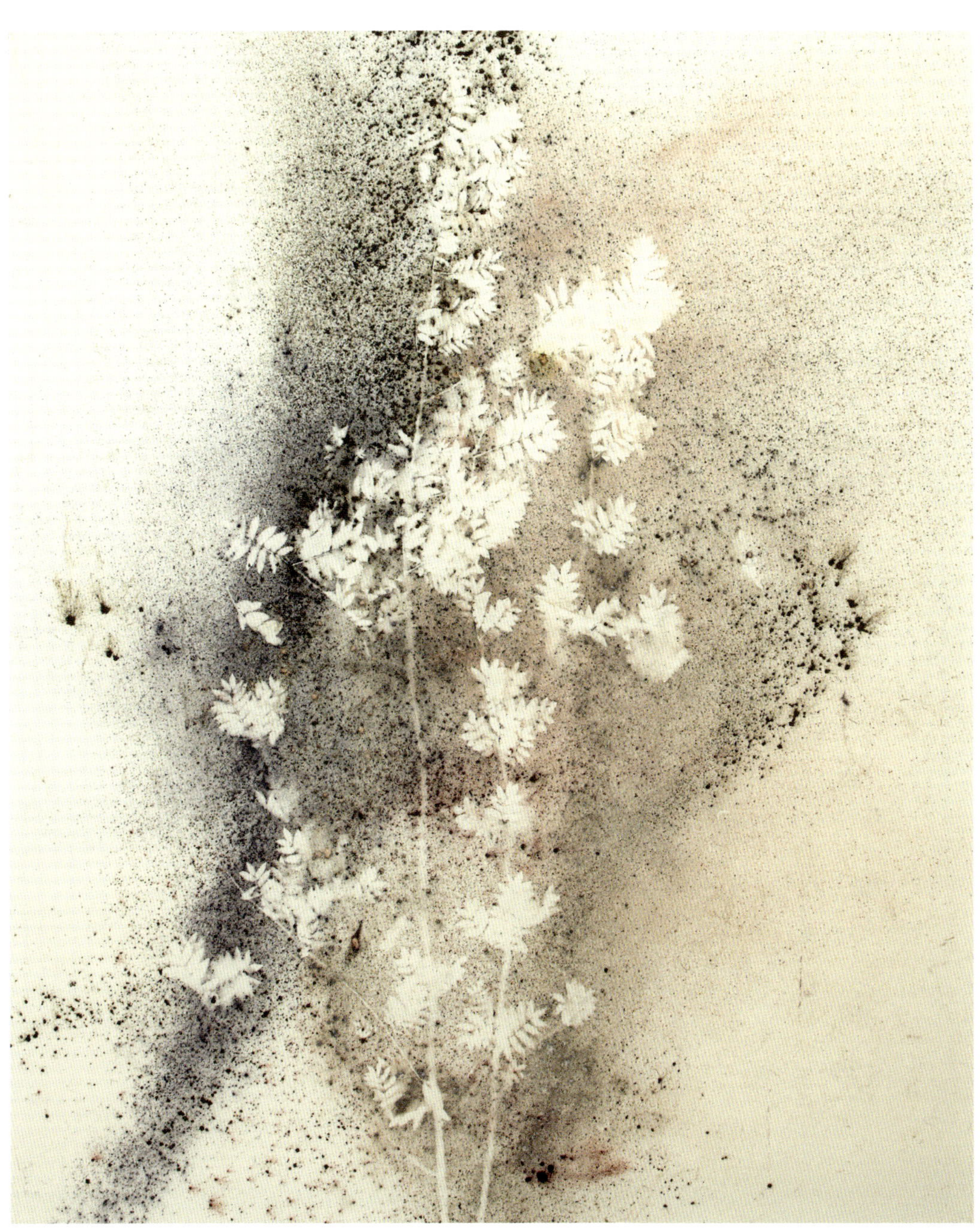

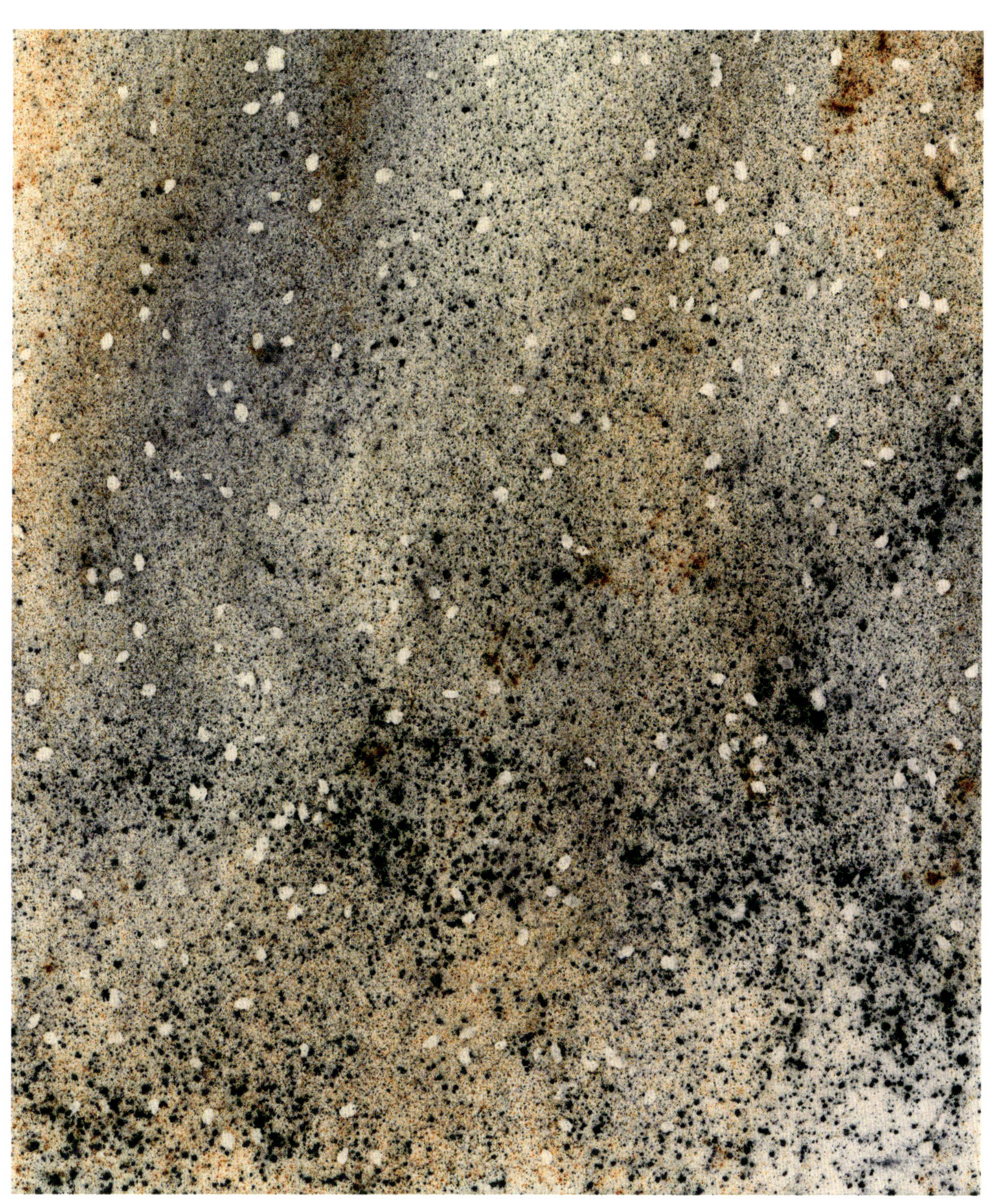

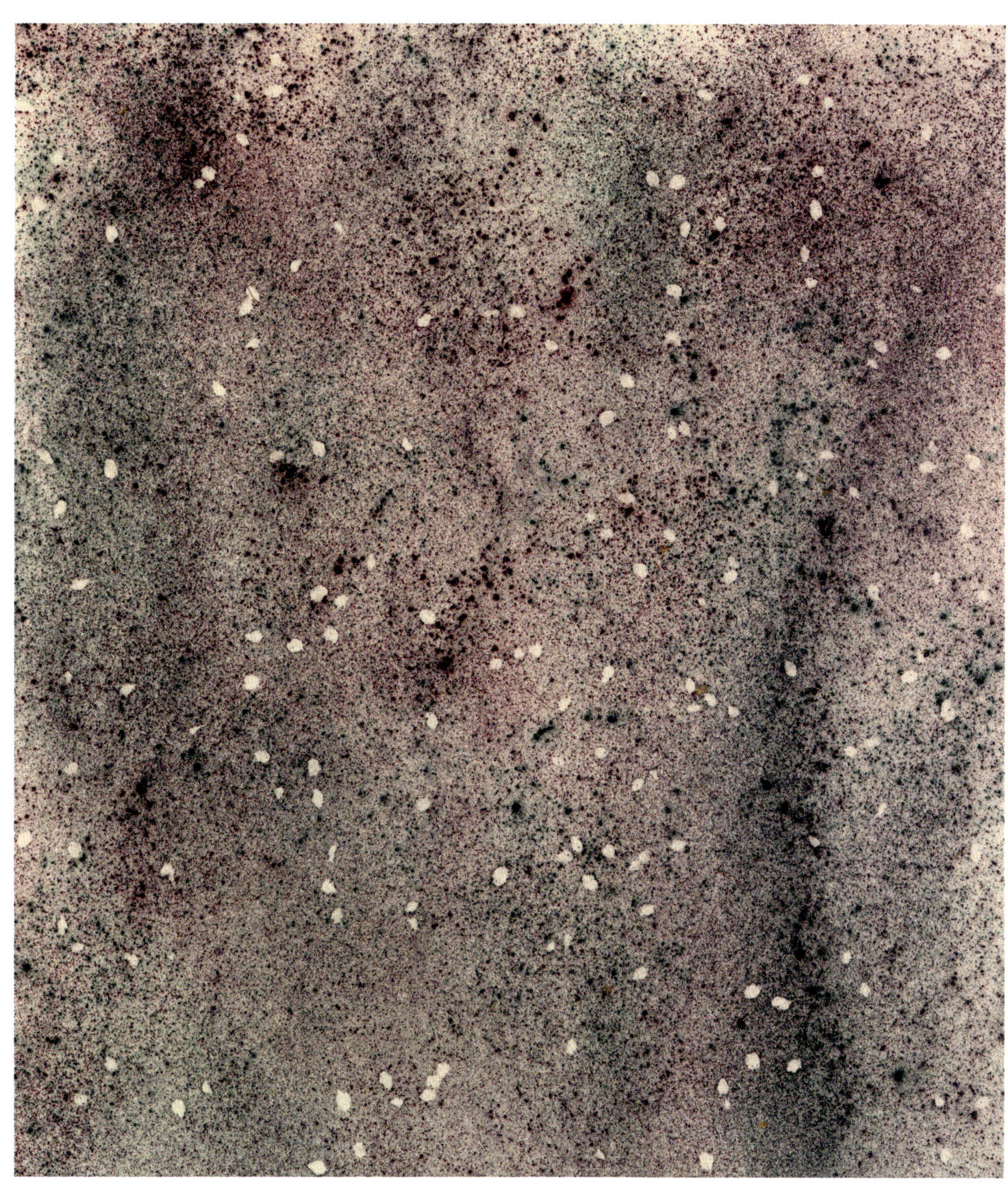

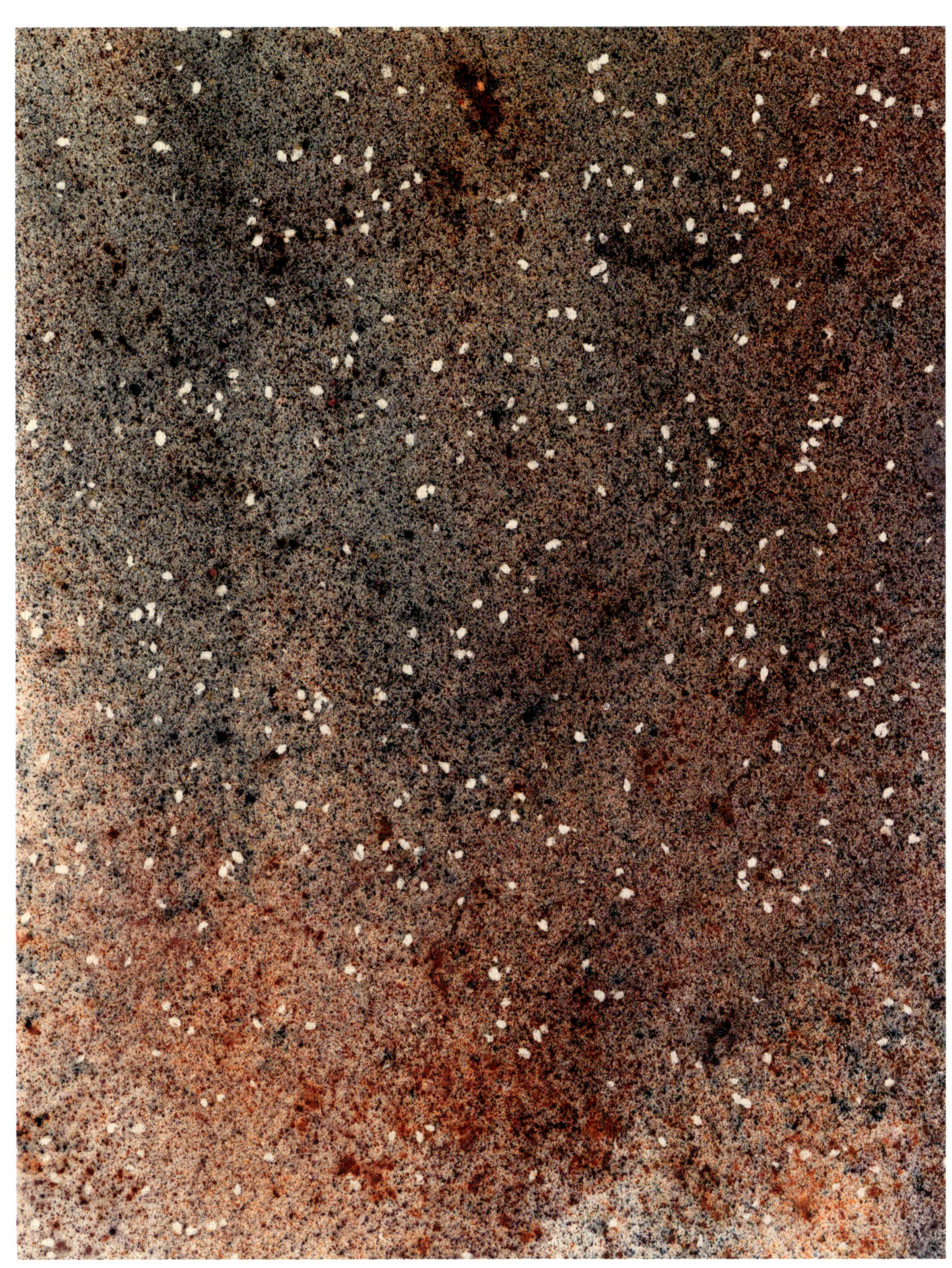

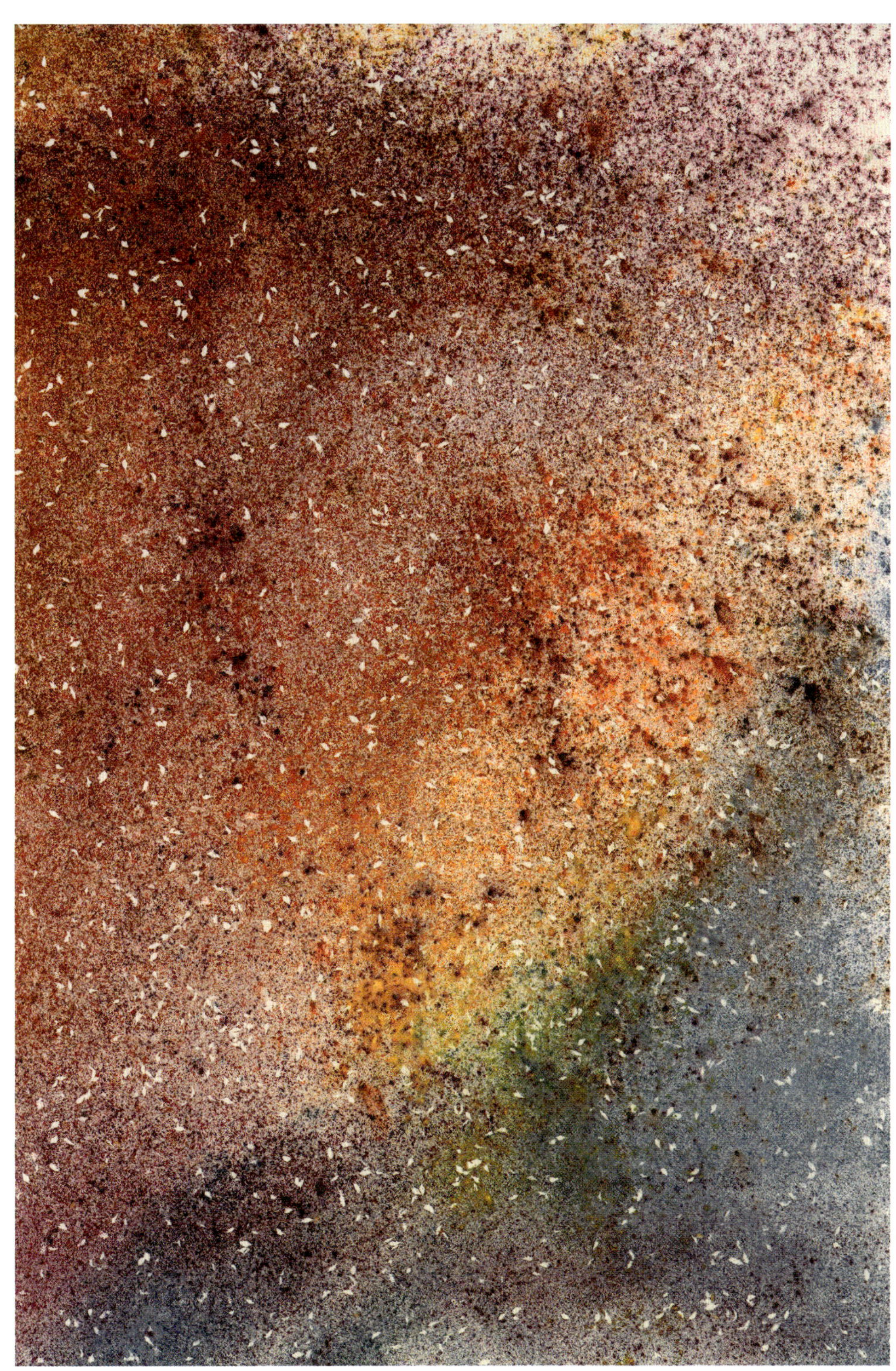

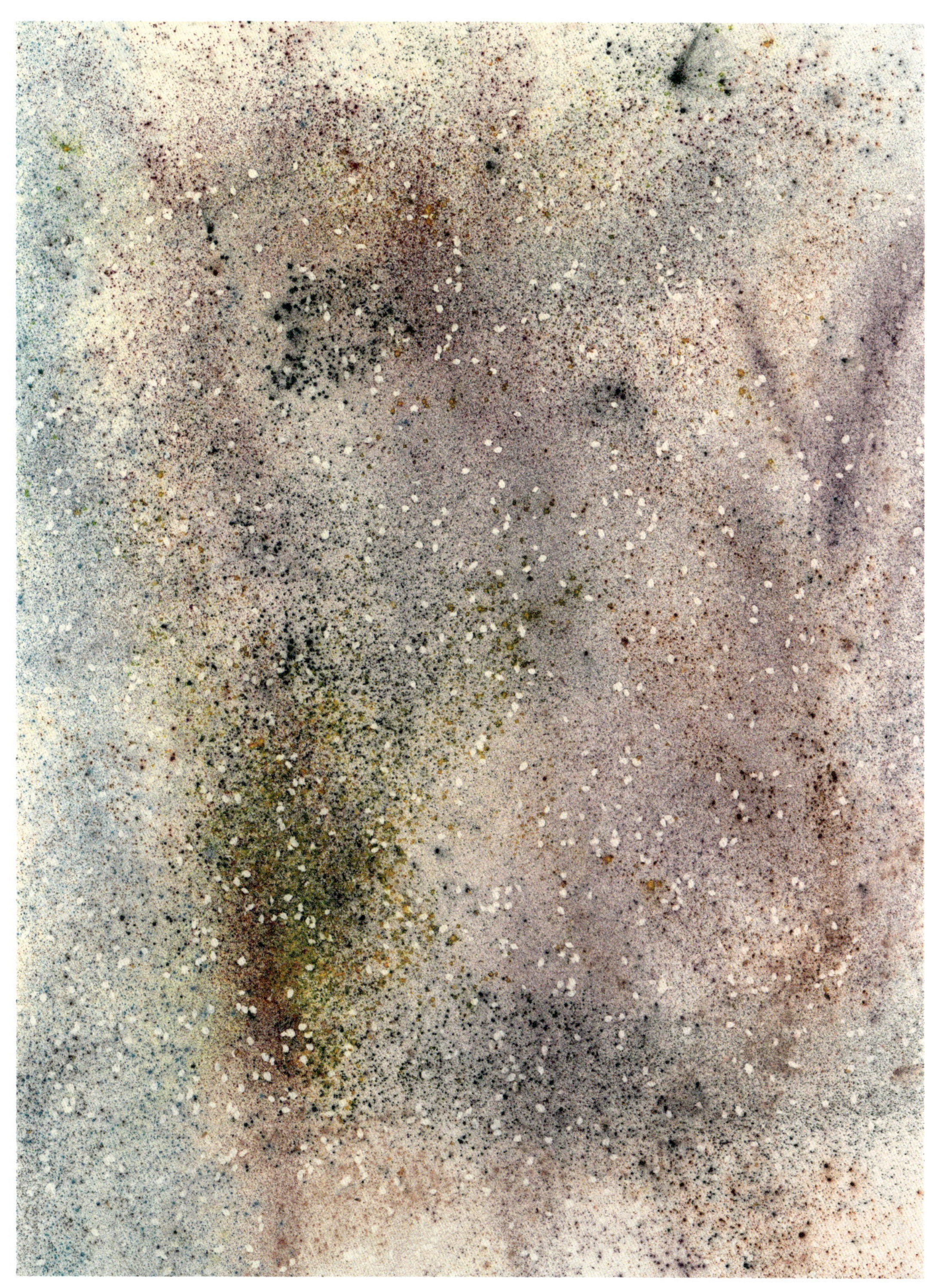

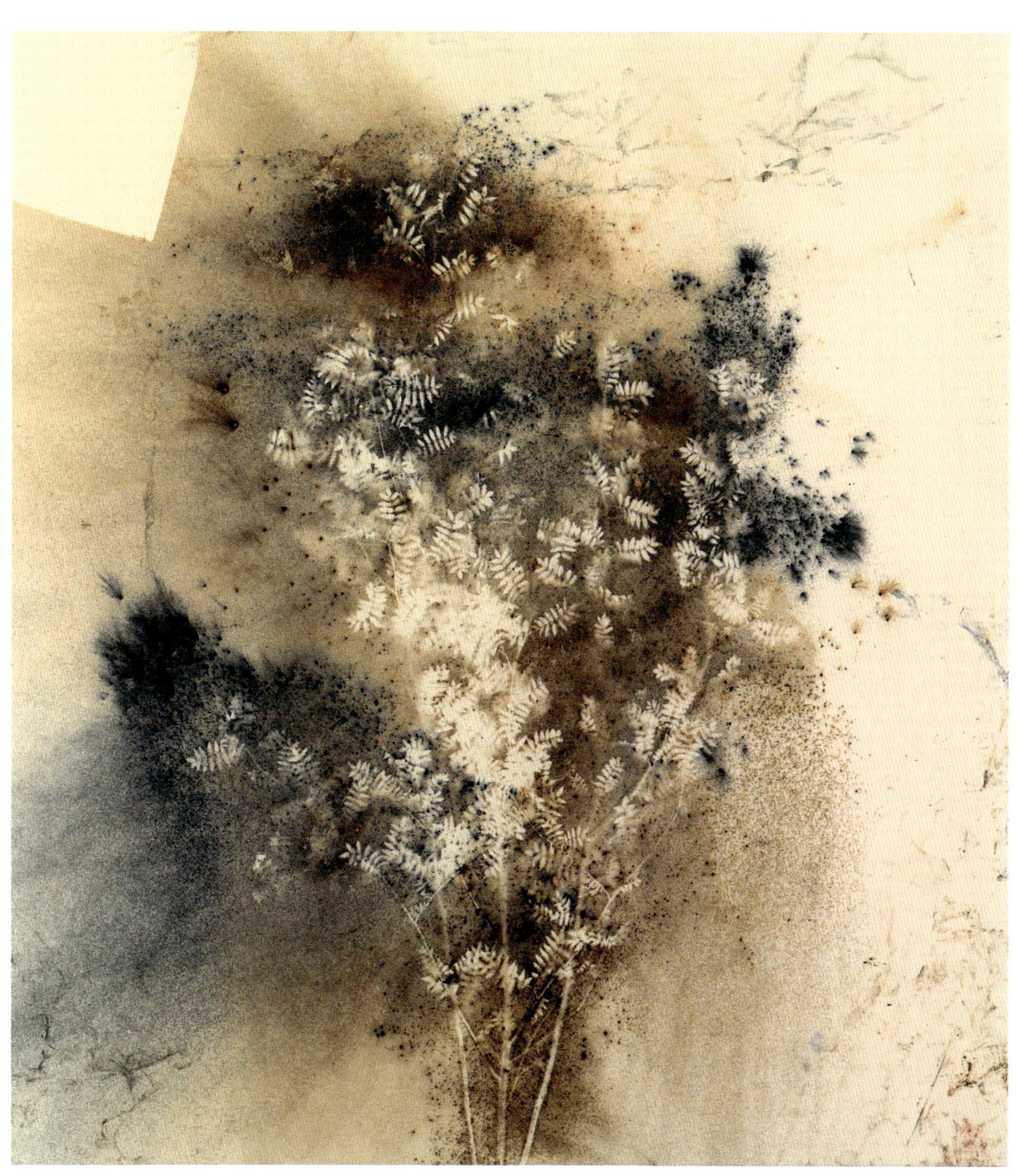

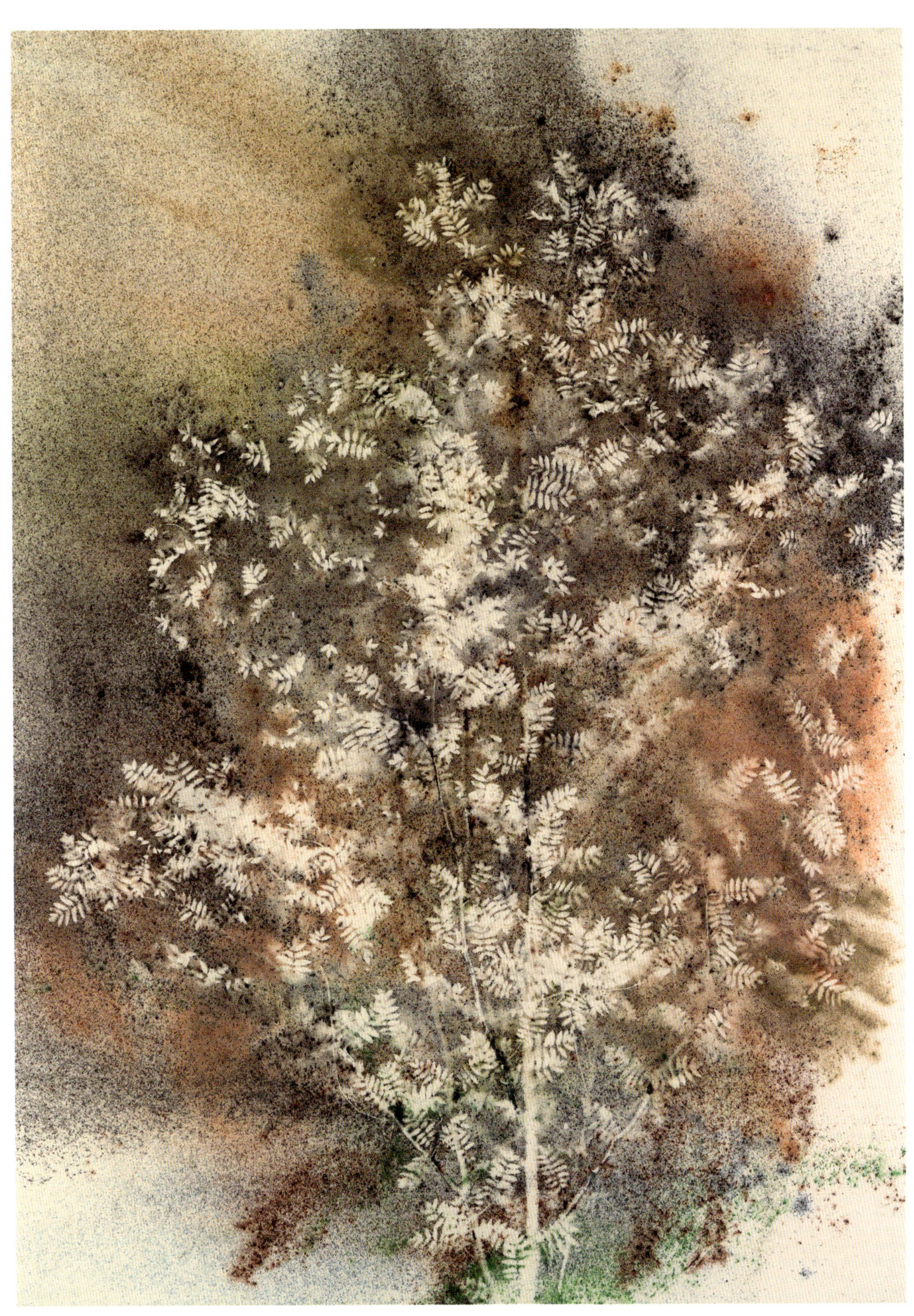

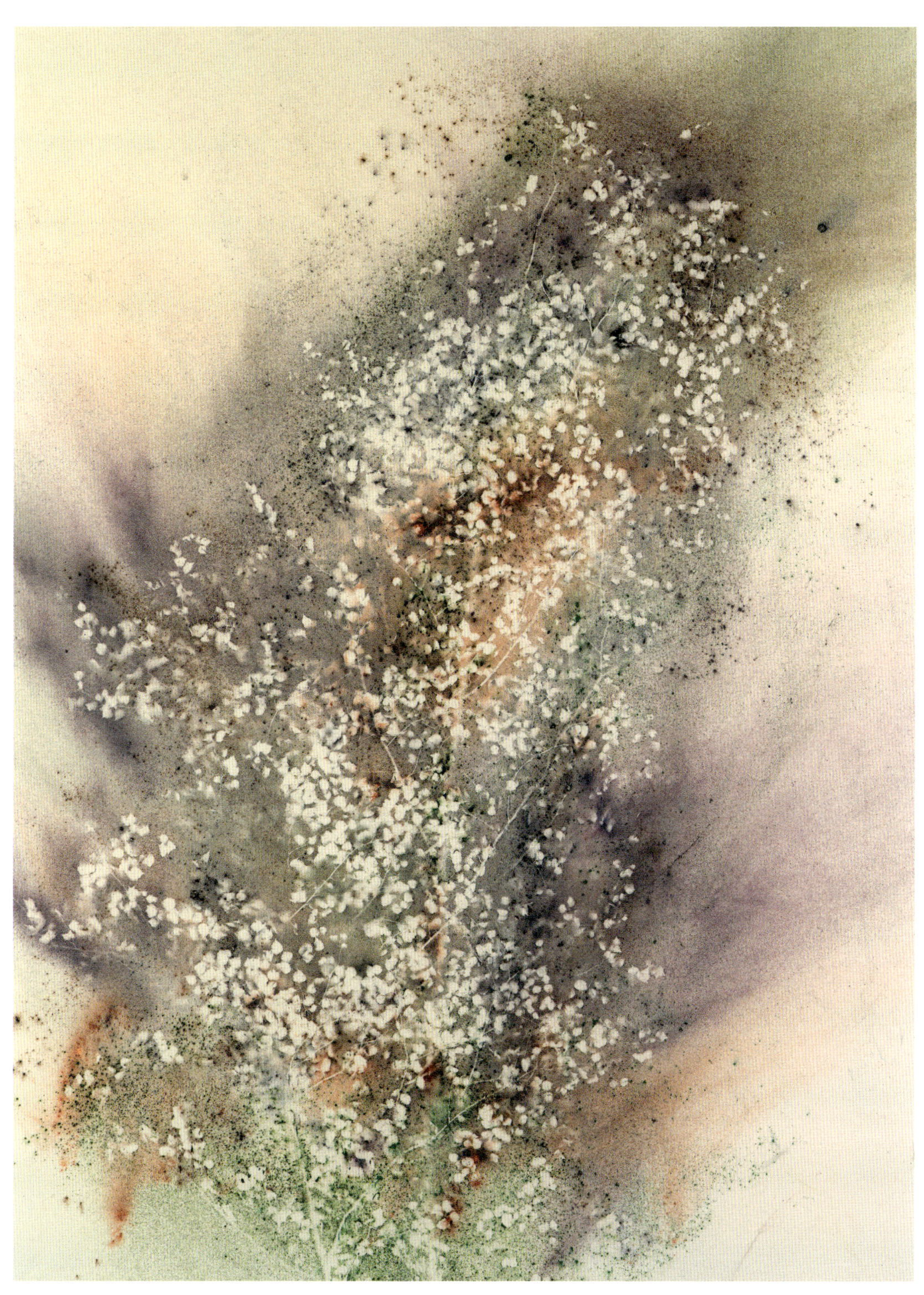

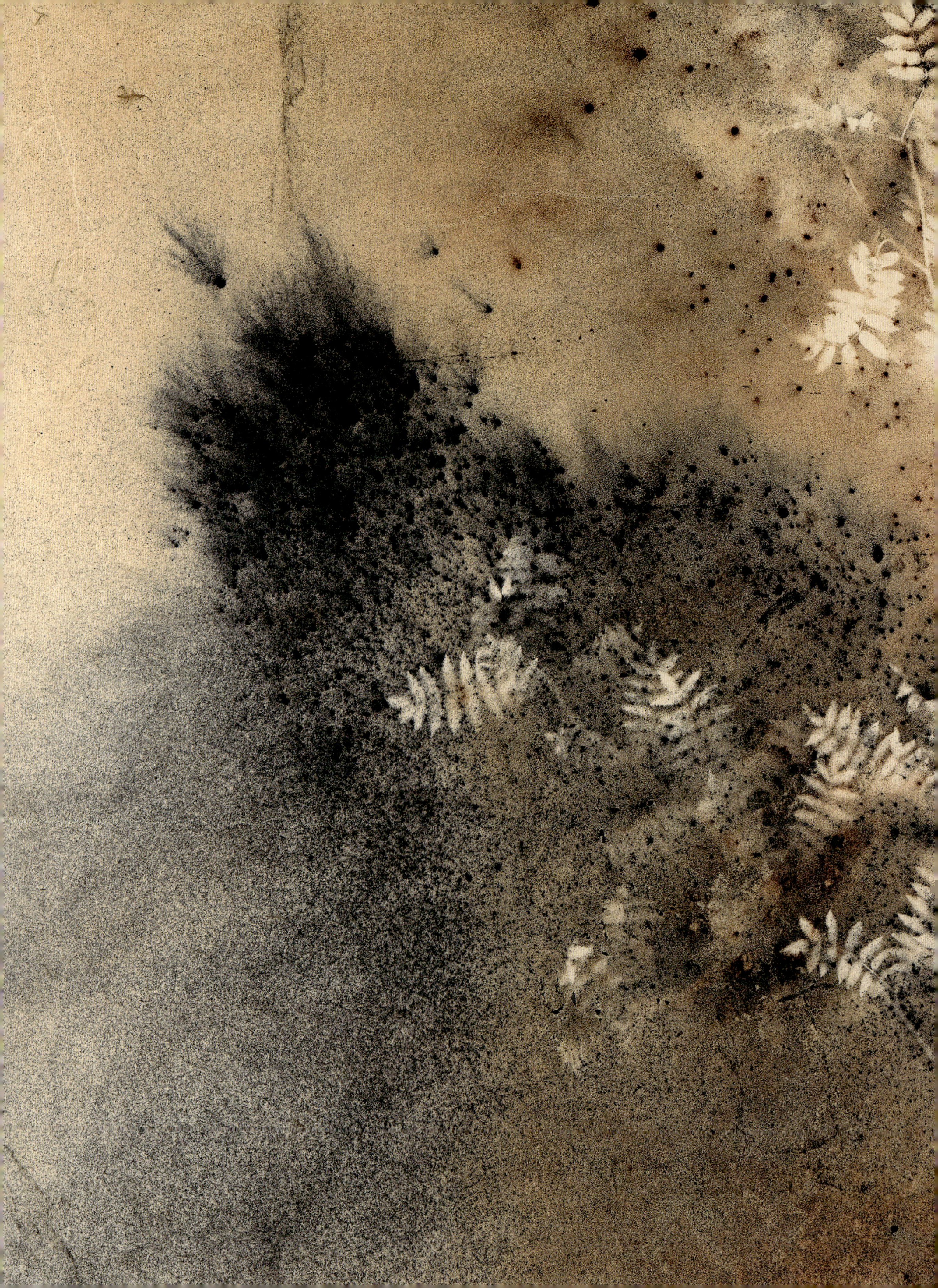

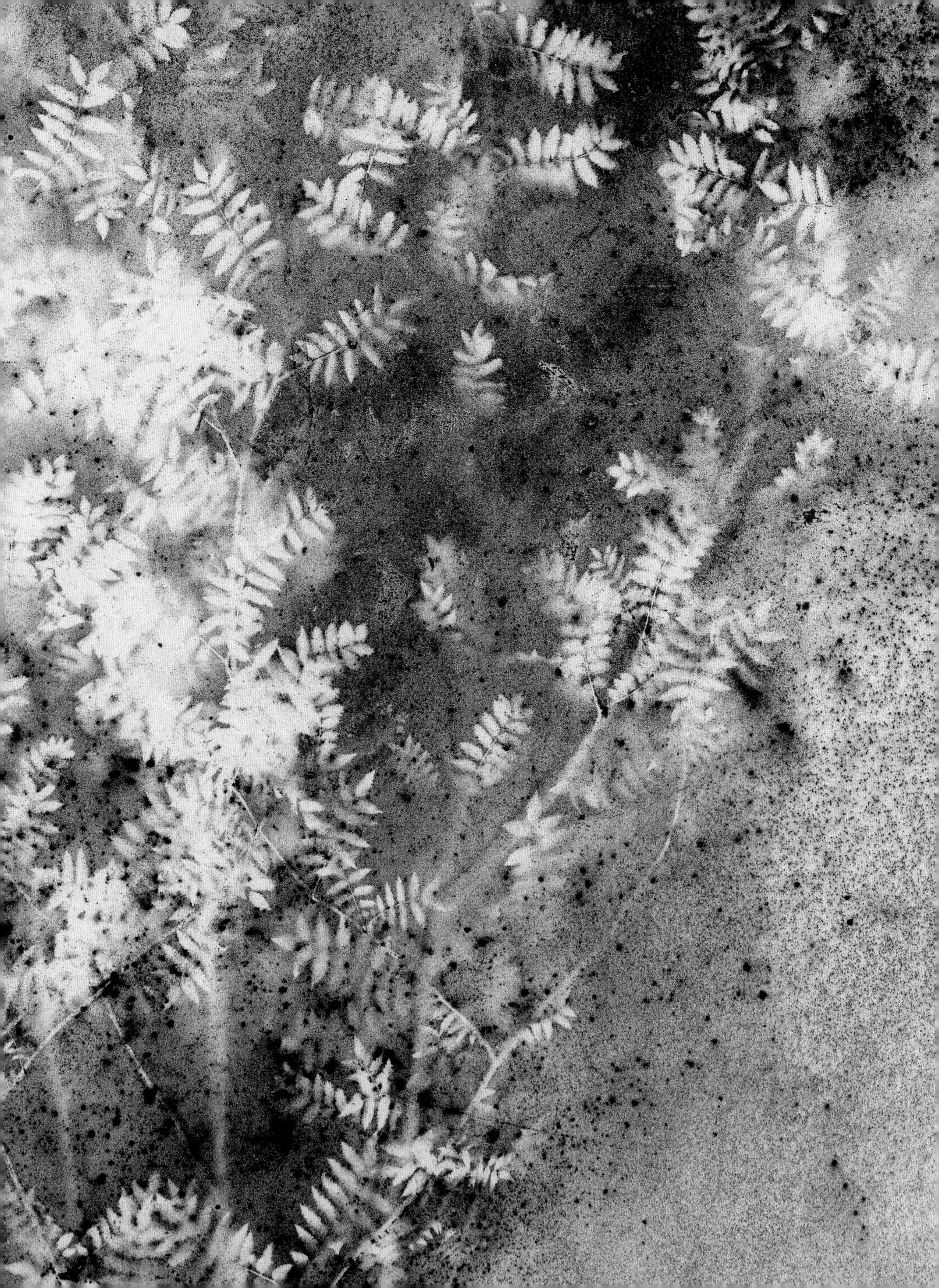

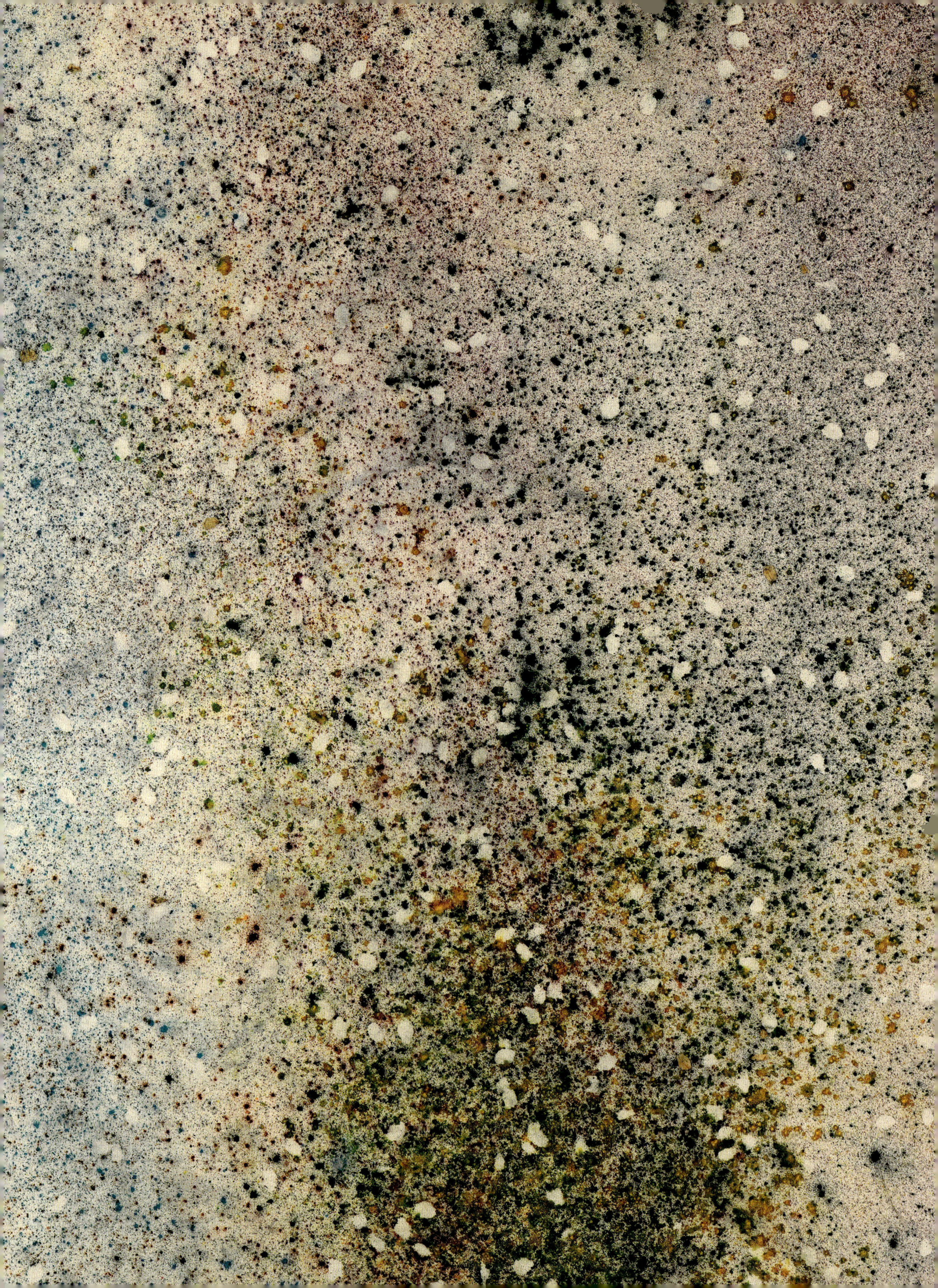

Galerie Eva Presenhuber
Zurich, Switzerland
Aug 30 – Oct 25, 2014

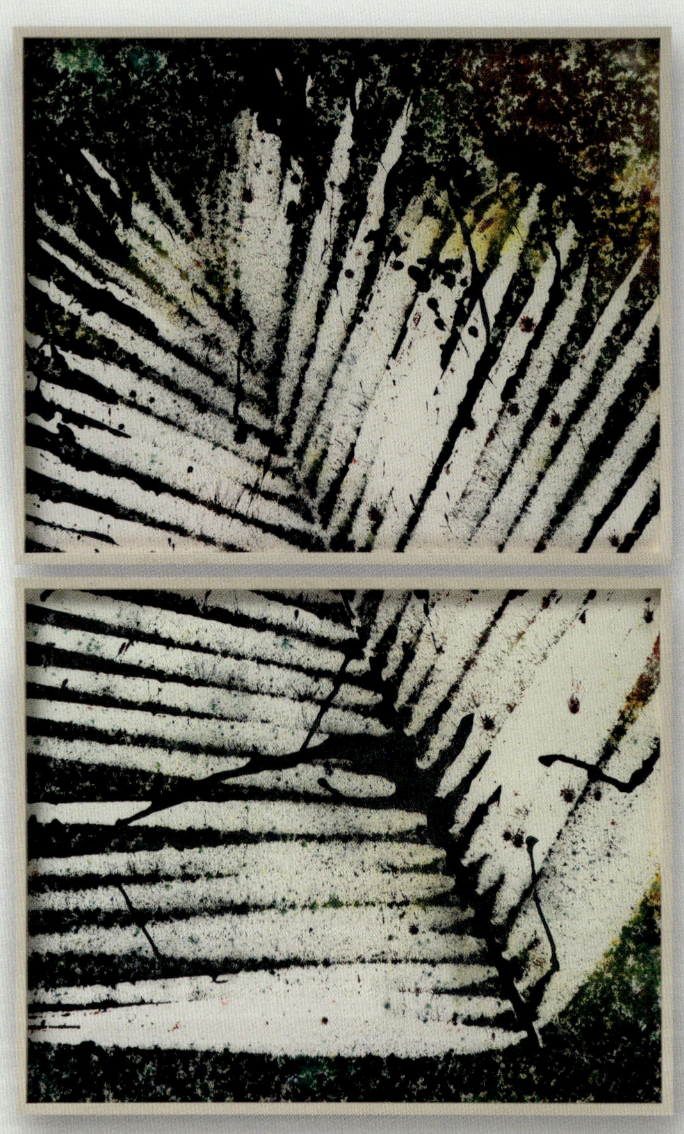

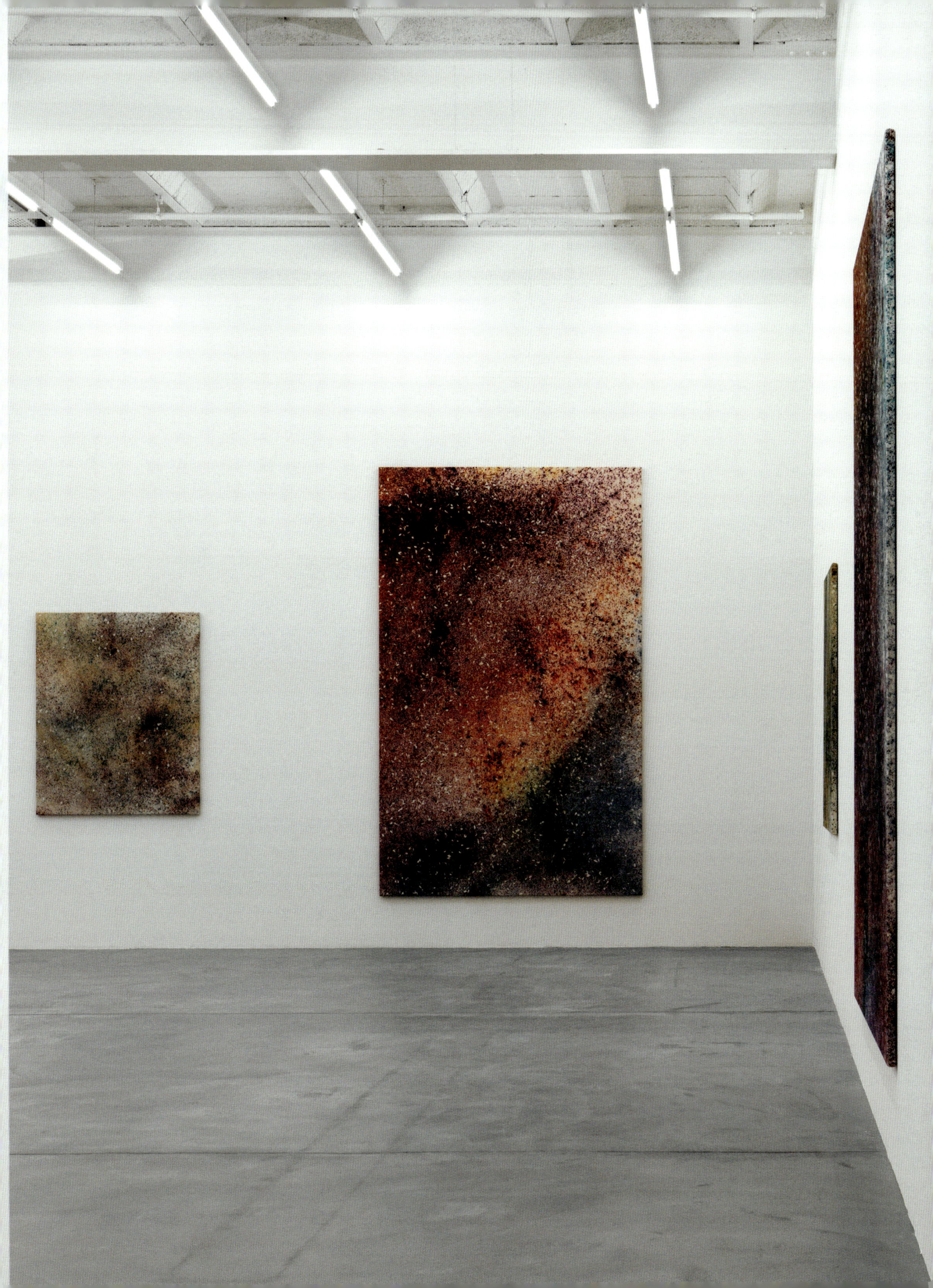

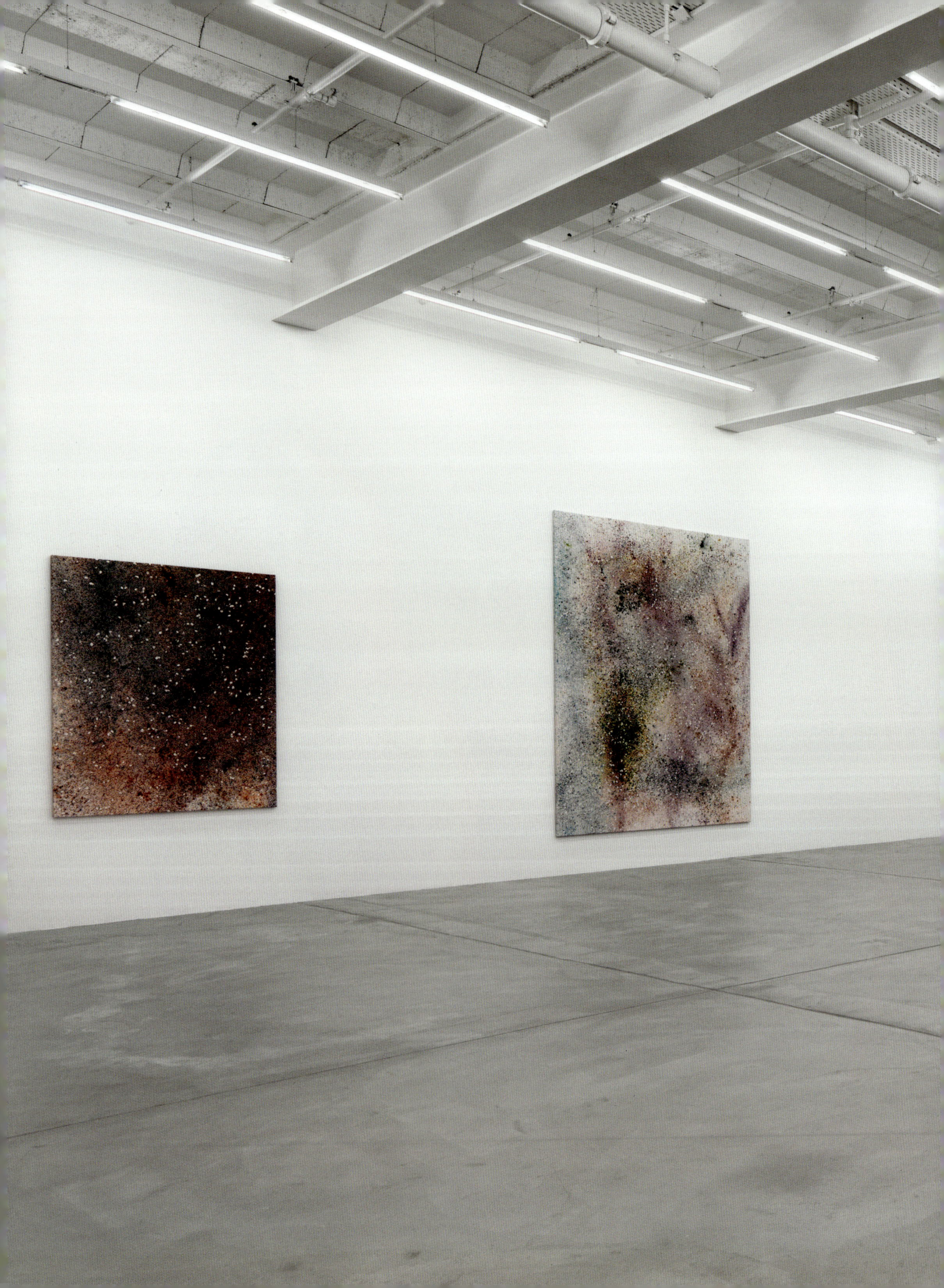

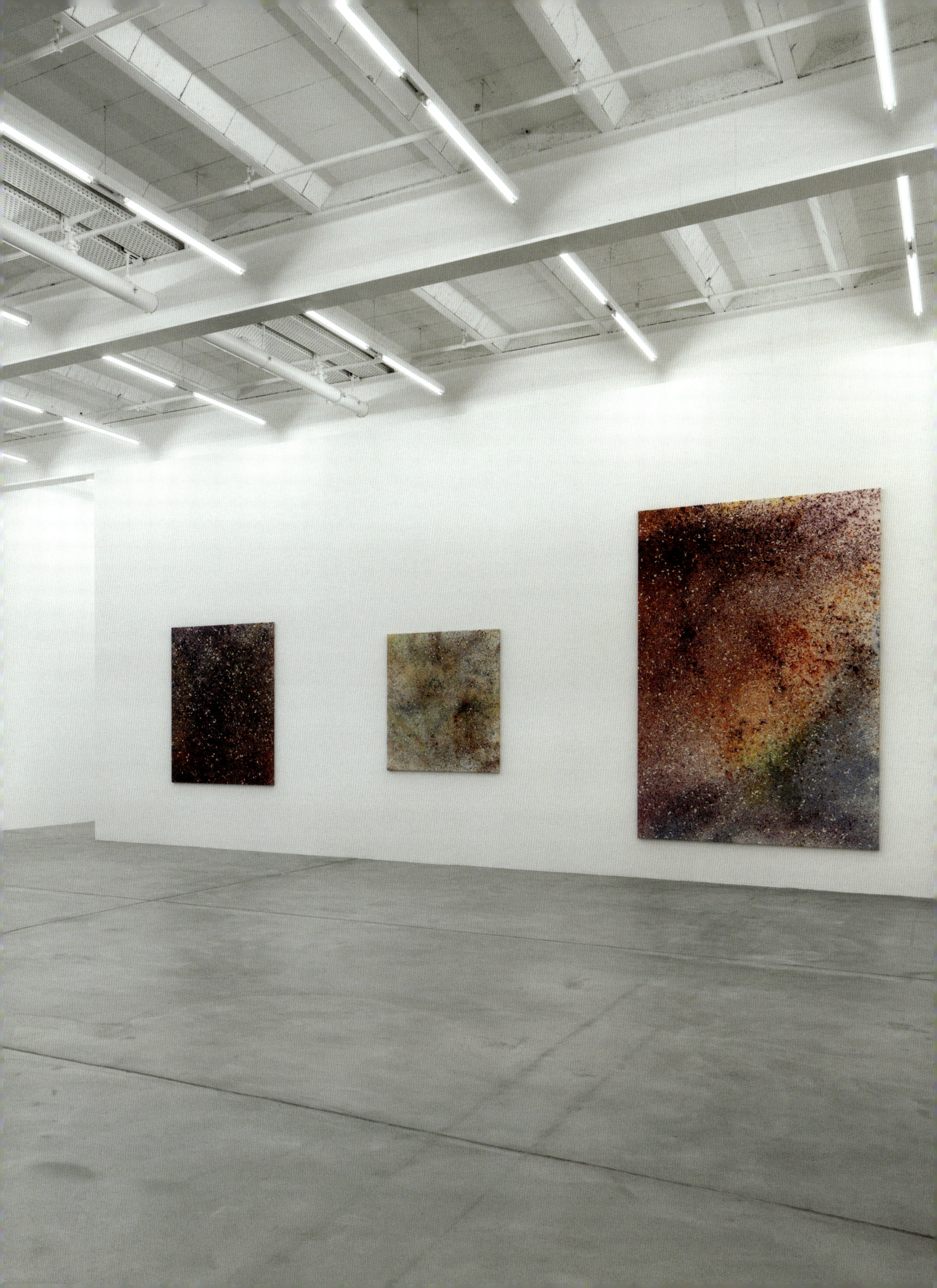

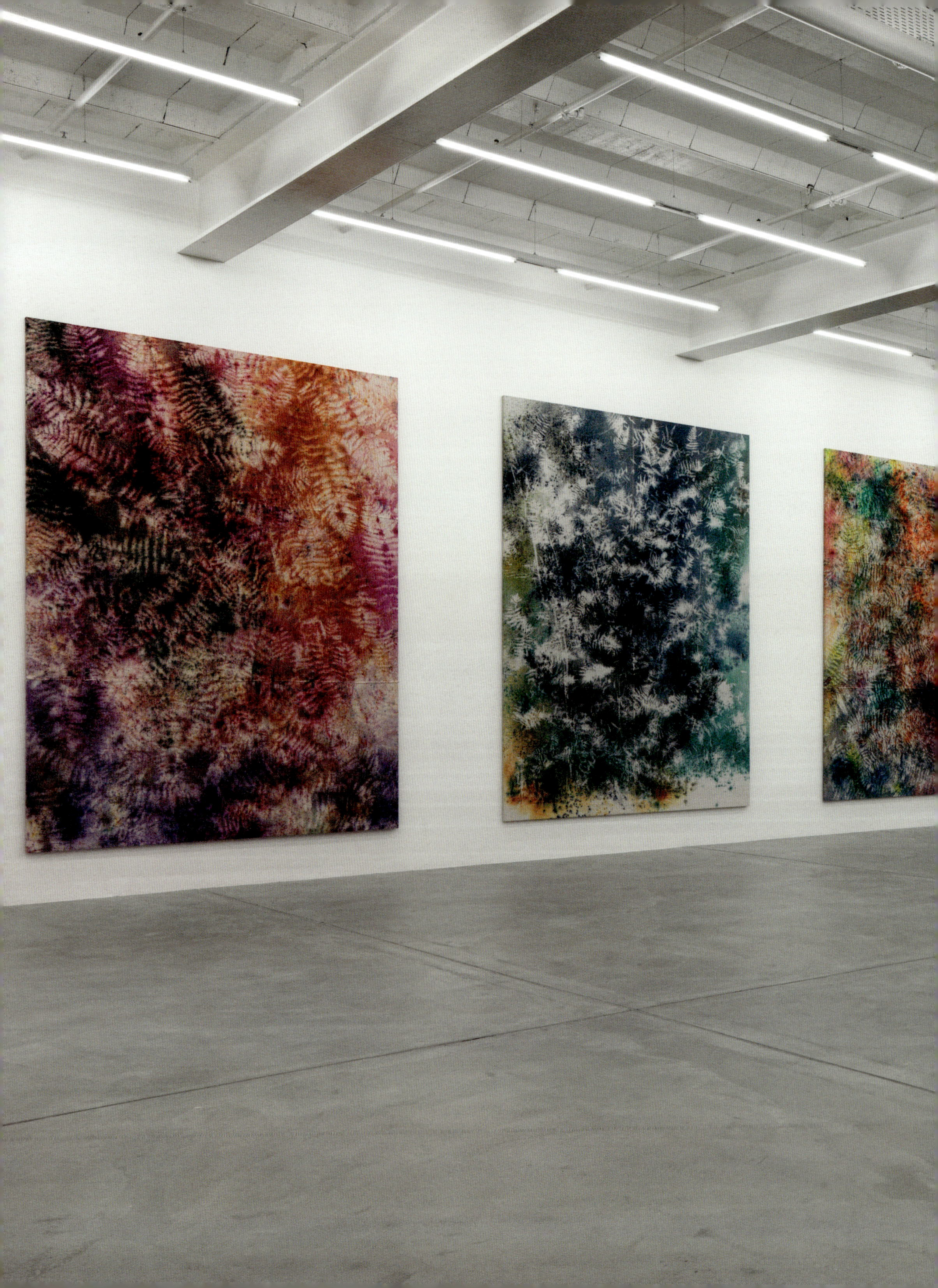

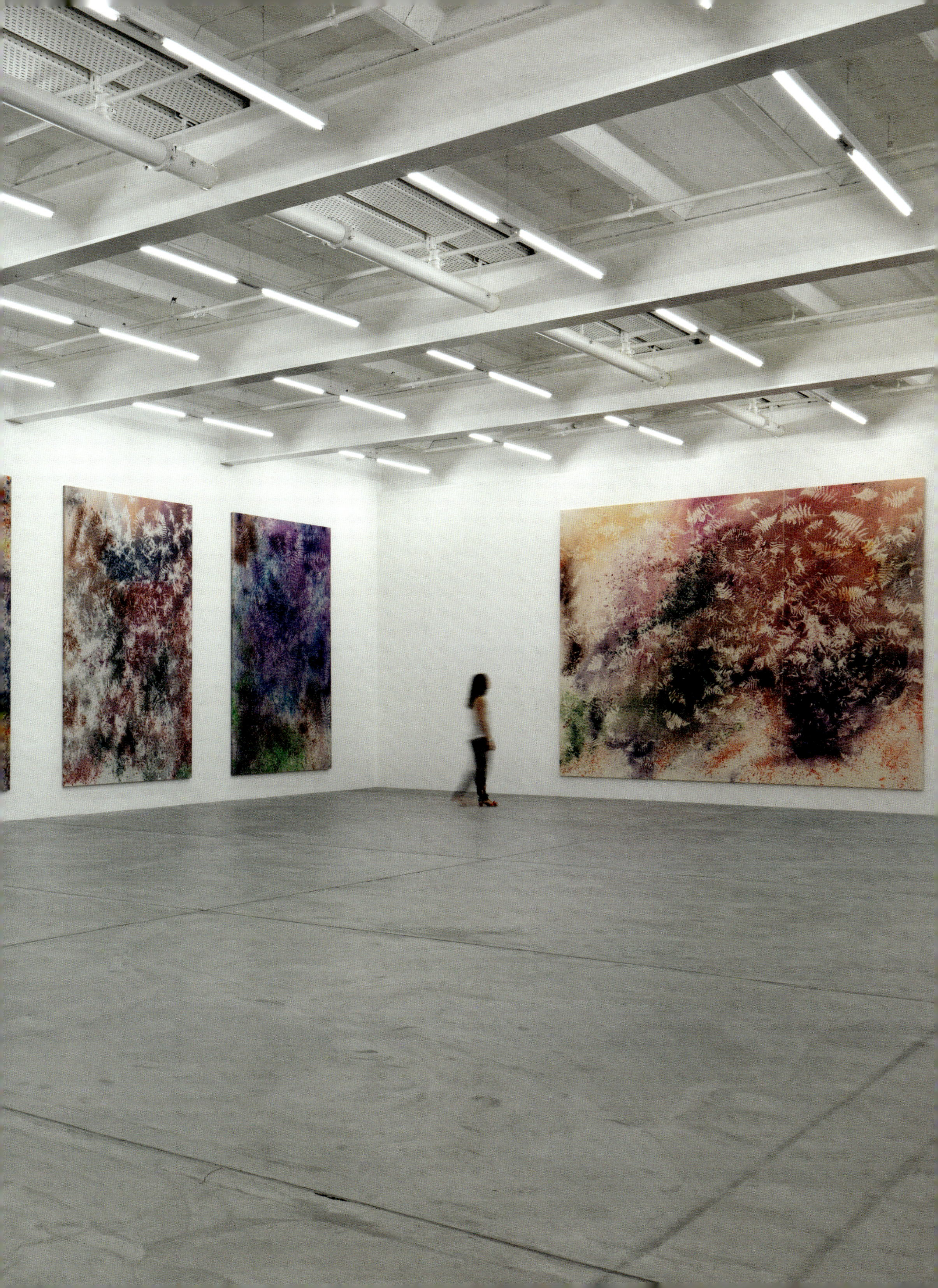

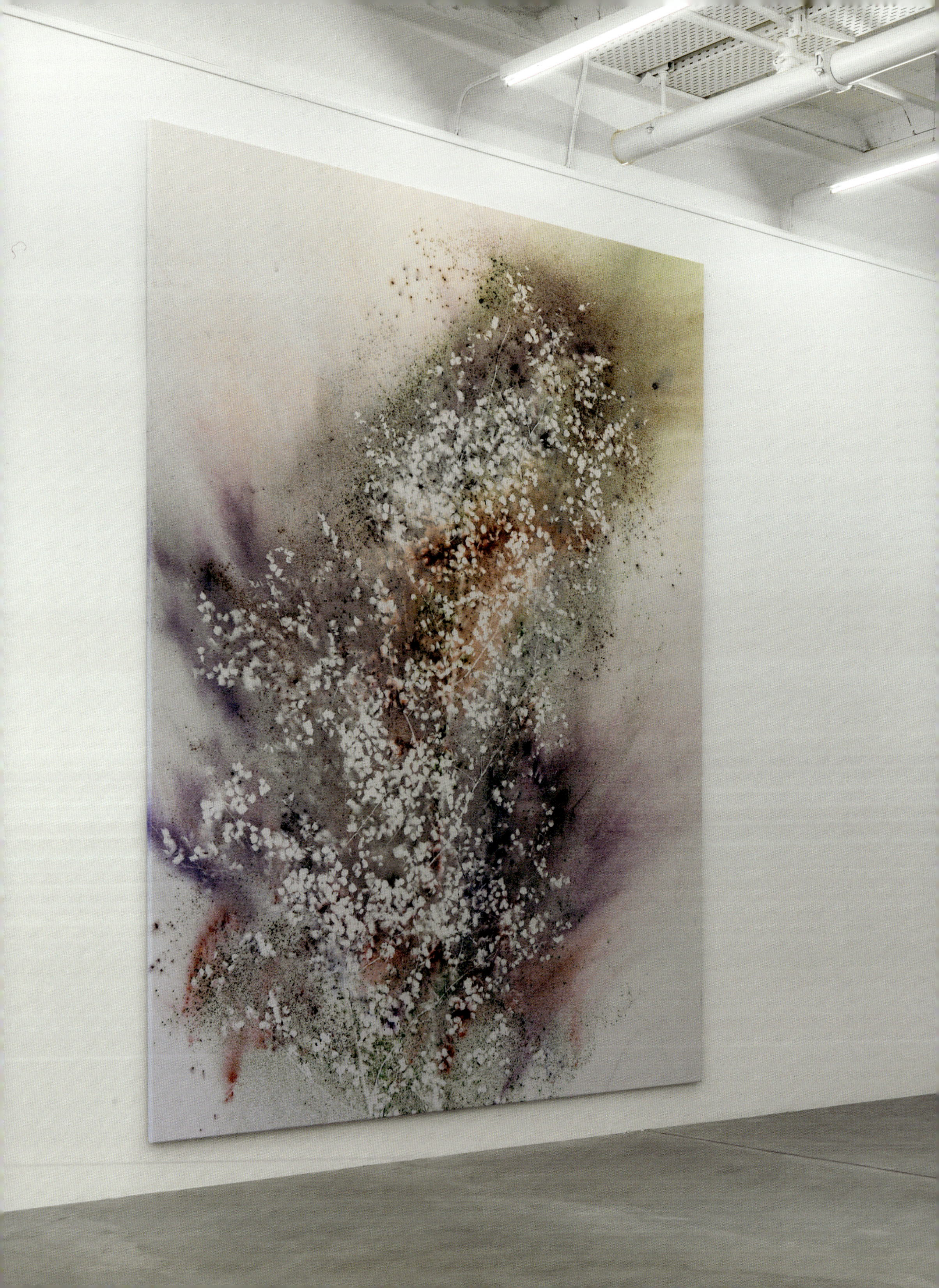

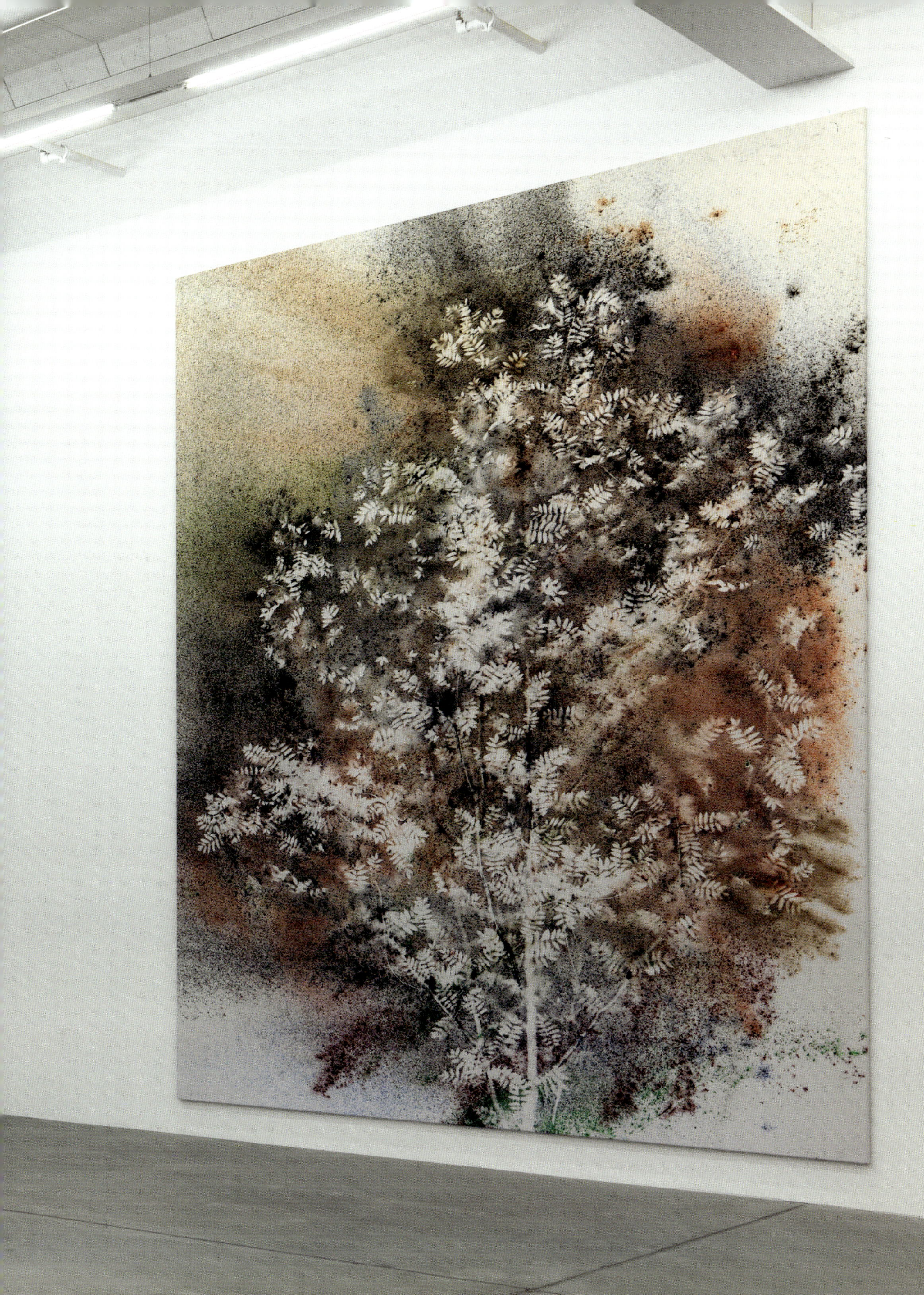

Pomona College
Museum of Art
Claremont, CA
Sept 2 – Dec 19, 2014

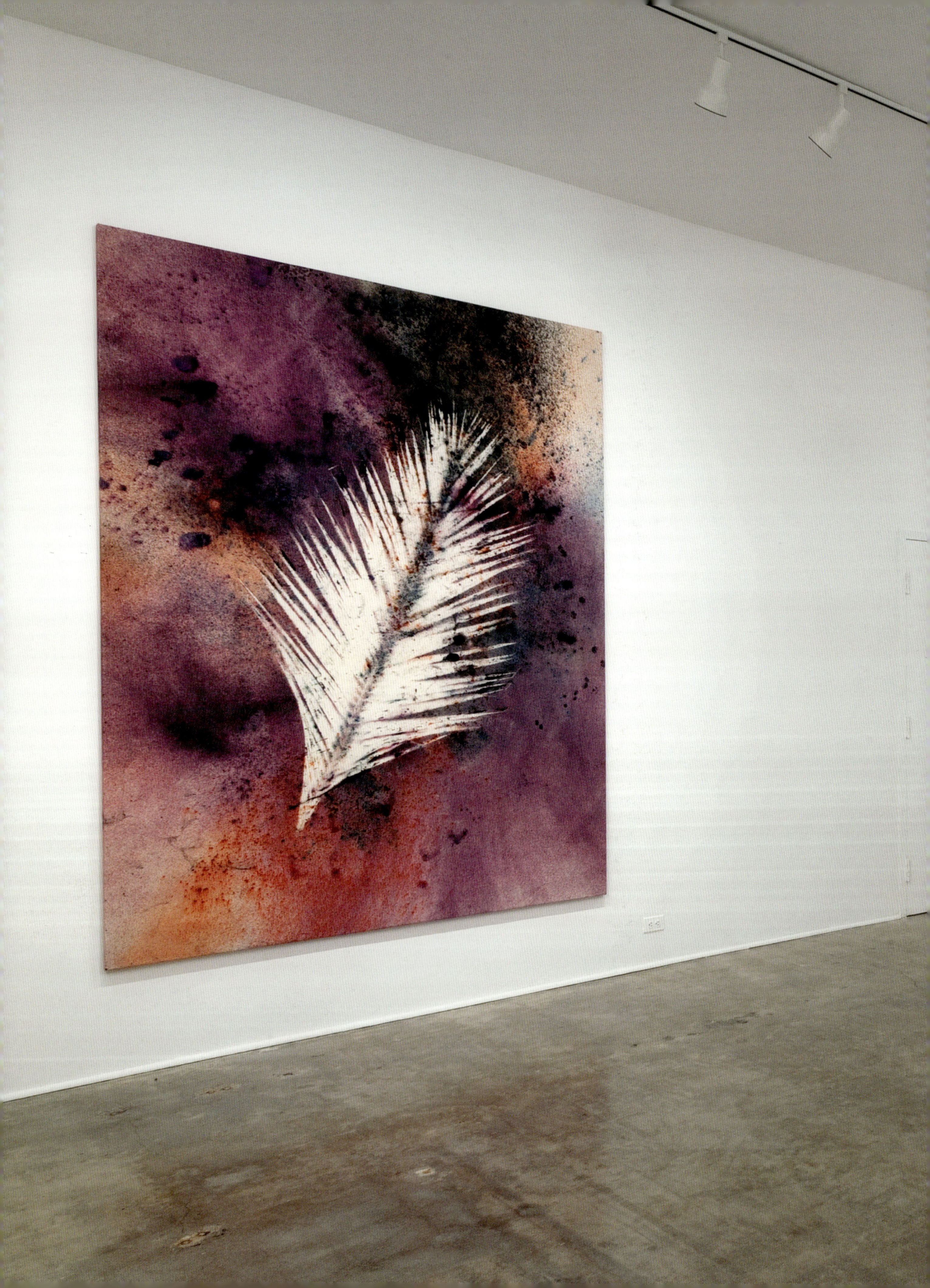

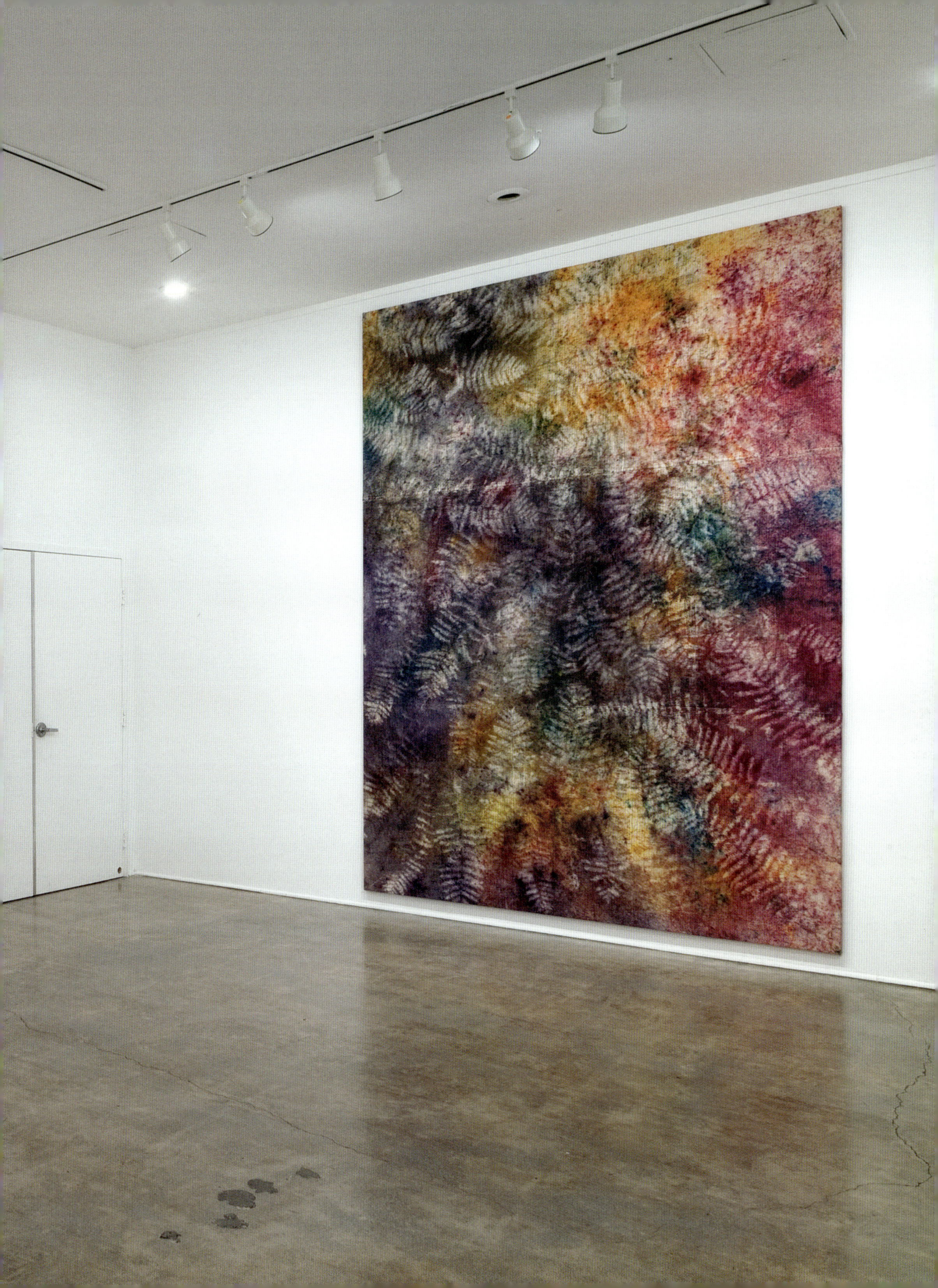

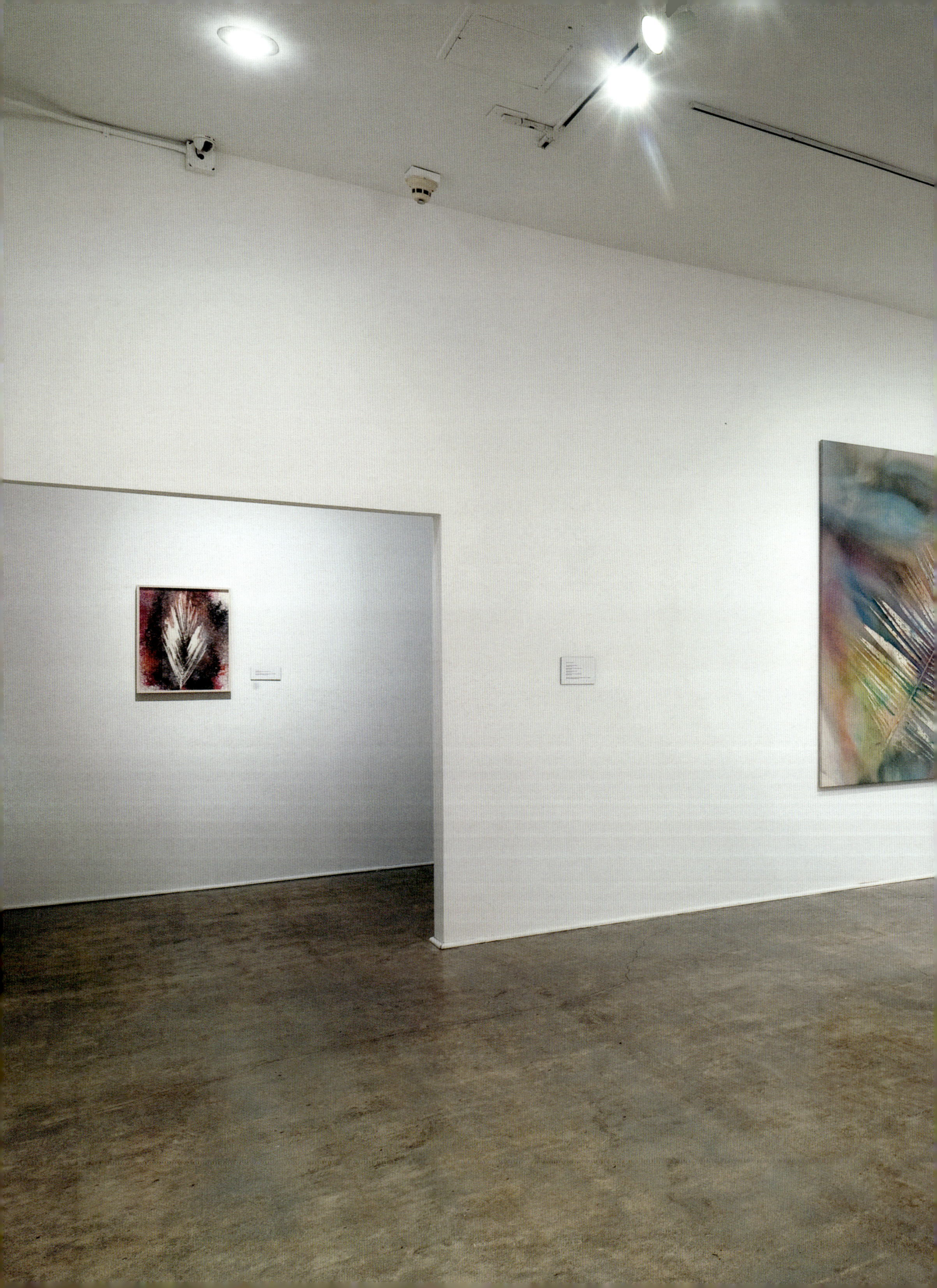

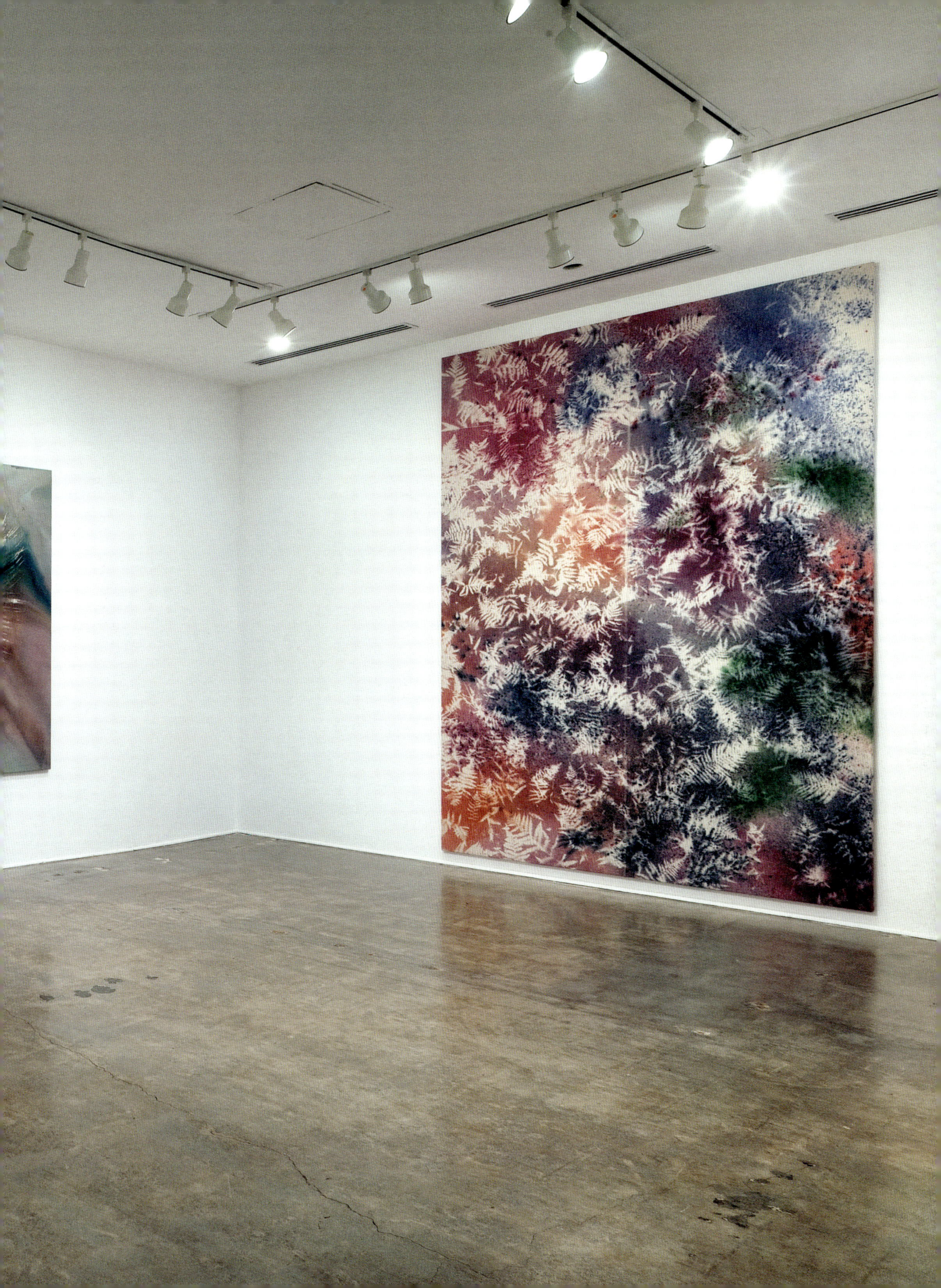

Hannah Hoffman Gallery
Los Angeles, CA
Sept 5 – Oct 25, 2014

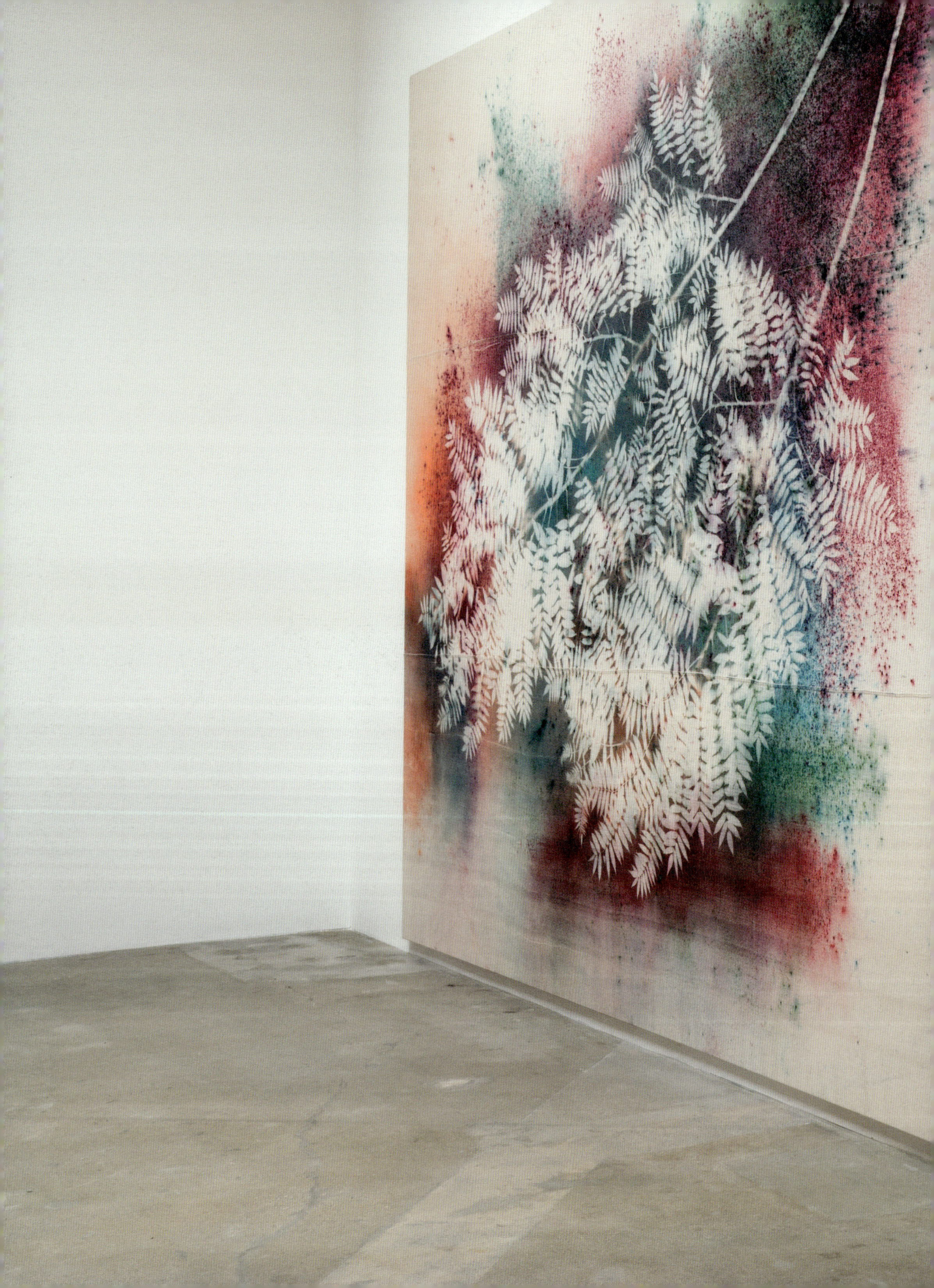

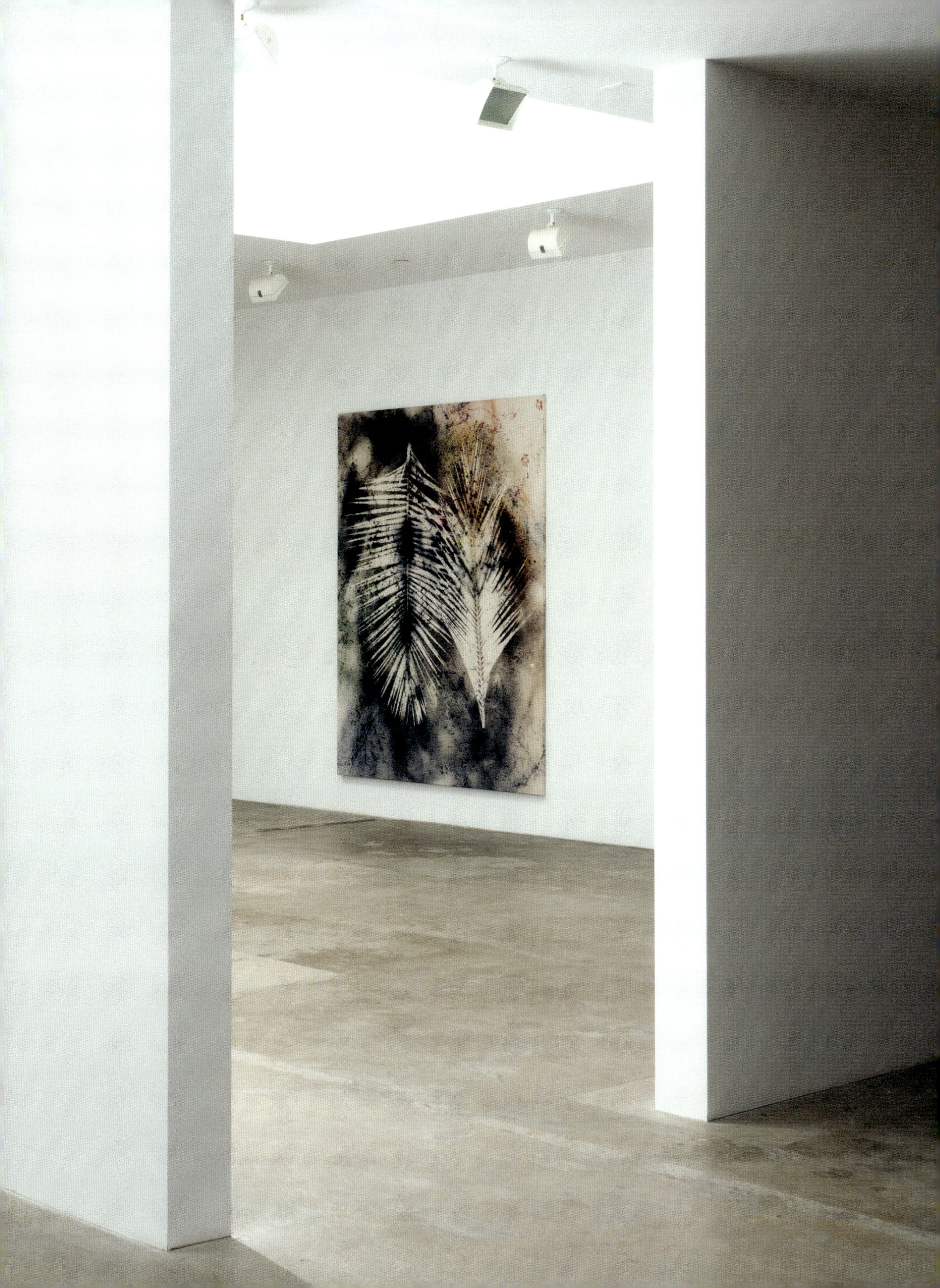

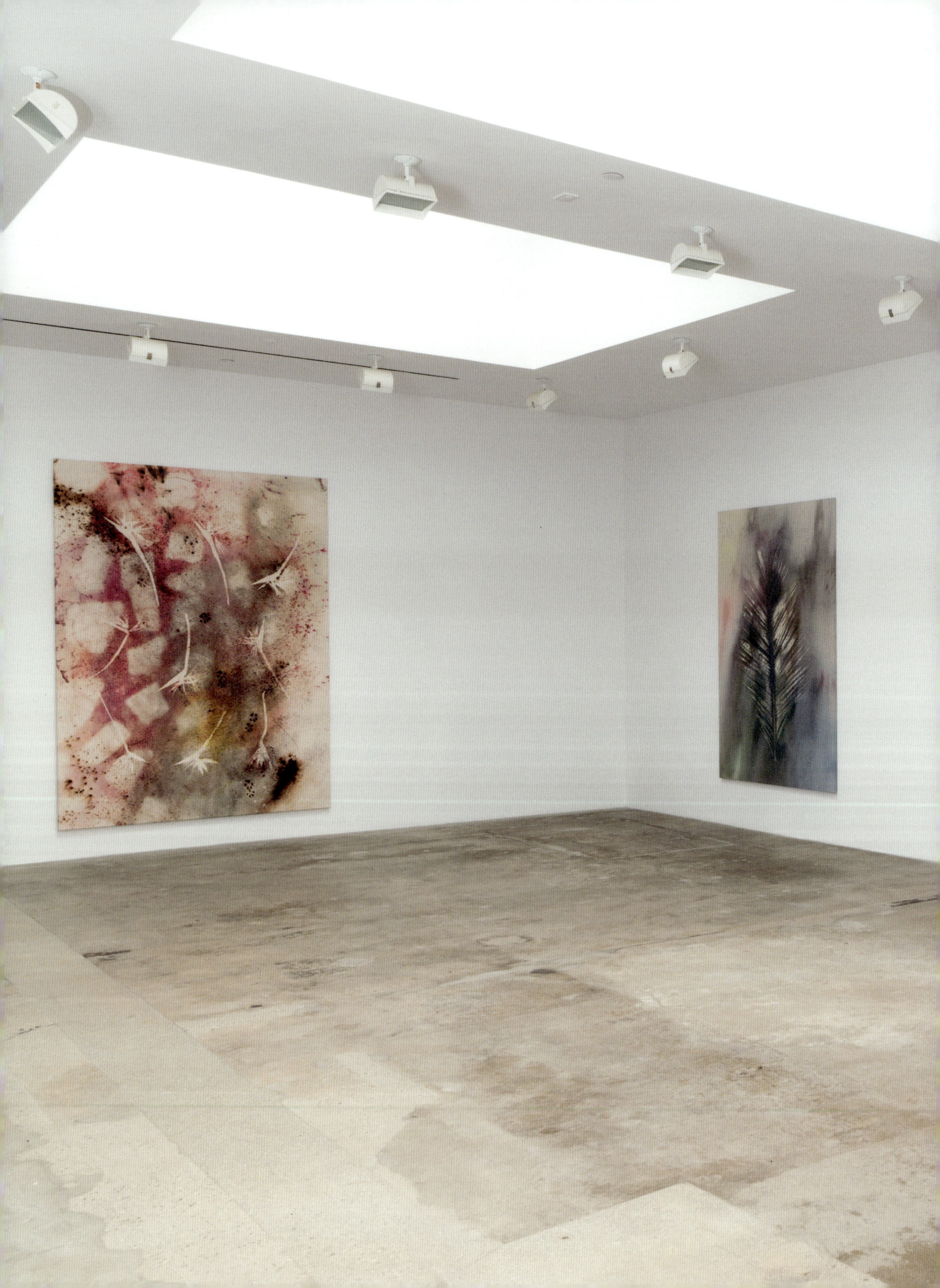

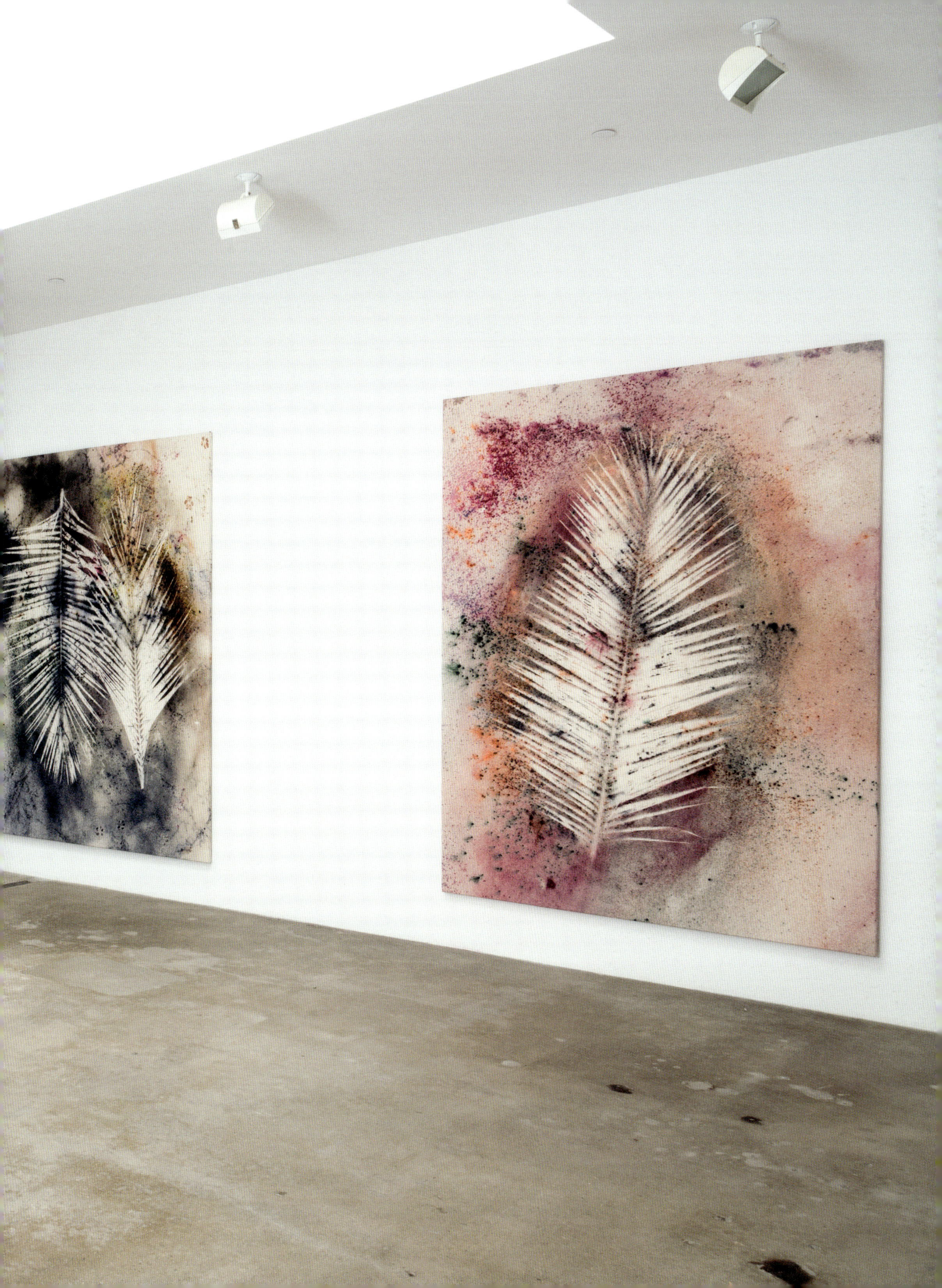

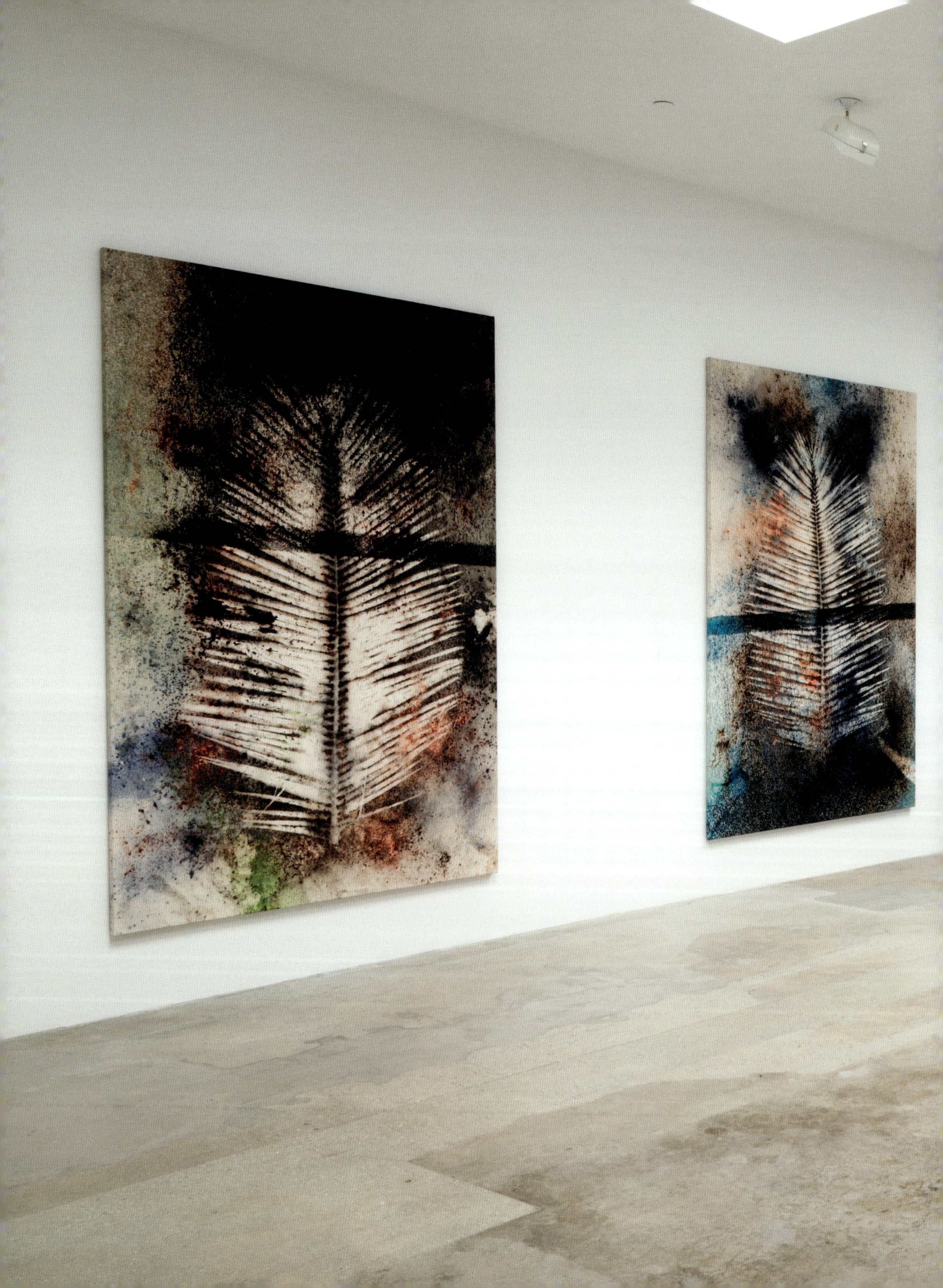

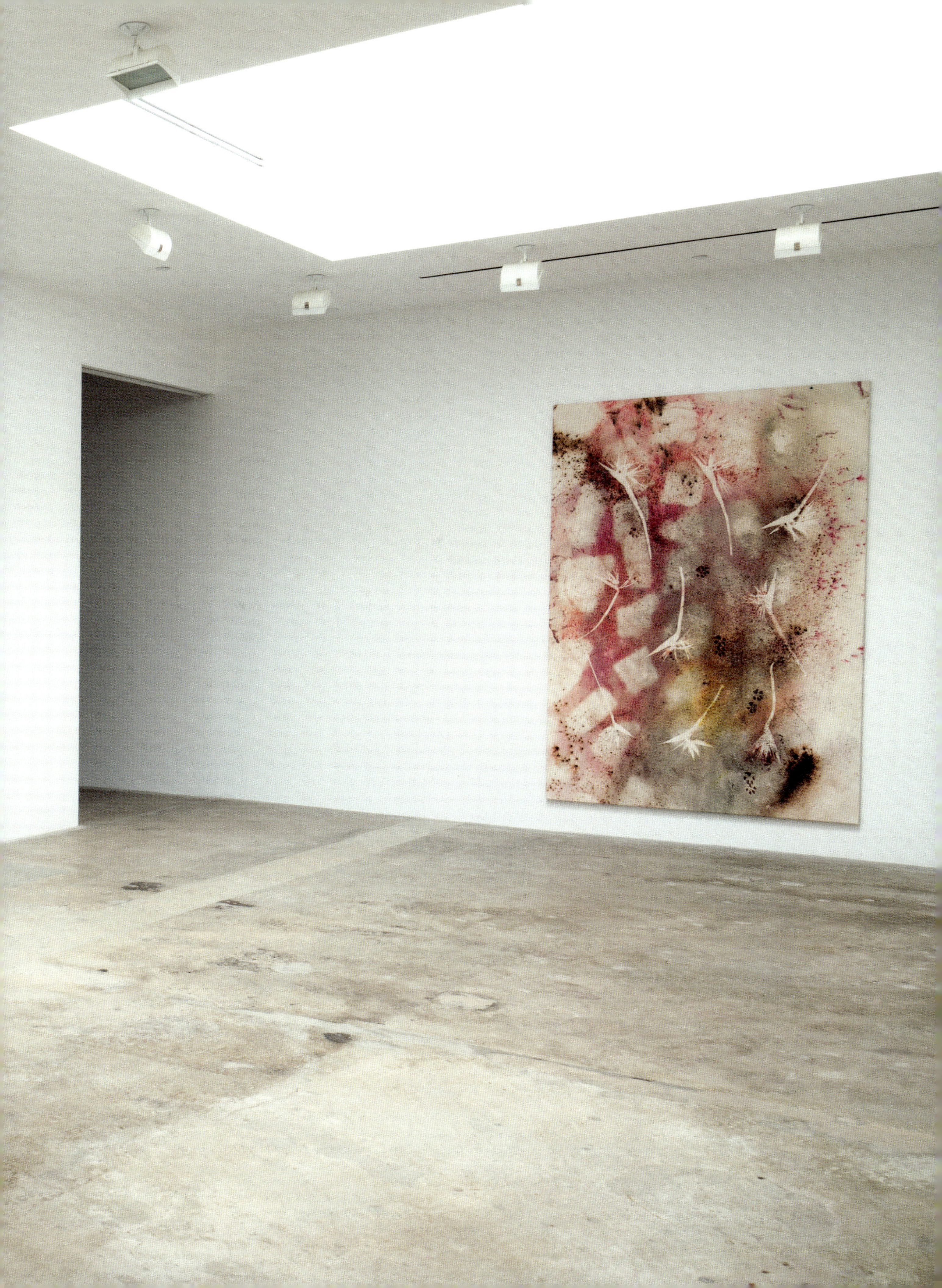

Karma
New York, NY
Jul 18 – Aug 23, 2014

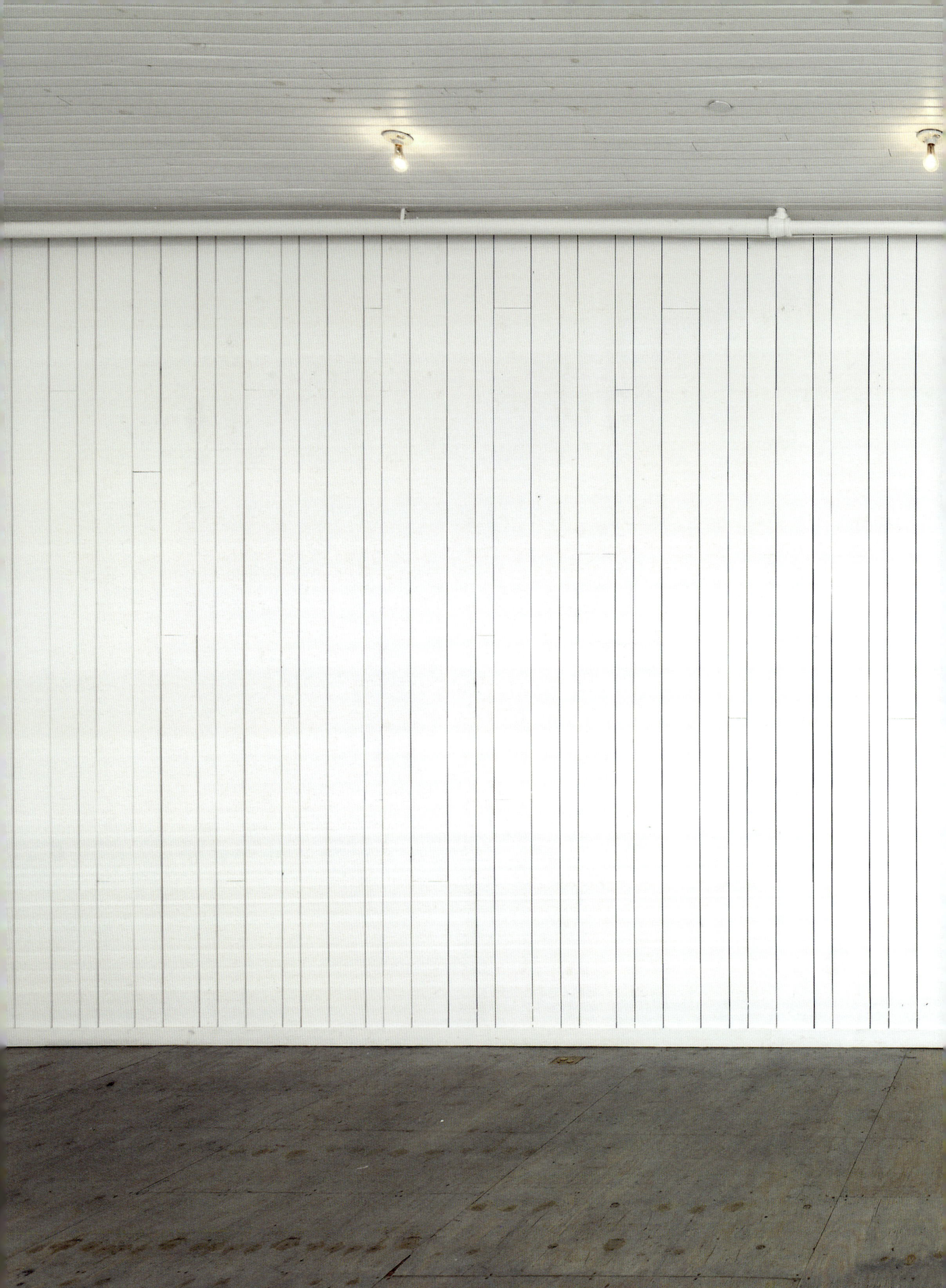

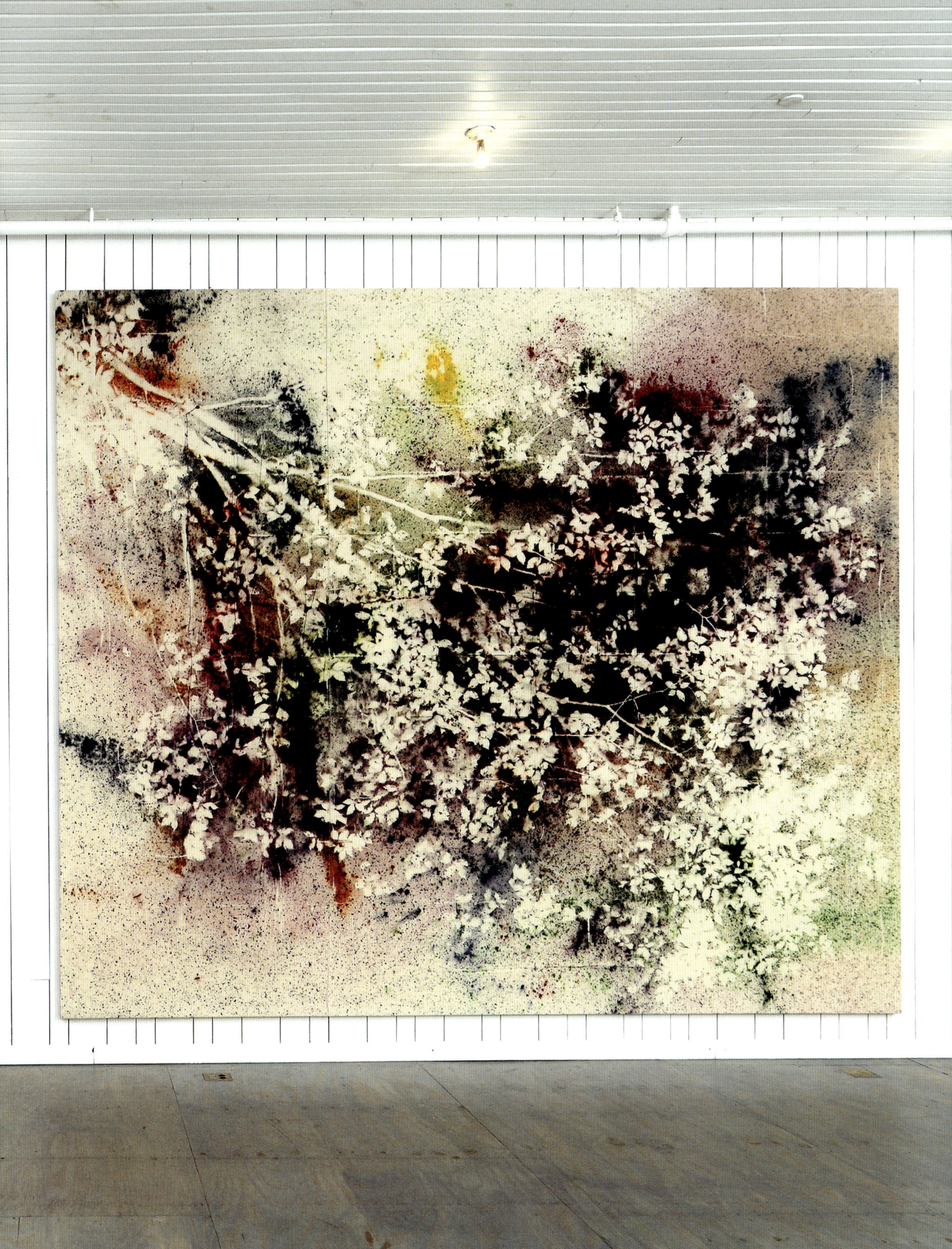

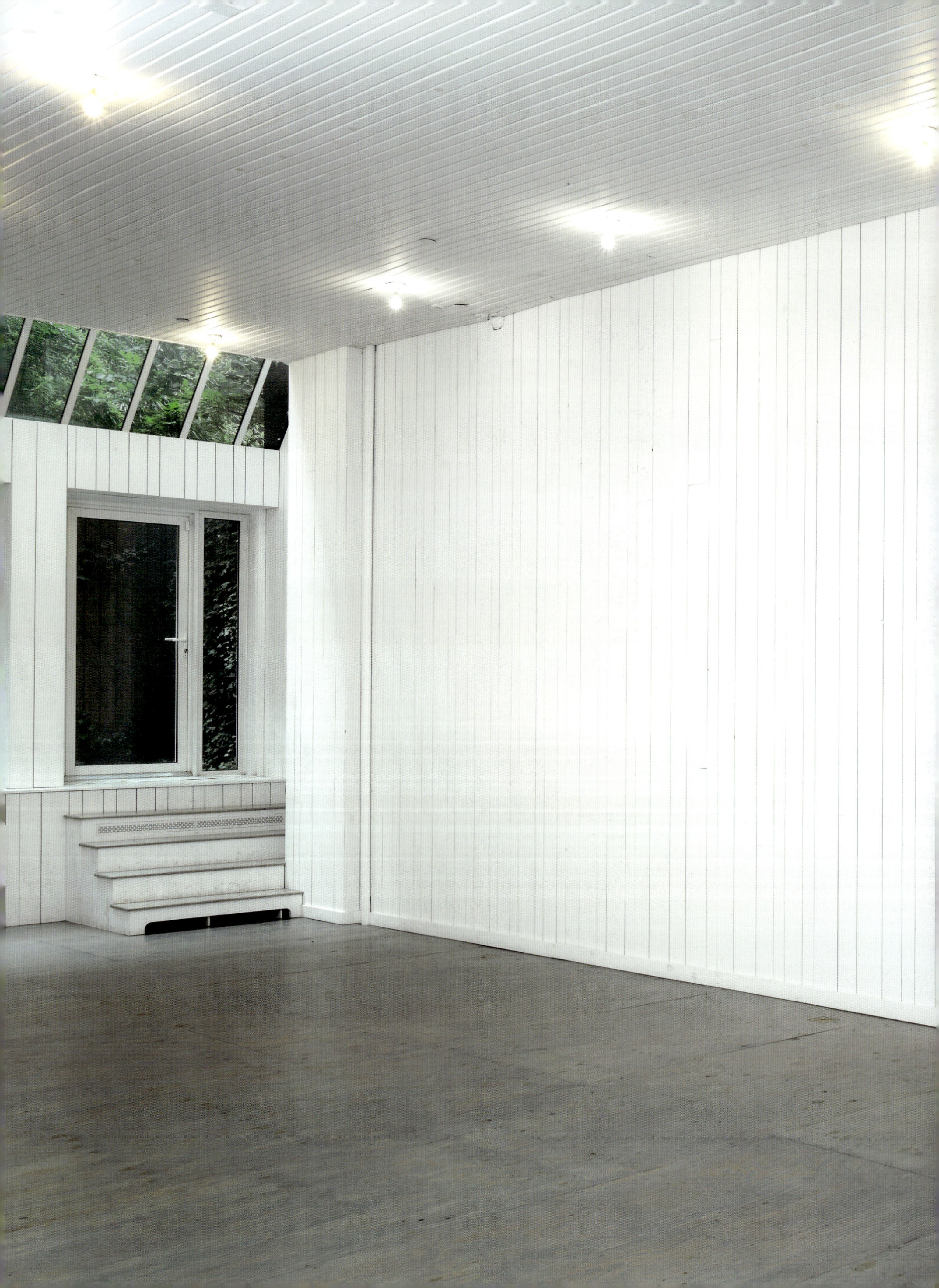

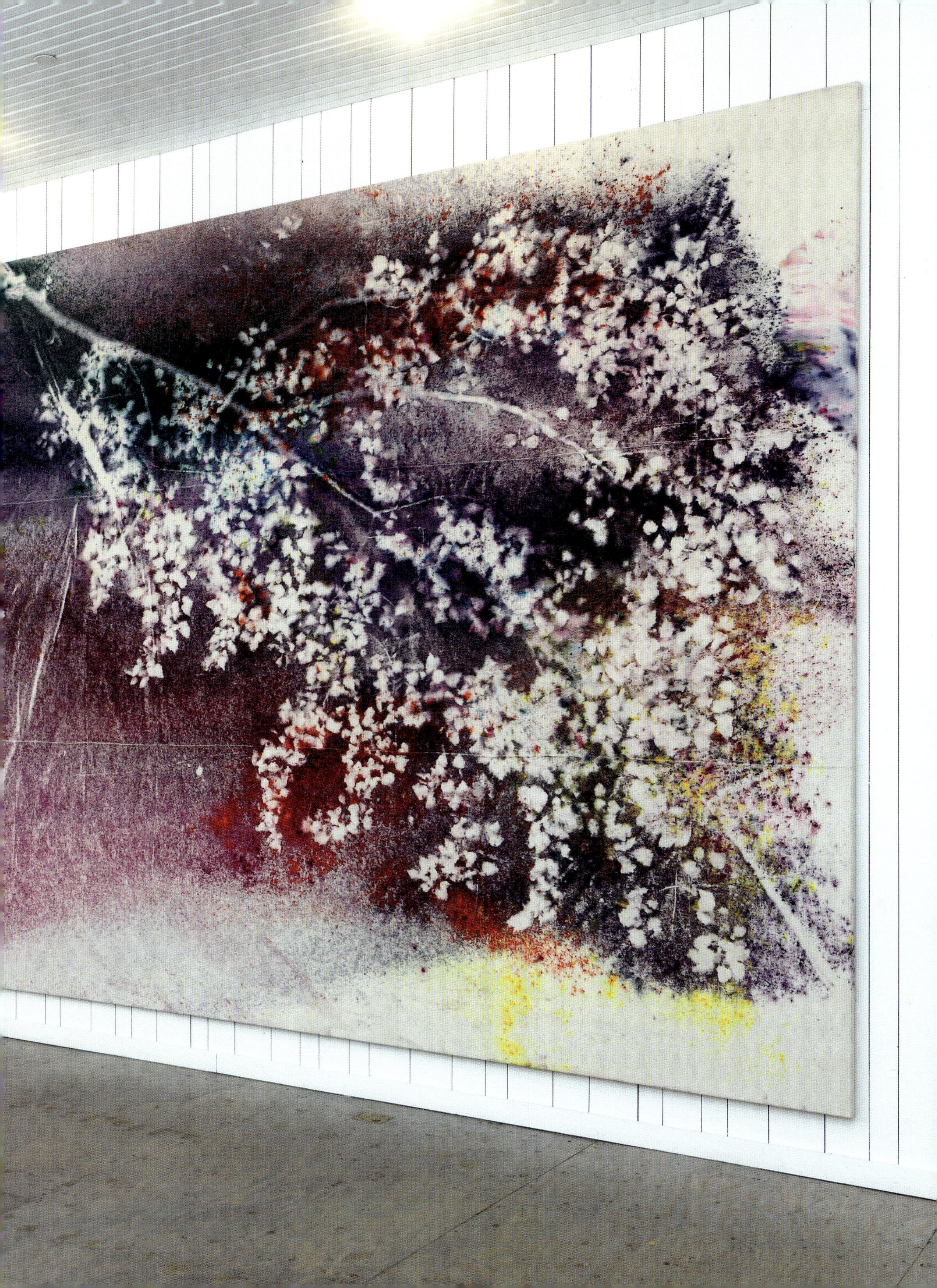

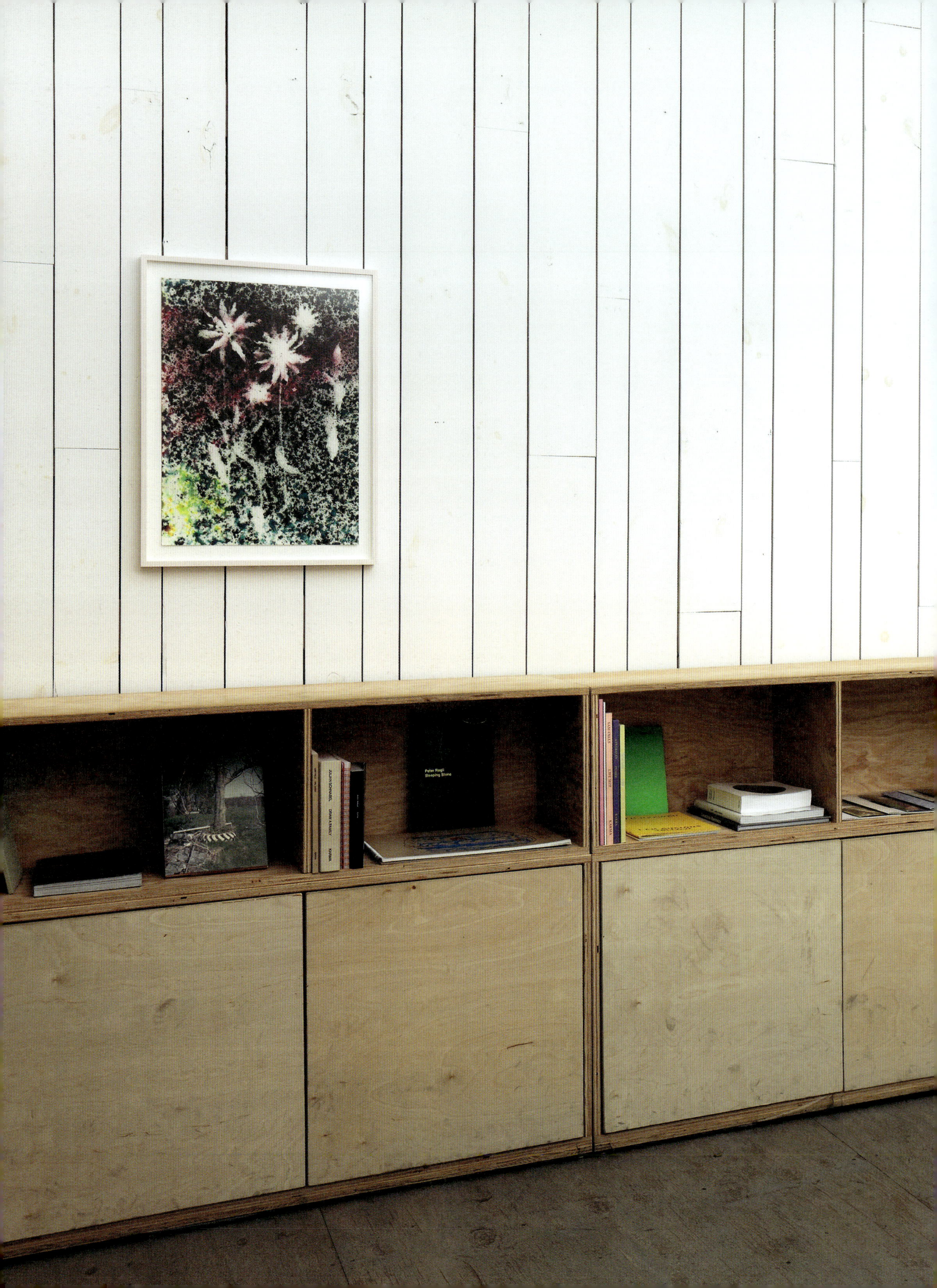
JULIAN SCHNABEL
DRAW A FAMILY
KARMA
Peter Regli
Sleeping Stone

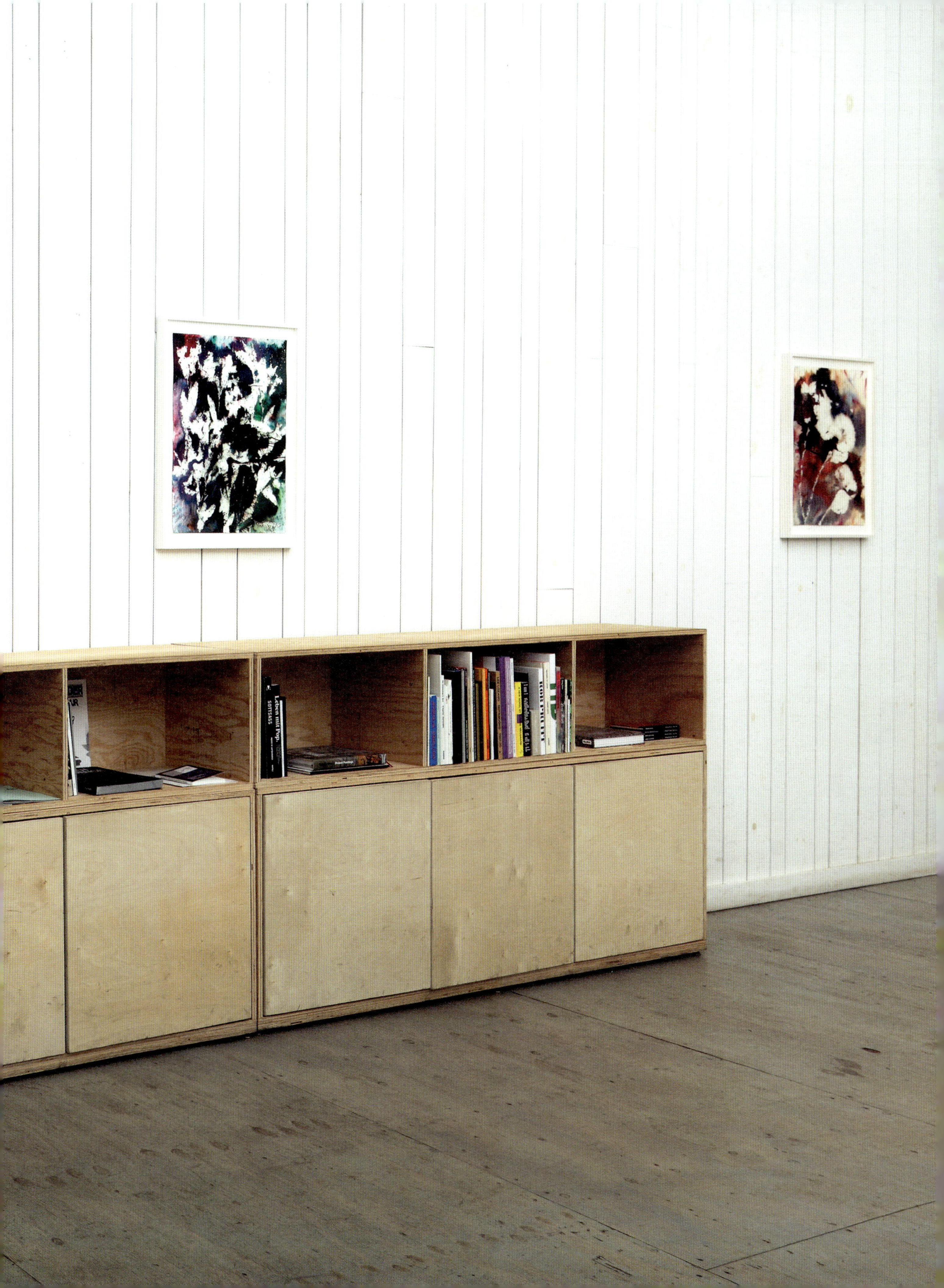

Sam Falls
Plein Air

Published by
Karma, New York

With generous support from:
Galerie Eva Presenhuber
Hannah Hoffman Gallery
Galleria Franco Noero

Edition of 1,500

© 2015 Sam Falls
and Karma, New York

Text © 2015
Aram Moshayedi

Photography:
Stefan Altenburger
Photography, Zurich
Thomas Mueller
Joshua White

ISBN: 978-1-938560-97-2